Lessons from a Dual Language Bilingual School

BILINGUAL EDUCATION & BILINGUALISM

Series Editors: **Nancy H. Hornberger** *(University of Pennsylvania, USA)* and **Wayne E. Wright** *(Purdue University, USA)*

Bilingual Education and Bilingualism is an international, multidisciplinary series publishing research on the philosophy, politics, policy, provision and practice of language planning, Indigenous and minority language education, multilingualism, multiculturalism, biliteracy, bilingualism and bilingual education. The series aims to mirror current debates and discussions. New proposals for single-authored, multiple-authored, or edited books in the series are warmly welcomed, in any of the following categories or others authors may propose: overview or introductory texts; course readers or general reference texts; focus books on particular multilingual education program types; school-based case studies; national case studies; collected cases with a clear programmatic or conceptual theme; and professional education manuals.

All books in this series are externally peer-reviewed.

Full details of all the books in this series and of all our other publications can be found on http://www.multilingual-matters.com, or by writing to Multilingual Matters, St Nicholas House, 31–34 High Street, Bristol, BS1 2AW, UK.

BILINGUAL EDUCATION & BILINGUALISM: 144

Lessons from a Dual Language Bilingual School

Celebrando una década de Dos Puentes Elementary

Edited by
Tatyana Kleyn, Victoria Hunt, Alcira Jaar, Rebeca Madrigal and Consuelo Villegas

MULTILINGUAL MATTERS
Bristol • Jackson

DOI https://doi.org/10.21832/KLEYN7380
Library of Congress Cataloging in Publication Data
A catalog record for this book is available from the Library of Congress.
Names: Kleyn, Tatyana, editor.
Title: Lessons from a Dual Language Bilingual School: Celebrando una década de Dos Puentes Elementary/Edited by Tatyana Kleyn, Victoria Hunt, Alcira Jaar, Rebeca Madrigal and Consuelo Villegas.
Description: Bristol, UK; Jackson, TN: Multilingual Matters, 2024. | Series: Bilingual Education & Bilingualism: 144 | Includes bibliographical references and index. | Summary: "Celebrating ten years of Dos Puentes Elementary School in New York City, this book showcases the lessons, successes and challenges of developing a fully bilingual school. It centers the voices of those directly involved in the school community while researchers discuss the implications for the field of bilingual education"—Provided by publisher.
Identifiers: LCCN 2024006302 (print) | LCCN 2024006303 (ebook) | ISBN 9781800417373 (paperback) | ISBN 9781800417380 (hardback) | ISBN 9781800417403 (epub) | ISBN 9781800417397 (pdf)
Subjects: LCSH: Dos Puentes Elementary School (New York, N.Y.) | Education, Bilingual—New York (State)—New York. | Education, Elementary—New York (State)—New York. | Community and school—New York (State)—New York.
Classification: LCC LC3733.N5 L47 2024 (print) | LCC LC3733.N5 (ebook) | DDC 372.65/1097471—dc23/eng/20240325
LC record available at https://lccn.loc.gov/2024006302
LC ebook record available at https://lccn.loc.gov/2024006303

British Library Cataloguing in Publication Data
A catalogue entry for this book is available from the British Library.

ISBN-13: 978-1-80041-738-0 (hbk)
ISBN-13: 978-1-80041-737-3 (pbk)

Multilingual Matters
UK: St Nicholas House, 31–34 High Street, Bristol, BS1 2AW, UK.
USA: Ingram, Jackson, TN, USA.

Website: https://www.multilingual-matters.com
X: Multi_Ling_Mat
Facebook: https://www.facebook.com/multilingualmatters
Blog: https://www.channelviewpublications.wordpress.com

Copyright © 2024 Tatyana Kleyn, Victoria Hunt, Alcira Jaar, Rebeca Madrigal, Consuelo Villegas and the authors of individual chapters.

All rights reserved. No part of this work may be reproduced in any form or by any means without permission in writing from the publisher.

The policy of Multilingual Matters/Channel View Publications is to use papers that are natural, renewable and recyclable products, made from wood grown in sustainable forests. In the manufacturing process of our books, and to further support our policy, preference is given to printers that have FSC and PEFC Chain of Custody certification. The FSC and/or PEFC logos will appear on those books where full certification has been granted to the printer concerned.

Typeset by SAN Publishing Services.

Para nuestra querida profesora, mentora y amiga:

Dra. María Torres-Guzmán

Contents

Contributors	xi
Acknowledgements	xvii
Foreword	xix
Ofelia García	
Dos Puentes Elementary: An Introduction	1
Tatyana Kleyn and Victoria Hunt	

Pillar 1: *Bilingüismo, Biliteracidad y Multiculturalismo*

	Introduction *Rebeca Madrigal*	17
1	Celebrating *Dos Lenguajes* *Jason Horowitz and Armando Lopez*	29
	Researcher Commentary *Cecilia M. Espinosa*	35
2	Translanguaging: Moving Beyond *"los dos" Lenguajes* *Diane Figueroa and Karina Malik*	38
	Researcher Commentary *Laura Ascenzi-Moreno*	44
3	Building Biliteracy through Educators, Resources and Curricula *Lara Ginsberg*	47
	Researcher Commentary *Carmen M. Martínez-Roldán*	51
4	Bilingual Activism *a Través de la Lectoescritura* *Ashley Busone-Rodríguez and Karen Mondol*	55
	Researcher Commentary *Luz Yadira Herrera*	61

5	Critical Collaboration to Support the Bilingualism and Biliteracy of Children with Disabilities *Sabrina Poms and Teresita Prieto*	64
	Researcher Commentary *María Cioè-Peña*	70

Pillar 2: *Las Familias son* Partners, Leaders and Advocates

	Introduction *Consuelo Villegas, Yesenia J. Moreno and Tatyana Kleyn*	73
6	Families as Educators, Leaders and Advocates *Stephanie Ubiera, Adriana Cando and Ained Casado*	83
	Researcher Commentary *Ivana Espinet*	88
7	Bridging Home and School *Sacha Mercier and Amy Withers*	91
	Researcher Commentary *Carmina Makar*	97
8	Family Diversity as a Strength and a Challenge *Annette Fernandez*	100
	Researcher Commentary *Kate Menken*	105
9	Building *Comunidad* *Elga Castro Ramos*	109
	Researcher Commentary *Bertha Pérez*	114
10	Socioemotional Learning and Support *Irving Mota and Kimberly Bautista*	118
	Researcher Commentary *Mary Mendenhall*	123
11	Remote Learning through a Pandemic *Aaron Sidlo*	127
	Researcher Commentary *Devon Hedrick-Shaw*	132

Pillar 3: *Investigaciones* and Hands-on Learning

    Introduction   137
    Alcira Jaar

12 *Exploraciones en* Early Childhood   147
    Elizabeth Menendez and Catherine Velásquez-Leacock

    Researcher Commentary   153
    Dina López

13 Transition to Investigations and Inquiry in the Upper Grades   157
    Hazel Garcia-Banguela, Michelle Madera Taveras and Carmen Morel

    Researcher Commentary   164
    Gladys Y. Aponte

14 Learning Science through Hands-on Experiences and Animals   168
    Karín DeJesus and Yesenia J. Moreno

    Researcher Commentary   175
    Patricia Martínez-Álvarez

15 Field Trips as *Paseos* to Real World Connections   178
    Peggy McQuaid and Kristen Minno-Bingham

    Researcher Commentary   184
    Sara Vogel

Pillar 4: Partnerships with Universities, Organizations y La Comunidad

    Introduction   187
    Victoria Hunt

16 University Collaborations: Service and Research Projects   199
    Wendy Barrales, Patricia Martínez-Álvarez, Maite T. Sánchez, Belinda Arana and Victoria Hunt

    Researcher Commentary   207
    Nancy Stern

17 University Partners: Bilingual Student Teaching   211
    Rebeca Madrigal, Silvia Peña and Jennifer Aquino Peña

    Researcher Commentary   217
    Sharon Chang

18 Expanding the Arts through Partnerships and Passion   221
    Clara Bello and Lorene Phillips

   Researcher Commentary   226
   Heather H. Woodley

19 Center-Based Learning: Partnerships with Staff
    Developers and Schools   229
    Queila Cordero and Joyce Veras

   Researcher Commentary   235
   Crissa Stephens

20 Connections with the Community and Beyond   239
    Katherine Higuera-McCoy and Maggie Orzechowski

   Researcher Commentary   245
   Kate Seltzer

   A Student's Closing Remarks   248
   Raphael S. Kollin

   Afterword   250
   Carmen Fariña and Manuel Ramirez

   Index   252

Contributors

Editors

Tatyana Kleyn is Professor of Bilingual Education and TESOL at The City College of New York and co-founder of Dos Puentes Elementary School. She received an EdD from Teachers College, Columbia University in International Educational Development with a focus on Bilingual/Bicultural Education. Tatyana is Principal Investigator for the City University of New York Initiative on Immigration and Education (CUNY – IIE). She served as President of the New York State Association for Bilingual Education (NYSABE) and was a Fulbright Scholar in Oaxaca, Mexico. Tatyana has authored books and articles on bilingual education, translanguaging and immigration. Her latest book is titled *Living, Learning and Languaging Across Borders: Students Between the US and Mexico*. Tatyana's work in film as a producer and director includes the *Living Undocumented* series, *Una Vida, Dos Países: Children and Youth (Back) in Mexico*, the *Supporting Immigrants in Schools Series* and the *Not Too Young: Immigration in Elementary Schools* video series. Tatyana was an elementary school teacher in San Pedro Sula, Honduras and Atlanta, Georgia. For more information see TatyanaKleyn.com

Victoria Hunt is the current and founding Principal of Dos Puentes Elementary School. Prior to being a principal, Dr Hunt was an assistant principal for six years in two New York City public schools with dual language bilingual programs. She was also a bilingual elementary school teacher in New York City for 10 years, as well as in Houston, Texas and Washington, DC. Dr Hunt received her doctorate in leadership and bilingual education from Teachers College, Columbia University. Her dissertation, titled *Transformative Education: A Comparative Study of Three Established Dual Language Programs,* received the AERA Bilingual Education Research SIG dissertation award in 2010. She loves being a principal and respects the privilege of serving her students and their families.

Alcira Jaar is Assistant Principal and a founding staff member of Dos Puentes Elementary School; a dual language bilingual K-5 school located in the Washington Heights neighborhood of Manhattan. There she also held the role of movement and science teacher. She received her Master's and Doctorate of Education from Teachers College, Columbia University and an Advanced Certificate in School Leadership from Bank Street College of Education. Dr Jaar has been an educator in the New York City Public Schools for over 20 years. She is a proud bilingual daughter of Dominican immigrant parents who lives in Washington Heights with her two daughters, husband and two cats.

Rebeca Madrigal is a founding bilingual teacher of Dos Puentes Elementary and mother of Raphael S. (Raffi) Kollin, a graduate of Dos Puentes. She has taught kindergarten through 5th grade, often in the Spanish component of dual language bilingual programs. She has over 20 years of experience in the NYC Public Schools and has presented nationally on multicultural and bilingual education. Her experience as a Mexican immigrant and educator has been the focus of several academic and mainstream news articles. In 2015, she was awarded recognition by the New York State Association for Bilingual Education (NYSABE) with the Bilingual Teacher of the Year Award. She earned a Master's degree in Bilingual Education at Teachers College, Columbia University.

Consuelo Villegas was the founding Parent Coordinator at Dos Puentes Elementary School for the first 11 years. She has also worked in two other New York City elementary schools: PS 75 in Manhattan as a family assistant, and office manager of the afterschool program and family worker in PS 64 in the Bronx. She immigrated to the US from Colombia without papers, where she studied and worked as a bookkeeper and accountant. In spite of her immigration status, she began taking English classes at Teachers College, Hunter College and other organizations. Consuelo also attended The City College of New York for bookkeeping and accounting. Consuelo has been honored for her work by the NYC Department of Education for Civil Service and by NYSABE with the Bilingual Support Personnel of the Year Award.

Authors

Gladys Y. Aponte is a New York City teacher educator and a Postdoctoral Research Scholar with the Children's Equity Project at Arizona State University.

Jennifer Aquino Peña is a 4th-grade teacher at Dos Puentes.

Belinda Arana is an Assistant Adjunct Professor of Bilingual/Bicultural Education at Teachers College, Columbia University.

Laura Ascenzi-Moreno is Professor of Bilingual Education and Bilingual Program Coordinator at Brooklyn College, City University of New York.

Wendy Barrales is an ethnic studies educator, activist and Postdoctoral Associate at New York University (NYU).

Kimberly Bautista is a bilingual special education teacher at Dos Puentes Elementary and member of the School Leadership Team who also provides early intervention services in NYC.

Clara Bello is the dual language dance educator at Dos Puentes who also serves as the arts liaison for the school.

Ashley Busone-Rodríguez is a bilingual 3rd-grade teacher at Dos Puentes who is also a project researcher for the CUNY Initiative on Immigration and Education (CUNY-IIE).

Adriana Cando is an immigrant from Ecuador and mother of a Dos Puentes graduate who served for two years on the School Leadership Team.

Ained Casado is a proud parent to a Dos Puentes graduate who served as Co-President of the Parent Association.

Elga Castro Ramos was part of the Dos Puentes community for six years as the mother of Elena, serving as the PA President, and is an Adjunct Professor at Barnard College.

Sharon Chang is a Senior Lecturer and Coordinator of the Student Teaching/Practicum in the Bilingual/Bicultural Education Program, Teachers College, Columbia University.

María Cioè-Peña is an Assistant Professor in Educational Linguistics at Penn GSE, who as a neurodiverse, bilingual and biliterate researcher, examines the intersections of disability, language, school-parent partnerships and education policy.

Queila Cordero is a dual language educator at Dos Puentes who is currently serving as Dean and Math Specialist.

Karín DeJesus is the lower-grade science teacher at Dos Puentes who also serves on the consultation committee, instructional leadership team and grade leaders team.

Ivana Espinet is an associate professor in the education program at the City University of New York (CUNY), Kingsborough Community College.

Cecilia M. Espinosa is Professor of Early Childhood/Childhood Education at CUNY, Lehman College, and is the co-author of the book: *Rooted in Strength: Using Translanguaging to Grow Multilingual Readers and Writers*.

Annette Fernandez is Valentina Lugo's mother (a Dos Puentes graduate), a writer, a cannabis activist and entrepreneur.

Diane Figueroa is a first-generation bicultural and bilingual educator who serves as a grade leader for 3rd grade.

Hazel Garcia-Banguela is a bilingual early-childhood special education teacher at Dos Puentes.

Lara Ginsberg is a 4th-grade ICT teacher and math study group facilitator.

Devon Hedrick-Shaw is a PhD candidate in Equity, Bilingualism and Biliteracy at the University of Colorado Boulder and a former Dos Puentes Elementary teacher.

Luz Yadira Herrera is an Assistant Professor of Bilingual Education at California State University, Dominguez Hills.

Katherine Higuera-McCoy is the Community Coordinator at Dos Puentes who is part of the school's administration team and works with local partners in the Washington Heights area.

Jason Horowitz is a 4th-grade educator at Dos Puentes and a musician who takes pride in bringing influences from both into the classroom.

Raphael S. Kollin is a graduate of the 2021 class of Dos Puentes.

Armando Lopez is a 1st-grade Spanish component teacher at Dos Puentes.

Dina López is an Associate Professor and Program Director in Bilingual Education and TESOL at CUNY, City College of New York.

Michelle Madera Taveras is a bilingual special education teacher at Dos Puentes who is also the 5th-grade team leader and a member of the instructional leadership and student leadership teams.

Carmina Makar is Adjunct Professor of Bilingual Education and TESOL at CUNY, City College of New York.

Karina Malik is an early-childhood special education teacher at Dos Puentes who is also a doctoral candidate at Teachers College, Columbia University.

Patricia Martínez-Álvarez is an Associate Professor and the director of the program in Bilingual/Bicultural Education at Teachers College, Columbia University.

Carmen M. Martínez-Roldán is Associate Professor of Bilingual/Bicultural Education at Teachers College, Columbia University.

Peggy McQuaid has taught the English component of the 1st and 2nd grades at Dos Puentes since 2016.

Kate Menken is Professor of Linguistics at CUNY, Queens College, and a Research Fellow at the CUNY Research Institute for the Study of Language in Urban Society.

Mary Mendenhall is Associate Professor of International and Comparative Education at Teachers College, Columbia University, leading research on education and forced migration, and mother of two Dos Puentes alumni (2019 and 2023).

Elizabeth Menendez is a veteran kindergarten teacher who serves as the grade leader and is on the instructional leadership team.

Sacha Mercier is a 1st-grade general education teacher at Dos Puentes who is also one of the proud coaches of the America Scores Dos Puentes Soccer Team.

Kristen Minno-Bingham has been a teacher at Dos Puentes for nine years and proudly opened the school's 1st and 3rd grades.

Karen Mondol is a 5th-grade language arts teacher at Dos Puentes.

Carmen Morel taught the 2nd and 4th grades at Dos Puentes.

Yesenia J. Moreno is the 4th- and 5th-grade bilingual science teacher and upper-grade math interventionist.

Irving Mota is a bilingual teacher at Dos Puentes who has taught the 4th and 5th grades in addition to being part of the social emotional study group.

Maggie Orzechowski is a Dos Puentes mother and connector who weaves together ideas, people, resources, and stories to produce actionable outcomes that center justice and connection.

Angela Paredes Montero is a cultural mediator and master's candidate in global mental health at Teachers College, Columbia University.

Silvia Peña is a bilingual special education teacher at Dos Puentes Elementary.

Bertha Pérez is Professor Emerita of Biliteracy at the University of Texas San Antonio, where she continues her research on biliteracy practices in dual language education.

Lorene Phillips is the music teacher at Dos Puentes and is an Orff Schulwerk practitioner.

Sabrina Poms is an early-childhood bilingual special educator who leads teacher study groups around Universal Design for Learning and bilingual phonics practices.

Teresita Prieto is a bilingual special education teacher at Dos Puentes who serves as the IEP teacher and supports the School Intervention Team and Special Education Department

Maite T. Sánchez is Associate Professor of Bilingual Education at CUNY, Hunter College.

Kate Seltzer is an Assistant Professor of Bilingual and ESL Education at Rowan University in New Jersey, where she works with pre- and in-service teachers of bilingual students.

Aaron Sidlo is father of two Dos Puentes graduates and is also an English as a New Language (ENL) teacher at Wright Brothers School in New York City.

Nancy Stern is a professor in the Programs in Bilingual Education and TESOL at CUNY, City College of New York, and the project director of B-SEAL for Multilingual Learners (Building Secondary English Learner Educator and Administrator Leadership).

Crissa Stephens is Assistant Professor of Teaching in the Program in Educational Transformation at Georgetown University and co-PI of Project ELEECT, which exists to train antiracist, culturally and linguistically sustaining teachers for multilingual learners in Washington DC.

Stephanie Ubiera is a special education teacher at Dos Puentes who is also a founding teacher.

Catherine Velásquez-Leacock was a kindergarten and 1st-grade teacher at Dos Puentes.

Joyce Veras is a 1st grade teacher at Dos Puentes.

Sara Vogel is Research Director of Computing Integrated Teacher Education Initiative at CUNY, and a researcher of (especially multilingual) learning environments that support conversations about, with, through, and against technology.

Amy Withers is, most importantly, mother to two amazing graduates of Dos Puentes, as well as an instructor and advisor at Bank Street College and a math education consultant.

Heather H. Woodley is Clinical Associate Professor of TESOL, Bilingual and World Language Education at NYU Steinhardt and director of the programs in Childhood Education and Teacher Residency in Inclusive Childhood Education.

Acknowledgements

This book was a tremendous undertaking for us as editors. Four of the five of us work full-time at Dos Puentes Elementary, and this is our first book project. We were joined by 40 Dos Puentes community members and 20 researchers for a total of 65 authors!

We want to thank the teachers and families who shared their experiences and expertise as chapter authors, even when it was something they never imagined doing. We are grateful to the researchers who made it possible for us to connect school practices to the literature in the field via this unique authoring partnership.

We are indebted to Pamela D'Andrea Martínez for her careful reading of this manuscript to ensure the book is consistent and accessible and, while being mostly in English, still connects with the *bilingüismo* of our school. We are also thankful to Nancy Stern for her critical reading of our introduction chapter.

Finally, we must say *gracias* to each and every family of the 670 current students and graduates for their *confianza* and trust with their children, because without them there would be no Dos Puentes.

Con cariño,
Tatyana, Victoria, Alcira, Rebeca and Consuelo

El Camino Traveled: Ten Years of Community Building: A Foreword

Ofelia García

This foreword introduces readers to the actions of the many people who have been making camino/paths as a community builds a school. In so doing, the traditional educational route is reversed. It is not simply the educators making the *camino* for a community regarded as poor and deficient. It is a rich bilingual comunidad of families, educational leaders and staff, students, community organizers who have fearlessly stepped into a *camino* that started out with Dos Puentes to bridge 'idiomas, culturas y mundos' and has ended up as a promising and rich bilingual comunidad in 'The Heights'. This monumental book highlights the philosophy, practices, and experiences of all the different actors to create this bilingual community, because as a Latina mother says in Chapter 8, 'community is created and nurtured; it does not just come from placing diverse people in the same space or school' (p. 101).

The school's philosophy of critical collaboration among diverse people is reflected in the ways that this book is structured and written. It is edited by a team made up of a university professor and co-founder (Kleyn), the founding principal of the school (Hunt), the founding assistant principal (Jaar), a founding teacher (Madrigal), and the founding parent coordinator (Villegas). Most research in bilingual education has been conducted and authored by academic researchers. This book, however, is authored by school leaders, teachers, student teachers, mothers, fathers, community advocates, and university professors and researchers, with all their diverse voices and lenses shaping an equitable community of scholars. In fact, this book emerges from a different locus of enunciation (Mignolo, 2020) – not from the scholars or the university partners, but from the comunidad itself, thus opening up a process of 'decolonizing research' (p. 3). The decolonizing work evident in this book's horizontal collaboration among equal participants demonstrates a commitment to addressing inequities in the production of knowledge. Decolonizing academic work by inverting the power relationships in a school has the effect of unsettling traditional ideologies about bilingualism, race, and class, as it reveals the potential and strength of complex multilingual comunidades. By acknowledging what Grosfoguel (2007) calls the 'silenced knowledge' of families and teachers, possibilities of an education 'otherwise' emerge.

As a decolonizing enterprise, the writing of this book has been inclusive of all voices and epistemologies, and has not shied away from the tension that exists when building a diverse community that centers language-minoritized children and families, their language and cultural practices, and knowledge. Teachers describe how their educational practices reflect their critical stances on equity, immigration, inclusion, race, bilingualism and biliteracy; and yet, how they must negotiate with family members who may question some of their beliefs and practices. Families recognize the disparities that exist between Latinx families and white families who live on the other side of the Broadway divide of Washington Heights, the side that is undergoing rapid gentrification. With honesty, differences are acknowledged and raciolinguistic ideologies are called out. The people making camino in these chapters make clear that what upholds this diverse comunidad is their shared meaning of bilingually and equitably educating the children of the Heights. The lens of this book is neither the center nor the periphery, but a network of complex relationships among equal partners.

Bilingual education in this book is not simply about language, for 'linguistic objectives exist *alongside* but never *instead of* curricular goals' (p. 179) and alongside an activist stance. In many ways, the commitments of this comunidad go back to the very beginnings of US bilingual education before models and language allocation policies had been defined by external educational authorities. Guided by the community and haciendo camino al andar, [making the path upon walking], the curriculum and educational practices and policies in this school have been shaped from the ground up. A decade of joint paseos and wanderings/wonderings through curricula, policies and practices have enabled them to 'shift, modify, stretch and expand' (p. 48). The original strict language allocation policies have made way for translanguaging spaces in order to give students the freedom to use their full linguistic and semiotic repertoire purposefully. Rigorous balanced literacy practices have given way to center-based learning, as the effects of the pandemic started to be felt. Strict class schedules now make room for Holding Space time to accommodate the experience of immigrant families who have been separated, for students and families who feared deportation after Trump's election, as well as the socioemotional experiences of all. Books used are multilingual/multicultural/multiracial-centered, adding to the many rich stories of everyone in the comunidad. Structures that support families have been strengthened and are many - Family Fridays, Welcome Potluck, Home Visits, Language Exchanges, Rincón Hispano. And yet, as the comunidad walks, sometimes with different rhythms, it has remained committed to a joint purpose - the education of a racialized bilingual community.

For me, this book offers much more than ideas about policies and practices. It offers lived experiences, thoughts, feelings. It does not just name and list educational policies and structures or pedagogical practices. It does not do so from the perspective of the teacher on the one hand, or of the student on the other, but from the totality of the comunidad. It brings the reader into the experience holistically. For example, it does not just describe how field trips connect to the curriculum. It takes us in actual paseos, and allows us to live them through the experience of teachers, students, and community members. It does not tell us about the difficulties of remote teaching and learning during COVID. It brings us into the life of a father, struggling with his children. It does not name Family Friday as a useful structure to support families. It lets us see it and feel its effects through the actions of family members. It lets us as readers into a home to experience the home visits that staff members conduct prior to students enrolling in kindergarten.

In describing actual lessons, student voices are heard in classrooms: 'Yo tengo una conexión,' says a student during a literacy lesson. But that connection is not simply a curricular one; it is a lived one, fueled by the students' agency in this comunidad. For example, parent-teacher conferences are replaced by student-led conferences, where children show parents pieces of their own work, thus 'placing each child at the center of their learning' (p. 95). We see, hear and feel children, parents and teachers. A 2nd-grader expresses his pride in showing his work to his parents during the student-led conference – 'At first I was nervous', but then 'I felt proud'. His father shares how pleased he was to hear his child. This process not only shows the father what it is the child is learning, but also, as the father says, to 'vivir la experiencia' (p. 95).

For me, this is what makes this book so special to live the experiencia of a committed community of educators, family members, activists, students, university partners, as they make the road en conexión. The book takes us into the lives, languaging, experiences and vivencias of a community trying to shape a world of orgullo (pride) y activismo bilingüe for all. In so doing, the book paves the way for other comunidades wishing to forge new caminos to justly educate racialized bilingual children. It engages us in not only imagining, but in living a vision of other realities. Stepping into this space, we are liberated from the confinement of educational failure assigned to racialized bilingual communities. This book shows us the radical potential of a dual language bilingual school en conexión with community as it makes camino al andar.

References

Grosfoguel, R. (2007) The epistemic decolonial turn: Beyond political-economy paradigms. *Cultural studies* 21 (2–3), 211–223.

Mignolo, W.D. (2020) The logic of the in-visible: Decolonial reflections on the change of epoch. *Theory, Culture & Society* 37 (7–8), 205–218.

Dos Puentes Elementary: An Introduction

Tatyana Kleyn and Victoria Hunt

Dos Puentes Co-Founder and Founding Principal

Image I.1 The Dos Puentes Elementary School building in Washington Heights. Photo by Gerardo Romo

Dos Puentes Elementary School was founded in 2013 as a New York City Public School, a community school in the upper Manhattan neighborhood of Washington Heights. Every student who walks through its doors becomes part of its dual language bilingual program *en español* and English from kindergarten through 5th grade. As the school prepares to celebrate its 10th anniversary, its founders, the editors of this volume – Professor Tatyana Kleyn, Principal Victoria Hunt, Assistant Principal Alcira Jaar, *Maestra* Rebeca Madrigal and Parent Coordinator Consuelo Villegas – wanted to bring together the school's *comunidad* to reflect on the formation and development of Dos Puentes.

Dos Puentes (translated as 'Two Bridges') is a fully bilingual school where all students – regardless of home language(s), place of birth, (dis) ability and additional social and human differences – are viewed as fully capable and deserving of becoming bilingual and biliterate, and of developing critical consciousness of their community and world as a human and educational right (Cervantes-Soon *et al.*, 2017). Within Dos Puentes, everyone is part of an enriching program that integrates students who come from Spanish/English/bilingual homes, as well as those who speak Arabic, Haitian Creole, Korean and Russian (among other languages). There are no barriers to entry such as academic assessments, teacher recommendations, or other gatekeeping mechanisms that ban emergent bilingual students with identified disabilities from taking part in a program where both their (dis)abilities and language learning are addressed (Cioè-Peña, 2021).

The student body continues to reflect the local community, which is mostly made up of those who come from Latinx, immigrant and Spanish-speaking homes. There are also students who come from upper/middle-class white, Black, and Asian English-speaking families, who contribute to the school's heterogeneity. This brings with it positive aspects of integration where students who come from different racial, ethnic, cultural, socioeconomic and linguistic backgrounds can learn about each other in their daily classroom experiences rather than from a distance (via literature, film, etc.). The school's dual language bilingual program is a model intended to push back against oppressive educational structures for Latinx students. While the setup for positive integration is there, having a dual language bilingual program does not make decentering whiteness a given. Research has shown that, 'US schooling has white normativity at its core and thus schooling defaults to providing an inequitable education to students from marginalized groups, even with efforts like bilingual education that intend to make schooling more just' (Chávez-Moreno, 2019: 103). This means that even when bilingual education programs – like Dos Puentes – are made up of a majority of Latinx students and teachers, the foundation of white supremacy still creates the conditions for unequal balances of power and entitlement that reinforce racial hierarchies (Spring, 2016). Therefore, while having diverse students together in a school learning bilingually is important, it does not ensure they will all benefit in the same way without an eye toward equity and decentering whiteness.

While the school is in a neighborhood where Dominicans have been the majority for decades, the neighborhood is experiencing gentrification that permeates into its schools. The gentrification of dual language programs across the country has brought to light issues of power, access, and resource hoarding that are certainly not absent from Dos Puentes Elementary (Delavan *et al.*, 2021). The school's staff, faculty and administration have remained focused on the civil rights movement that serves as the root of US bilingual education policies as they work to center the families who are most vulnerable in our society and the school (Flores & García, 2017). This is done by paying attention to issues of race and racism, working toward linguistic equity in and out of the classroom, ensuring that leadership roles are available to Spanish-speaking and immigrant family members and focusing on equity – rather than equality – in terms of the needs and strengths of students and families. This work is undertaken with the goal of making these issues visible to the larger community, in order to counter how bilingual programs often remain centered on white and middle-class values and norms (Hadi-Tabassum, 2006).

This book offers case studies and longitudinal reflections from those who make up the school community. It is geared toward educators currently working in bilingual schools or programs, as well as those aspiring to be part of such a school to understand all that goes into developing and sustaining a bilingual school. Most of the text is written in English so that educators of all language backgrounds can access the content and make connections to bilingual programs in a variety of languages. However, *el español* is used throughout the chapters to reflect the bilingual approach of the Dos Puentes school, families and educators. The editors italicize Spanish words so that they stand out to readers who may not recognize them. The inclusion of Spanish in italics also allows for the book to reflect how languages are both integrated and separated in dual language bilingual programs. Names in Spanish and other languages are not italicized.

Decolonizing Research

Lessons from a Dual Language Bilingual School tells the story of the growth, successes and struggles of Dos Puentes directly from those who have made it their educational home. And just as the school does, the book brings to the forefront the varied voices and experiences of the whole community. In this way, the book works to decolonize research, which is often told through the lens of researchers, making the perspectives of educators and families tangential through quotes or text boxes. The reality is that some researchers have limited experience in the communities, schools and classrooms about which they write. As Ofelia García stated in the foreword, our approach to decolonizing educational research aims to center the voices of those often silenced, or left on the periphery, in research through an intentional approach that create more equal power structures among and between educators, families and researchers by forefronting the former. Therefore, the lessons of *una década de* Dos Puentes will be told directly by school community members, including the teachers, families, administrators and their university and community partners. The chapters also include student perspectives and work. Then, to contextualize the key ideas shared by the Dos Puentes community, researchers with expertise in the topic and/or with a connection to Dos Puentes as university partners, student teacher supervisors, professional developers, or collaborators offer a short commentary to highlight the connections between the Dos Puentes cases and the literature, and to discuss implications and next steps for the field of bilingual education.

There exists a range of powerful books about how to create bilingual programs (Freeman *et al.*, 2022; Hamayan *et al.*, 2013; Lindholm-Leary, 2001; Romero-Johnson, 2012; Soltero, 2016), understand the raciolinguistic experiences of bilingual students and families (Flores *et al.*, 2020; Rosa 2019), develop a translanguaging stance and build it into the pedagogy (García & Kleyn, 2016; García *et al.*, 2017; Sanchéz & García, 2022), teach towards biliteracy (Escamilla *et al.*, 2014; Espinosa & Ascenzi-Moreno, 2021; Pérez & Torres-Guzmán, 2001) and address issues of power and culturally sustaining practices (Dorner *et al.*, 2023; España & Herrera, 2020). This book aims to show how these areas come together within one bilingual school, and to do that from the voices of those who have been the most closely connected to Dos Puentes, some since its formation. The aim of the book is not just to share the trajectory and experiences of this singular and unique school, but to allow for prospective and current educators and leaders to think through how the work of Dos Puentes can connect to their own settings, and how they can inform and improve their context as well.

The Road to Dos Puentes Elementary: A Principal's Journey

Experience and opportunity

'Have you ever thought about starting a school?' the email read. It was the summer of 2012. These were the years of New York City (NYC) Mayor Bloomberg. Upon gaining mayoral control of the public schools, Mayor Mike Bloomberg felt that longtime 'failing' schools – meaning those with low standardized test scores – should be closed and reopened with a new administration, new staff and a new focus. While I (Victoria) was unsure about the legitimacy of this philosophy, the idea of starting a fully bilingual school that would use language as an asset, build from educators with many collective decades of teaching experience in bilingual settings and collaborate with like-minded educators in a city rich in resources, cultures and opportunities, was more than intriguing. 'Our whole school will support full bilingualism in Spanish and English. We will treat parents as partners. We will use inquiry and hands-on learning to support deep thinking and language development. And we will partner with Teachers College, Columbia University and The City College of New York to ensure current teachers continue to deepen their craft as they also prepare future bilingual teachers', read the proposal submitted. After many pitches, interviews and panel presentations, the proposal was accepted, and the school was born.

I was the person who received the email six months prior and wrote the initial proposal. I had not grown up bilingual. After graduating from college, I moved to Chimbote, Perú to do volunteer work and learned Spanish through immersion in a new culture and community where no one spoke English. I worked in a school with very limited resources and created a summer program for children when school was on break. As I struggled in Spanish and made many mistakes, the education I brought with me was never questioned. My privilege as a white, English-speaking US citizen certainly contributed to the assumption that I was educated. Over time, I could share and build from my knowledge base as I learned to communicate in Spanish. A few years later, I was given the opportunity to teach in Houston, Texas in a transitional bilingual program. I told the representative from the district that my Spanish was not great. I could speak but my Spanish literacy was lacking. The person hiring replied, 'It's okay, you don't really need to teach much Spanish, as the goal of our program is to teach children English – the Spanish doesn't matter much'. How could this be? These children's Spanish was rich and beautiful. They brought with them so much knowledge and confidence in their language. Why would anyone not want to build from that? As Latinx children they were not afforded the privileges offered to me in Chimbote.

My experience in Perú and Houston was what led me to pursue a master's and then a doctorate in bilingual education and leadership. I learned about the power of building on students' home language and culture, as well as the power of full bilingualism and biliteracy (Nieto, 2002). At Teachers College (TC), Columbia University, I was introduced to dual language bilingual education as an approach to supporting students to continue to develop their home language as they acquire a new language. In a dual language model, children learn to use their home language to build on or develop literacy and other academic skills as they develop these same skills in an additional language. At Dos Puentes our dual language program combines children from different linguistic and cultural backgrounds to support children's learning from each other as they serve as language models (Torres-Guzmán, 2002). By systematically alternating languages in the classroom, the power dynamic between linguistic groups can be shared. On any given day, some children are leaders due to their language skills and the language of the day. Then, the following day, the other group are leaders as the language switches. But even within these structures there is space for linguistic flexibility and freedom via translanguaging (García *et al.*, 2017, see Chapter 2). I saw the power of this model prior to starting Dos Puentes through my experience as a dual language bilingual teacher for ten years and an assistant principal for six years in schools that housed a dual language program as a strand within the larger school.

The proposal for a brand new fully bilingual school was built not only from my experiences as an ever-developing bilingual educator, but also as a person who knows that there is so much to be gained through collaboration. My teaching experiences over the past 20 years were exponentially deepened by working with others. Initially, I collaborated with Tatyana Kleyn and Alcira Jaar, two longtime colleagues, through various stages of the new school proposal. Tatyana brought research and her deep connections as a professor of bilingual education at The City College of New York, CUNY. We had studied for our doctorates together at TC where we were both mentored by Professor María Torres-Guzmán. Alcira brought multiple years of teaching and curriculum knowledge and dual language pedagogy. We had taught together in two different NYC public schools, one with a bilingual strand, and we also shared similar training at TC. Once the proposal for the school was approved, we quickly reached out to Consuelo Villegas, a person with many experiences working with families and schools who was very sensitive to the challenges of migration and raising children as an immigrant. We also reached out to Rebeca Madrigal, a committed and award-winning bilingual teacher with deep roots in supporting Spanish development and teaching practices that center families in their children's education. Rebeca was also a teaching colleague who shared the same training from TC. This rounded out the five co-founders whose collective expertise, experience and passion laid the foundation for Dos Puentes.

Image I.2 The five co-founders at the Dos Puentes 10th Anniversary Gala. From left to right: Rebeca Madrigal, Victoria Hunt, Consuelo Villegas, Alcira Jaar and Tatyana Kleyn

In December 2012, our school was approved by the New York City Public Schools, and a building had been promised. However, there was no location, no staff, no budget, no furniture, no curriculum and no name for a school that was supposed to start in August 2013. Over the next four months, I attended the New School Institute with 39 other future principals who were chosen to open new public schools throughout the New York City school system. We learned a lot about budgets, unions and enrollments. We were taught leadership skills, personnel management, and teacher observation tools. We were also taught how to 'brand' our future schools, including marketing tools and how to compete with the many, many charter schools that were opening during the Bloomberg mayoral administration. While I had been an assistant principal of an elementary school for six years, and had completed my doctorate on leadership in dual language bilingual settings, opening up a new school was an exercise in building each individual piece from the ground up, within a context of school competition.

Image I.3 Principal Victoria Hunt explaining the school's values to prospective families. Photo by Gerardo Romo

By March 2013 we were given a location to house our new school. We would be a zoned community kindergarten-to-5th-grade elementary school, and co-located, meaning we would share a building with another long-existing elementary school. A zoned school meant our first priority was to serve the children in the surrounding blocks of the neighborhood. Our building was a 100-plus-year-old structure in Washington Heights, a vibrant neighborhood in northern Manhattan that consists of many families with Latinx roots. The location of the school was to be in the NYC Public Schools' District 6, which has among the highest number of students in the city labeled as 'English Language Learners' (ELLs). As a new dual language school, we were in a position to build from the strong cultural and linguistic roots of the community. Additionally, Alcira had grown up a few blocks away from the school and had deep ties to the neighborhood. All five initial members were very excited (and relieved) about our geographic placement.

Building a bilingual school

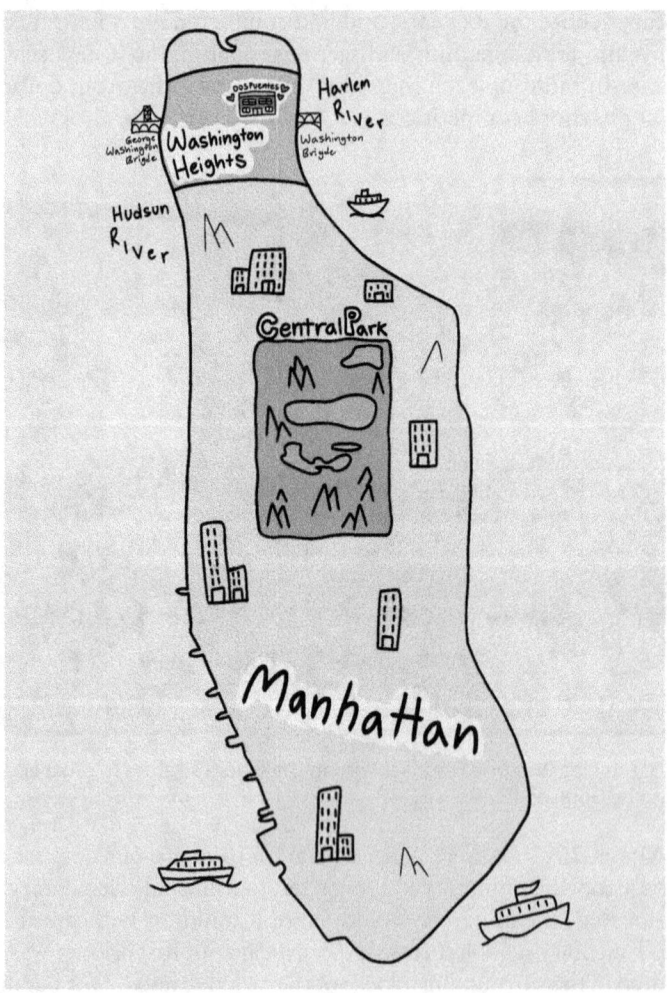

Image I.4 A map of Manhattan that shows the location of Dos Puentes Elementary School and its nearby bridges. Map created by Aliana Ellington

Now that we were officially a NYC Public School, we needed to create a name. On a Sunday morning in March 2013, I, as the future principal, sat with Alcira and Tatyana in a Starbucks three blocks from the future school site. We wanted a name that would embrace the multicultural community, and pay tribute to both Spanish and English. We also hoped to recognize the location of Washington Heights, and the potential strength and opportunities of an education that supports two languages. Geographically, the school sits between the Washington Bridge connecting upper Manhattan to the Bronx across the East River, and the George Washington Bridge crossing the Hudson River to connect Manhattan to New Jersey. Alcira nailed it when she suggested, 'Dos Puentes Elementary!'. Then, we added 'Bridges between languages, cultures and worlds'. From that fateful moment Dos Puentes Elementary became our name. Soon after, we chose a logo to represent our bridges *entre idiomas, culturas y mundos*.

Image I.5 The Dos Puentes Elementary logo, which can be seen in color on the book cover, includes the bilingual name of the school in red, and a representation of the *dos puentes* or two bridges in blue and green. These colors represent flags connected to the origins of many of the school's immigrant families. The red and blue pay tribute to the students of Dominican heritage, and the red and green pay tribute to the students of Mexican heritage.

Over the next five months, our team of five chose curricula, hired and trained staff and bought furniture and supplies. We also had to recruit students. Flyers about our new school were posted in apartment buildings, hair salons, churches, restaurants and laundromats. We visited street fairs and local preschools. On weekends, we set up a table in front of our building to recruit families. Over time, we registered enough brave families to open our doors to our first group of children: three classes of bilingual dual language kindergarten students. Two of the classes were general education dual language classes and the third was a dual language integrated co-teaching class (ICT). The ICT structure supports up to 40% of students in the class with an Individualized Education Plan (IEP), considered full-time special education students, alongside 60% of general education students. We were committed to being an inclusive community that embraces the different ways children learn and build from their individual strengths. Over the next five years we grew the school one grade level per year to have 18 classes, with three classrooms per grade from kindergarten to 5th grade. We graduated our first class in June 2019, and now in our tenth year as a school (2023), Dos Puentes serves 437 students, all through a Spanish-English dual language bilingual model.

I am very proud to be the founding principal of Dos Puentes, but I am more proud of the collective efforts of all who have contributed along the way, and of our continued ability to transform.

Our Students, Families and Washington Heights Community

Three fourths of our student body are from a Latinx background. Depending on the year, 22 to 40% of these students are designated as 'English Learners Learners' and the overwhelming majority speak Spanish as their home language. Twenty percent of our students identify as white or mixed race and speak English in their homes. The remaining 5% of students identify as African American or Asian and generally speak English in their homes, though we have had students who speak Russian, Portuguese, Arabic, Italian, French, Haitian Creole, Korean, Hebrew and other languages. The demographics of our neighborhood make Spanish an important and integral part of all our lives. When one walks down the street in front of our school, Spanish is often seen and heard in the store displays, campaign posters, street domino games and music escaping from apartment windows. Interactions with many street vendors and the corner *bodega* are often exclusively in Spanish, which is a vibrant and rich part of our surrounding community. It is also important to note that many of our bilingual students might be dominant in English even though they live in bilingual homes where other languages, mostly Spanish, are often spoken.

The multilingualism and multiculturalism of our school and surrounding community is something we view as a source of strength and pride. However, we are also aware of the imbalance of power that our families face in society, and subsequently in our school. The ripples of gentrification penetrate our interactions, and allow some family members a sense of privilege while others feel silenced, especially when they are Spanish speakers, in spite of being part of a bilingual school. There are tensions that arise based on differences in culture and values that require difficult conversations and deep listening, especially for those who are accustomed to having the loudest voices. These realities are not only something we aim to remain aware of, but to address explicitly with students and families. Thereby we can push back against the ways that 'bilingual education programs often predominantly serve the interests of the white English-speaking majority' (Chávez-Moreno, 2019: 107).

Our Educators

The vast majority of the Dos Puentes faculty are bilingual, and they hold bilingual teaching certification (what New York State calls a bilingual extension). Our staff is reflective of our students; about three fourths identify as Latinx, a fifth identify as white and the remainder are African American. While English can easily become the language of dominance, we strive to deepen Spanish by holding some professional development in Spanish, and we use Spanish within our community and with the whole student body. When working with families, we try to say everything in Spanish first, and then follow up with translation into English in order to prioritize the value of Spanish. The recent influx of immigrants, refugees and asylum seekers from Venezuela and Central America being welcomed into New York City has increased our overall student population, with many more new immigrant Spanish speakers than in the past. As an established dual language bilingual school, we are ready to support these newly arrived children and their families.

The Dual Language Bilingual Approach

The implementation of the dual language bilingual program at Dos Puentes primarily follows a 50/50 model of Spanish and English. In general, we alternate languages each day, one day in Spanish and the following day in English. Across grades this is implemented with slight modifications. In kindergarten and all ICT classes, the children stay in the same room and the teachers switch languages day to day. Monday and Wednesday are in Spanish; Tuesday and Thursday are in English. In kindergarten, the model begins with a 60/40 distribution where Friday is fully in Spanish to develop a strong base for our youngest students. This helps the Spanish-dominant students build from their base with early literacy skills being introduced in Spanish, while the more English-dominant students benefit from a strong consistent foundation in Spanish. By contrast, the ICT classrooms from 1st through 5th grade split Friday with Spanish in the morning and English in the afternoon to maintain the 50/50 model. In the non-ICT general education classes, students follow the side-by-side 50/50 model. Within the side-by-side model, a child has two teachers, one who teaches in one language and the other who teaches the second language in two separate classrooms (Freeman *et al.*, 2022). The children alternate teachers and classrooms to receive instruction bilingually across both languages.

At Dos Puentes, in our two general education classes in 1st through 4th grade, one teacher teaches in Spanish and the other teaches in English. The students switch between the Spanish and English component classes every other day. The teachers work as a team to always extend the content across the languages, rather than repeat it. The 5th grade general education students also have two teachers, but they divide the instruction by content and both alternate languages day by day. One 5th grade general education teacher teaches language arts, and the other teaches math and social studies through inquiry. On Monday, Wednesday and half of

Friday, they both provide instruction in Spanish, and then Tuesday, Thursday and half of Fridays they both teach in English (see Table I.1). All children subsequently have two teachers either in one classroom (kindergarten and all ICT) or two teachers across two classrooms. While there are different ways that we implement the language balance within the school, the goal is always to ensure both languages are used to promote full bilingualism and biliteracy.

Table I.1 Language distribution across grade levels in ICT and general education classes. Created by Sabrina Poms

Kindergarten General Education & ICT				
Self-Contained Bilingual Model (60/40)				
Students stay in one classroom with the same teacher(s) and alternate languages daily				
Monday	Tuesday	Wednesday	Thursday	Friday
el español	English	el español	English	el español

1st Grade – 5th Grade ICT				
Self-Contained Bilingual Model (50/50)				
Students stay in one classroom with the same teachers and alternate languages daily				
Monday	Tuesday	Wednesday	Thursday	Friday *Alternates weekly
el español	English	el español	English	el español / English

1st Grade – 4th Grade General Education									
Side by Side Bilingual Model (50/50)									
Students alternate between the Spanish and English component classrooms across a 2 week cycle									
	MON	TUE	WED	THU	FRI	MON	TUE	WED	THU	FRI
Class 101	el componente de español	English Component	el componente de español	English Component	el componente de español	English Component	el componente de español	English Component	el componente de español	English Component
Class 102	English Component	el componente de español	English Component	el componente de español	English Component	el componente de español	English Component	el componente de español	English Component	el componente de español

5th Grade General Education									
Departmentalized Bilingual Model (50/50)									
Students rotate mid-day between departments and alternate languages daily									
	Monday		Tuesday		Wednesday		Thursday		Friday	
	AM	PM	AM	PM	AM	PM	AM	PM	AM	PM
Class 501	Literacy el español	Math el español	Math English	Literacy English	Literacy el español	Math el español	Math English	Literacy English	Literacy el español	Math English
Class 502	Math el español	Literacy el español	Literacy English	Math English	Math el español	Literacy el español	Literacy English	Math English	Math el español	Literacy English

Dos Puentes has been intentional in identifying out-of-classroom teachers who are bilingual, so that dance and art can be taught completely in Spanish. Music is mostly in English because we first began working with Ms Lorene, our music teacher, through a community partnership that evolved into a full-time position. While Ms Lorene is not fluent in Spanish, she sings in Spanish and has learned a lot of Spanish over the past eight years that she has worked at the school. Our two science teachers alternate units in Spanish and English. Intervention and service providers such as speech and occupational therapy are done in the language(s) designated on students' IEPs. The ability for students to get these services in the language of need is critical in supporting the goals of our school as well as student needs. As we hire staff and create programs, bilingualism, language support and language planning are an integral part of our decision making.

Because we have students and staff with diverse backgrounds and countries of origin, we have the opportunity to explore, learn from and celebrate these linguistic and cultural differences. The variation in Spanish across different regions and countries is acknowledged and explored within the classroom, with each difference being seen as unique rather than correct or incorrect. While many of our faculty and students have ties to the Dominican Republic, many others are from Mexico, Honduras, Colombia, Puerto Rico, Venezuela, El Salvador, Peru, Argentina, Spain and more, as well as the United States and specifically New York City. Each person brings their own nuances to Spanish and from that we all exponentially grow.

The Four Dos Puentes Pillars

When all the founders of the school came together, we identified four areas that would anchor the vision of the school to keep everyone united and working toward the same goals.

Eventually, these areas became the pillars of the school's philosophy. First, we shared a common commitment to value the multilingualism and multiculturalism of the school community. We also committed to centering the experiences, knowledge and strength of families while supporting the bridge between home and school. Additionally, we agreed that learning had to be active, based on inquiry and exploration. This allows children to make connections and build from their different strengths, and prepares them to solve problems in their classrooms and beyond. Lastly, we were committed to building two-way partnerships to support and deepen the work of the school. These partnerships started with local universities to ensure staff continued growing and learning as we supported future bilingual educators. And it is these four commitments that became our four Dos Puentes pillars:

(1) *bilingüismo, biliteracidad y multiculturalismo*,
(2) *las familias son* partners, leaders and advocates,
(3) *investigaciones* and hands-on learning, and
(4) partnerships with universities, organizations *y la comunidad*.

These pillars are all written to emphasize *el bilingüismo*, woven throughout. They serve to unite us in working together to provide the foundation of what we do to support one another: students, teachers, staff, families, partners and the community. We regularly reflect upon and make changes to our practices, but we do so while maintaining our commitment to these overarching pillars.

While we are far from a perfect school, our four pillars ensure we remain committed to building from the strength of bilingualism and multiculturalism, and from our families, as well as from inquiry-based learning and partnerships.

Book Organization

This book will describe the challenges, successes and lessons that have been part of starting and growing a bilingual school for a decade. This is done through taking readers into the planning sessions, lessons, trips and school-wide activities that make up the Dos Puentes ecosystem. The cases are often enriched by photographs that feature the people, community and artifacts from the school. While the book is rich in stories, it is not a 'how-to' guide that outlines the steps to starting a (dual language) bilingual program or school. Nor do we provide an overview of central theories and pedagogies, although references in the commentary that follows each chapter can provide that information. Instead, we show readers the inside story of a bilingual school that is centered on four pillars that have been constant since the school was founded: *bilingüismo, biliteracidad y multiculturalismo, las familias son* partners, leaders and advocates, *investigaciones* and hands-on learning, and partnerships with universities, organizations *y la comunidad*.

Each section of the book begins with an introduction of each pillar and includes four to six short chapters by Dos Puentes community authors. The Dos Puentes authors employ a composite-case approach that allows them to highlight a topic by showing rather than telling, and integrating a range of key moments, experiences, years, grades and anecdotes that take us into the school (Willis, 2019). Then, each chapter is followed by a researcher's commentary.

This book was written *en comunidad* to celebrate, reflect upon and share the decade-long project of Dos Puentes Elementary. It features the perspectives and voices of families, educators and students who make up the school's members and serve as its experts. The process of bringing this book to publication was aligned with the way the school functions, through a shared leadership approach that permeates the ethos of the community. In other words, the book is not just *about* Dos Puentes, but it *is* Dos Puentes, and more specifically those who are at the heart of it. As you make your way from chapter to chapter you will hear directly from a bilingual special education teacher who has been at the school since it started, an immigrant Ecuadorian mother who herself was never able to earn a college degree but has much to teach educators, a teacher who started out at Dos Puentes as a student teacher and a father whose child graduated during the pandemic. These authors, and many more, aim to take readers inside the classroom walls as well as outside the school doors, to show how bilingual theories and pedagogies are enacted when they center the bilingual students, families and community. We hope that readers will draw from these cases, not for replication, but for consideration and comparisons with their own schools and settings.

Lastly, while this book addresses the four pillars of Dos Puentes, it in no way covers everything that happens within the school. We would need a few more books to address all the inner workings and activities of Dos Puentes, or any other school for that matter. However, we hope to share here the heart of what makes Dos Puentes unique, and to help readers think about the core principles that will make their own schools and programs thrive for decades to come.

References

Cervantes-Soon, C.G., Dorner, L., Palmer, D., Heiman, D., Schwerdtfeger, R. and Choi, J. (2017) Combating inequalities in two-way language immersion programs: Toward critical consciousness in bilingual education spaces. *Review of Research in Education* 41 (1), 403–427.

Chávez-Moreno, L.C. (2019) Researching Latinxs, racism, and white supremacy in bilingual education: A literature review. *Critical Inquiry in Language Studies* 17 (2), 101–120.

Cioè-Peña, M. (2021) *(M)othering Labeled Children: Bilingualism and Disability in the Lives of Latinx Mothers*. Multilingual Matters.

Delavan, G., Freire, J. and Menken, K. (eds) (2021) Thematic issue: Gentrification of bilingual, immersion and dual language education. *Language Policy* 20 (3).

Dorner, L., Palmer, D., Cervantes-Soon, C., Crawford, E. and Heiman, D. (eds) (2023) *Critical Consciousness in Dual Language Bilingual Education: Case Studies on Policies and Practice*. Routledge.

Escamilla, K., Hopewell, S., Butvilofsky, S., Sparrow, W., Soltero-González, L., Ruiz-Figueroa, O. and Escamilla, M. (2014) *Biliteracy From the Start: Literacy Squared in Action*. Caslon Publishing.

España, C. and Herrera, L.Y. (2020) *En Comunidad: Lessons for Centering the Voices and Experiences of Bilingual Latinx Students*. Heinemann.

Espinosa, C.M. and Ascenzi-Moreno, L. (2021) *Rooted in Strength: Using Translanguaging to Grow Multilingual Readers and Writers*. Scholastic.

Flores, N. and García, O. (2017) A critical review of bilingual education in the United States: From basements and pride to boutiques and profit. *Annual Review of Applied Linguistics* 37, 14–29.

Flores, N., Tseng, A. and Subtirelu, N. (eds) (2020) *Bilingualism for All?: Raciolinguistic Perspectives on Dual Language Education in the United States*. Multilingual Matters.

Freeman, Y.S., Freeman, D.E. and Mercuri, S. (2022) *Dual Language Essentials for Teachers and Administrators* (2nd edn). Heinemann.

García, O. and Kleyn, T. (2016) *Translanguaging with multilingual students: Learning From Classroom Moments*. Routledge.

García, O., Johnson, S.I., Seltzer, K. and Valdés, G. (2017) *The Translanguaging Classroom: Leveraging Student Bilingualism for Learning*. Caslon.

Hadi-Tabassum, S. (2006) *Language, Space and Power: A Critical Look at Bilingual Education*. Multilingual Matters.

Hamayan, E.V., Genesee, F. and Cloud, N. (2013) *Dual Language Instruction From A to Z: Practical Guidance for Teachers and Administrators*. Heinemann.

Lindholm-Leary, K.J. (2001) *Dual Language Education*. Multilingual Matters.

Nieto, S. (2002) *Languages, Culture, and Teaching: Critical Perspectives for a New Century*. Lawrence Erlbaum Associates, Publishers.

Pérez, B. and Torres-Guzmán, M.E. (2001) *Learning in 2 Worlds: An Integrated Spanish/English Biliteracy Approach* (3rd edn). Prentice Hall.

Romero-Johnson, S. (2012) *Implementing Dual Language Immersion Strand Programs: Challenges and Opportunities for School Leaders*. Lambert Academic Publishing.

Rosa, J. (2019) *Looking Like a Language, Sounding Like a Race: Raciolinguistic Ideologies and the Studies of Latinidad*. Oxford University Press.

Sánchez, M.T. and García, O. (eds) (2022) *Transformative Translanguaging Espacios: Latinx Students and their Teachers Rompiendo Fronteras sin Miedo*. Multilingual Matters.

Soltero, S.W. (2016) *Dual Language Education*. Heinemann.

Spring, J. (2016) *Deculturalization and the Struggle for Equality: A Brief History of the Education of Dominated Cultures in the United States* (8th edn). Routledge.

Torres-Guzmán, M.E. (2002) Dual language programs: Key features and results. *Directions in Language and Education* 14 (Spring). National Clearing House for Bilingual Education.

Willis R. (2019) The use of composite narratives to present interview findings. *Qualitative Research* 19 (4), 471–480. https://doi.org/10.1177/1468794118787711

Pillar 1 Introduction

Bilingüismo, Biliteracidad y Multiculturalismo

Rebeca Madrigal

Founding Dos Puentes Teacher

As one enters the Dos Puentes main office they are greeted with a hearty *buenos dias* from our parent coordinator Consuelo and our secretary Milly. Families sense the *confianza* that Spanish is welcomed in our school, and as an extension, our families are as well. *Bilingüismo, biliteracidad y multiculturalismo* are the heart of Dos Puentes Elementary School. From the inception, our mission has been to support students' bilingualism and biliteracy, whether they come from monolingual or multilingual homes. Bilingualism and biliteracy are leveraged through the powerful cultural and linguistic backgrounds that each family brings to make our school diverse. Care and focus are given to hiring staff, selecting and then adapting curriculum and identifying resources to provide high-quality instruction that builds the foundation for bilingual and biliterate development and multicultural perspectives and understandings.

This Pillar 1 introduction outlines the different elements that contributed to the Dos Puentes bilingual and biliteracy program, which was built around students and families, rather than a prescribed model. Located in the heart of Washington Heights, the majority of our students are from Latinx families. Many come from immigrant-origin families in Latin America and others are from the US. Some families are multilingual, whereas others are monolingual in Spanish or English. Our Spanish-speaking families want their children to learn how to read and write in their home language and become proficient communicators, readers and writers in both Spanish and English. Our English-speaking families aim for their children to become bilingual and biliterate to connect to their culture or to a new cultural group, as they prepare to be part of the local community as well as a globalized world. However, there are additional nuances that contribute to reasons families from different linguistic, cultural, racial and ethnic groups seek out bilingual programs. For Latinx Spanish-speaking families there is often a focus on their children connecting with their roots and communicating with family members. Thus, the bilingual program serves as a way for students to develop identities that transcend linguistic and cultural boundaries. Bilingual programs provide a context for students to bring their full selves and their families into the teaching and learning process by allowing them to celebrate the varied facets of their languages and cultures. Despite the best intentions of bilingual programs that emphasize the additional language, English holds its power and subsequently, non-English speakers can feel intimidated and/or excluded. For white English-speaking families, a bilingual program can be a way to expand their children's horizons. However, as they learn Spanish and participate in cultural activities connected to the language, learning Spanish may become more of a commodity for long-term economic benefit than a way to truly engage in two-way learning and co-constructing knowledge (Flores, 2017). There is also the danger that families bring a white savior complex into bilingual programs so that they are more focused on fixing things that don't align with their values than being part of a multilingual and multicultural school where hierarchies are challenged and broken down in the process of community building. Nevertheless, dual language programs provide the context to challenge these imbalances where both populations are represented in the school and support one another's language learning. For example, English-speaking students need Spanish speakers as a model and vice versa. Families of different linguistic, cultural and socio economic backgrounds are able to interact with each other to create an awareness of the uniqueness of one another when there exists a critical consciousness of these differences that is both acknowledged and challenged.

Beyond linguistic and cultural backgrounds, we welcome families from low-income homes as well as middle-class homes. Some families have limited prior opportunities for formal education whereas others have advanced levels of education, including doctorates and medical and law degrees. There are interracial and interfaith families. Collectively, the school supports the diversity of our community by developing *bilingüismo, biliteracidad y multiculturalismo* in all our students as they build a sense of cultural pride, exploration and connections. And simultaneously, we strive to develop critical consciousness in our students as they learn languages and cultures to also consider the power, hierarchy and privileges of certain speakers to address inequalities on a local and global scale (Palmer *et al.*, 2019).

Bilingüismo, Biliteracidad y Multiculturalismo at Dos Puentes

Bilingualism

We believe that students should have the opportunity to continue developing their home language as they learn their new language. Whether the home language is Spanish, English, both or another language, it is important that each family feels they have found a home in which their language practices are valued and integrated into the school. The 50/50 Spanish/English language allocation plays a fundamental role in our school structure because it ensures students receive instruction in both languages without minimizing either. The schedule of each classroom supports this by alternating languages every other day (see the Introduction and Table I.1 for an overview of the language allocation across grades and models). The content of instruction is always extended between the two languages without repetition to ensure the whole curriculum is covered, and children do not simply wait to participate on the day of their language of dominance.

To follow our language allocation policy, teachers work in self-contained, integrated co-teaching (ICT) or side-by-side classrooms with Spanish and English organized accordingly. In the self-contained kindergarten, ICT and 5th grade classrooms (where content areas are divided among teachers), displays, charts and student work are in Spanish and in English. In kindergarten through 2nd grade, text on charts and displays is color-coded to differentiate the languages, with red for Spanish and blue for English. By the time children are in 3rd grade the color coding is less evident as children easily identify the two languages of instruction. However, the side-by-side component classes maintain print to be in the language of the class. For example, in a Spanish classroom, displays, charts, books and teachers are speaking *en español*. This is the same in the English classroom. Appropriate scaffolds and prompts are used in all classrooms to encourage students to practice their new language to build their bilingualism and biliteracy. However, since most of our students are emergent bilinguals, this is a process. Depending on where each child is in their bilingualism, the teacher gauges when to push the new language and when to allow the child to use their dominant language, even if it is not the language of the day. Over time, our teachers encourage children to communicate, read and write in both languages.

While we support a clearly defined language separation, we are cognizant that within these structures there is flexibility for translanguaging so students are anchored to their bilingual identities, have opportunities to make cross-language connections and access content that may be challenging for them (García & Li, 2015). To that end, teachers also plan for spaces where students can translanguage to leverage their bilingualism and bring in features of languages other than Spanish or English. Translanguaging pedagogy allows students to develop bi- or multilingual products, consider how and why authors translanguage and see the power of creating ideas with their full linguistic repertoire (Sánchez *et al.*, 2019).

For a strong bilingual program, it's imperative to attract strong bilingual teachers that can connect with the community. Dos Puentes has a hiring committee made up of teachers, administrators and occasionally family members. The committee asks questions based on the different components of our mission: bilingualism, collaboration, inquiry, social-emotional aspects and ways a teacher might enact community partnerships. A critical part of the hiring process is the candidate must teach a math demo lesson in Spanish to show how language learning is incorporated into content-based instruction. The demo lesson allows us to analyze the candidate's Spanish level and teaching style as a potential match for the school community. By asking all candidates to do their demo lesson in Spanish (even if they are being considered for an English component position), we send a message that we take Spanish seriously for everyone as a central feature of our school.

Even though our school is committed to the implementation of our bilingual structures, we are aware of the power of English to disrupt our mission through a focus on English via standardized testing, greater availability of resources in English and how students often shift to English in informal spaces such as lunch and recess. We also take to heart the cautionary note from Guadalupe Valdés (1997) about the dangers of prioritizing white English-speaking students who are learning Spanish and overlooking Latinx students who are doing similar work to learn a new language. This occurs due to societal forces associated with white supremacy and xenophobia that do not make space to celebrate racialized students' emerging *bilingüismo y multiculturalismo*. Thereby Spanish can serve both as 'a deficiency in one context and then as a commodity in another context' (Pimentel, 2011: 351).

Countering these forces requires extra planning and attention to promote Spanish and its speakers to connect students to their culture or a new culture, the surrounding community and the world. We prioritize Spanish during specific assemblies and give this same opportunity to our families. All presentations and meetings with families are conducted in Spanish with English translations, rather than the reverse. Our parent coordinator established a club called El Rincón Hispano solely for Spanish monolingual parents. The group meets monthly to attend different types of trips or workshops exclusively in Spanish. There are workshops to guide families to support their children in literacy and math at home with the homework. These are just some examples of ways we create spaces in which all families and students can express themselves in a safe and comfortable environment where Spanish and its speakers are central and vital to our bilingual school community.

Biliteracy

When Dos Puentes started we had a small, but passionate and dedicated staff. What we lacked was a developed bilingual curriculum across content areas with accompanying classroom resources. At that time, the

New York City Public Schools adopted new literacy and math curricula based on the Common Core Standards. District administrators urged us to use the free basal literacy curriculum they were offering. We quickly discovered the reading levels were not appropriate for kindergartners, the materials were primarily in English and the scope and sequence were not compatible with a dual language context. The curriculum required written responses to texts but did not support young children to use their voices to write about their experiences, noticings or opinions. Further, the materials were not culturally responsive to our predominantly Latinx and multiracial students, nor reflective of our neighborhood. The NYC Public Schools curriculum became a major challenge for supporting our students both academically and linguistically. Teachers worked hard to align the prescribed programs to our bilingual students and setting, but quickly realized that these approaches were in many ways in opposition to our vision. As a result, our students were disengaged and our teachers had limited room for innovation or to put their professional bilingual training into practice.

Our short-lived experience with a top-down literacy curriculum revealed why it was crucial for us to plan and establish a biliteracy program from the ground up. Top-down literacy approaches assume that biliteracy is the sum of literacy in two languages or that literacy should occur in one language before it does in the other (Pérez, 2003). Instead, biliteracy is the dynamic process of learning to read as a bilingual person and it involves translanguaging and borrowing literacy knowledge from both languages in learning to read. We wanted a program that would support English language learners, Spanish language learners and bilingual students to develop academic skills as they became bilingual and biliterate. We wanted a curriculum that would build from children's strengths and meet their various reading levels in Spanish or English. We wanted children to choose Spanish, English and bilingual books that appealed to their interests as well as supported early literacy skills and independence. By the middle of the first year, the classroom teachers and principal decided to establish a child-centered biliteracy approach that would allow students to be inquisitive leaders and advocates for their learning.

We shifted to a balanced literacy approach that is pedagogically inclusive of a range of strategies. Namely, it's grounded in reading and writing workshops that include word study and phonics, read-alouds, shared reading, independent reading, guided reading, shared writing, independent writing and small group support (Chen & Mora-Flores, 2006). We adapted this approach to *el español*-English biliteracy within our school to draw from students' experiences and provide them space to build from their personal strengths, both linguistically and academically. Escamilla *et al.* (2014) refer to a holistic approach to biliteracy as 'concerned with complete systems rather than their analysis, treatment, or dissection into parts' and where instruction 'includes oracy, reading, writing and metalanguage' (2014: 7). Further, this approach allowed children to develop along an integrated language continuum, meaning the progression would differ depending on the students and their language and literacy backgrounds.

By following a balanced biliteracy approach students had multiple opportunities for language modeling and teachers embedded various strategies and structures to support vocabulary and context across languages. For example, when students were considering character traits in a read-aloud in Spanish, a book like *Sorpresa de Navidad para Chabelita* by Argentina Palacios could be used. Then, the same character traits are deepened and expanded in English when the class reads a book such as *Peter's Chair* by Ezra Jack Keats. Aligning books across languages to focus on a theme also helps to develop concepts and vocabulary across languages.

To support our balanced biliteracy approach we partnered with the Teachers College Reading and Writing Project (TCRWP). Although we could not find a curriculum that was written to support two languages simultaneously, we felt the program built on our prior experience and training, allowed us to benefit from the time we invested into translating and adapting resources for our population and aligned with our stance that balanced literacy was a viable approach to support students in becoming biliterate. TCRWP curriculum units provide multiple opportunities for children to read books of interest, as their curriculum does not prescribe specific texts for all students. The units themselves were neither written in Spanish nor were there many Spanish book titles. On a larger scale, our administration and teachers were familiar with this approach and clear on the in-house planning required to teach literacy in Spanish as part of a bilingual program. When a school joins the TCRWP, program staff developers are assigned to work with teachers in the school to support instruction through modeling lessons, considering data and making adjustments to support the school (see Chapter 19 on FACIL). While our staff developers are not bilingual, they worked closely with us during professional development days throughout the year to develop our units in Spanish as well as adapt the English instruction to fit within the dual language structures.

The realignment of the Teachers College Reading and Writing Project (TCRWP) curriculum has taken years to ensure consistency in both Spanish and English. Adjustments included aligning terminology in Spanish. For example, a 'student checklist' is used for each unit to help students address the standards to revise their writing. In Spanish, we decided to call it *'lista de verificación'*. Kindergarten teachers introduce this terminology and we continue reinforcing it through 5th grade as a way to maintain consistency. Obtaining Spanish texts has been another challenge. Initially, we reprinted and copied Spanish books from an online printable app called Reading A to Z (Raz-Kids) to mirror the English libraries provided in the curriculum. This ensured children had access to literature in Spanish at home and in the classroom. However, over the last five years, book publishers have increasingly supported Latinx writers to publish more authentic literature for bilingual classrooms. Over time, the TCRWP also focused on producing some of their resources in Spanish and they have recently hired bilingual staff who create bilingual templates such as character maps, word banks and checklists for reading responses. Teachers now can create more Spanish and bilingual classroom libraries with reduced labor. This gives students more opportunities to take books home as they are exposed to authentic literature that increases engagement and personal connections.

In addition to the TCRWP reading and writing curriculum, we have used phonics programs in both languages to support students as they develop phonological awareness to ensure a fully inclusive literacy approach. Since our first year, we have implemented *Estrellita* for Spanish and *Fundations* for English. *Estrellita* has a strong approach to support students' reading strategies from basic print to reading complete sentences. It is used in kindergarten through 2nd grade. Second grade teachers use *Estrellita* in the Fall and then introduce *Lunita* as a sequential program to support fluency, comprehension and vocabulary development (See Image P1.1). *Fundations* supports phonics in English through a structured, progressive approach. It focuses on reading, writing and handwriting to develop print concepts, spelling, word recognition and word families. Beginning in 3rd grade, children move into Words their Way with its Spanish equivalent *Palabras a Su Paso*. In addition to these phonics programs, in the last two years, we have added *Heggerty*, a phonemic awareness program to address sounds, blends and syllables. It is taught daily for 10 minutes, one day in Spanish and the next in English following the language of the day. Finding programs that support our philosophy of building from children's strengths and interests as well as supporting literacy in two languages required us to be both critical and creative with the curricula available to adapt them to our dual language bilingual program.

Multiculturalism

The unique backgrounds of our community members is a wonderful strength that is prioritized and celebrated within our school. This diversity provides the context for children to build pride in their own experiences, to learn from each other in authentic ways and embrace differences. As outlined earlier, our school's diversity is demonstrated in our families' languages, countries of origin, socio economic statuses and educational and religious backgrounds. It also presents itself in our students' learning profiles, non/gender-conforming identities and more. Throughout our classrooms and school, we strive to be inclusive and

Image P1.1 *Maestra* Rebeca Madrigal teaches Spanish phonics via the Lunita Program from Estrellita. Photo by Silvia Peña

support children to celebrate who they are, where they come from and what they hope to become. This work is situated in the inclusion of our families through the work we do school-wide to promote the Spanish language – including all of its varieties and connected cultures – as well as in the classroom where spaces are created for children to share and learn from each other.

Multiculturalism is promoted by creating opportunities for families to share their backgrounds and experiences. Family Fridays were established in our first year as a school and occur one to two times a month. Families are invited to visit their child's classroom for collaborative learning experiences during the first period of the day. They are conducted primarily in Spanish, with the exception of the English component classrooms. This allows the Spanish-speaking families to feel more confident and comfortable to participate in the activities and demonstrates to the English-dominant families the rigor and abilities of their children to use their new language (see Chapter 9). Cross-cultural conversations are highlighted during the sharing of traditions, countries of origin and individual likes and dislikes. Another event that highlights the cultures of our school community is our annual 'Welcome Potluck' that occurs in September. Families come to share food, get to know each other and bring in the new school year. Potluck dishes in any given year include empanadas, chow fun, masala dosa, fried rice, plátanos, arroz con gandules or habichuelas, kimchi, lasagna, flautas, papa a la huancaina, pizza, fried chicken and rice, all kinds of salad and lots of sweets from all parts of the world. Food always brings a sense of pride and community.

Multiculturalism is also shown by supporting events within the school to promote Spanish and the multiple cultures within our community. Our CARES (Cooperation, Assertiveness, Responsibility, Empathy, and Self-control) assemblies are based on different social and emotional competencies. Each grade is in charge of presenting one specific competency as a class via a video or a skit. The MCs and the students speak primarily in Spanish to remind the community that we belong to a bilingual program and that we need to recognize Spanish as a language that can be celebrated on stage in a public manner. Reading is also highlighted in March, through March Reading Madness. We sing Spanish songs to motivate students to read in both languages and to remind children that they are powerful because they are bilingual. Though our school neighborhood is very bilingual, the dominance of English as the language of power within the US and New York City means that Spanish needs to be highlighted, uplifted and practiced publicly as an equally powerful language in Dos Puentes and beyond.

Multiculturalism is also embraced within the classrooms as teachers make time to get to know their students and help them better relate to one another as well. Children's literature is used to share experiences from different perspectives. Class discussions provide space for students to identify connections and differences as topics in the curriculum foster these links. For example, the family unit in kindergarten allows children to share who they each identify as family members and the various languages spoken in their home. Second graders take part in a two-month unit on identity that includes their likes and dislikes, as well as linguistic backgrounds, countries of origin, religion and gender identification. Fourth graders interview family members about their youth and traditions and then share them with their classmates in presentations that include artifacts such as photographs and maps. These particular units allow children and families to identify and share themselves with others through a topic in which they are the experts. This pride builds confidence in children as it creates a context for others to ask questions and learn more about their peers. Children share themselves in ways that their characteristics and backgrounds are brought to life authentically and help others to appreciate their similarities and differences. These spaces for celebration can sometimes lead to instances of cruelty.

Unfortunately, there are times when words are used in hurtful or exclusionary ways. But addressing them and building on the foundation of acceptance makes taking responsibility for them a lot easier. Additionally, our students develop an awareness of critical consciousness as it relates to inequity and how power can be unequally distributed within and beyond the school community.

Bilingüismo, biliteracidad y multiculturalismo all support each other and are deeply embedded in our school community and curriculum as a way to promote our students' development and success. Collectively, they provide the tools that support the first and perhaps the guiding principle of Dos Puentes. Over 10 years, we have grown our structures and supports to embed *bilingüismo, biliteracidad y multiculturalismo* in all we do. At the same time, we continually make space for reflection so that each aspect of this pillar is utilized collectively to ensure the constant transformation of our dual language bilingual school.

Overview of Chapters

This section includes five chapters, all authored by Dos Puentes teachers, to show how the pillar *bilingüismo, biliteracidad y multiculturalismo* is intentionally built into school structures, classroom practices and larger events. In the first chapter, 'Celebrating *Dos Lenguajes*', Jason Horowitz and Armando Lopez explain how students feel empowered by learning about cultural traditions and music and constantly celebrating *español* as part of their bilingualism and biliteracy in our school events. In Chapter 2, 'Translanguaging: Moving Beyond *"los dos" Lenguajes*', Diane Figueroa and Karina Malik present translanguaging as a catalyst for students to promote and embrace their dynamic bilingualism. They highlight classroom activities that allow students to build their linguistic repertoire *en español*, English and additional languages as well. In Chapter 3, 'Building Biliteracy through Educators, Resources and Curricula', Lara Ginsberg demonstrates how choosing appropriate instructional materials for read-alouds engages students through cultural connections and classroom discussions. In Chapter 4, 'Bilingual Activism a *Través de la Lectoescritura*', Ashley Busone-Rodríguez and Karen Mondol introduce an essential element at Dos Puentes: activism. Being bilingual is a journey where one encounters barriers and hostility, but we empower our students to confront such obstacles by advocating for their right to be bilingual, biliterate and multicultural. Finally, in Chapter 5, 'Critical Collaboration to Support the Bilingualism and Biliteracy of Children with Disabilities', Sabrina Poms and Teresita Prieto illustrate how Dos Puentes serves and advocates for bilingual students with disabilities. They explain how the integrated co-teaching (ICT) model is composed and how the two teachers collaboratively plan to serve the needs of their emergent bilinguals with and without disabilities. Collectively these chapters demonstrate how *bilingüismo, biliteracidad* y *multiculturalismo* live and develop within Dos Puentes.

References

Chen, L. and Mora-Flores, E. (2006) *Balanced Literacy to English Language Learners, K-2*. Heinemann.

Escamilla, K., Hopewell, S., Butvilofsky, S., Sparrow, W., Soltero-González, L., Ruiz-Figueroa, O. and Escamilla, M. (2014) *Biliteracy from the Start: Literacy Squared in Action*. Caslon Publishing.

Flores, N. (2017) From language as resource to language as struggle: Resisting the Coke-ification of bilingual education. In M.-C. Flubacher and A. Del Percio (eds) *Language, Education and Neoliberalism: Critical Studies in Sociolinguistics* (pp. 62–81). Multilingual Matters.

García, O. and Li, W. (2015) Translanguaging, bilingualism, and bilingual education. In W.E. Wright, S. Boun and O. García (eds) *The Handbook of Bilingual and Multilingual Education* (pp. 223–240). Wiley-Blackwell.

Palmer, D., Cervantes-Soon, C., Dorner, L. and Heiman, D. (2019) Bilingualism, biliteracy, biculturalism… and critical consciousness for all: Proposing a fourth fundamental principle for two-way dual language education. *Theory Into Practice* 58 (2), 121–133. https://doi.org/10.1080/00405841.2019.1569376\

Pérez, B. (2003) *Becoming Biliterate: A Study of Two-way Bilingual Immersion Education*. Taylor & Francis Group.

Pimentel, C. (2011) The color of language: The racialized educational trajectory of an emerging bilingual student. *Journal of Latinos and Education* 10 (4), 335–353.

Sánchez, M.T., García, O. and Solorza, C. (2018) Reframing language allocation policy in dual language bilingual education. *Bilingual Research Journal* 41 (1), 37–51.

Valdés, G. (1997) Dual-language immersion programs: A cautionary note concerning the education of language-minority students. *Harvard Educational Review* 67 (3), 391–430.

1 Celebrating *Dos Lenguajes*

Jason Horowitz and Armando Lopez

Dos Puentes Teachers

Every morning at Dos Puentes, Habiba, our school security guard and an immigrant from Bangladesh, greets the staff as we file into the building, just as she also sees us off each afternoon. One Friday afternoon she shouted '¡*Hasta lunes*!' followed by 'I'm learning Spanish'. Dos Puentes is a multilingual learning space, and everyone makes a concerted effort to celebrate all languages and cultures. '¡*Buenos días* Dos Puentes!' 'Good Morning Dos Puentes!' The collective morning chant can be heard by anyone passing near the schoolyard, as the school staff, families and students engage in a back-and-forth bilingual greeting. Every day begins with a definitive celebration of *orgullo bilingüe* (See Image 1.1).

Image 1.1 The scene at morning arrival where the bilingual greeting between students, families and staff can be heard. Photo by Armando Lopez

The Dos Puentes community takes pride in celebrating all students on their journey to multilingualism, rather than just celebrating their acquisition of English. Our school offers students opportunities to connect with the cultures, identities and values that exist in their homes and hearts. The celebration of *dos lenguajes y multiculturalismo* compliments the day-to-day immersion through bilingual instruction. This chapter will highlight how the school invites students to develop their identities and imagine a co-constructed space where they can celebrate their cultural, linguistic and racial diversity.

A School Culture of Multilingualism

We live in a country and state that does not have an official language. Yet, in the US English is still disproportionately celebrated, while the bi/multilingualism of racially minoritized students is often discounted. The multilingual focus of the school-wide bilingual program at Dos Puentes works to counteract this message that permeates our society, by taking a decidedly multilingual stance to celebrate and center the multilingual and multicultural members of our community.

Our commitment to our students and families embraces several essential experiences, through which we celebrate and applaud their cultures and accomplishments. The teachers at Dos Puentes serve as bilingual models for our students, as we intentionally speak, read and write in both English and Spanish. We seek to create joy and learn with a passion that values our identities as cultural beings. Our work implores us to fuse academic progress with the development of socioemotional and cultural consciousness. This process demands an environment where students experience bilingualism through the recognition and appreciation of their linguistic and cultural strengths and differences. In this chapter, we share some of the ways Dos Puentes connects bilingual learning to cultural pride and joyful celebrations.

Bridging Languages and Cultures in the Classroom

Each classroom at Dos Puentes has an amazing kaleidoscope of personalities that offers teachers opportunities to bring classes together to celebrate *bilingüismo, biliteracidad y multiculturalismo*. In the lower grades (kindergarten-2nd), our students take part in a multicultural journey to represent *la alegría de ser bilingüe* by expressing their culture through biliteracy. To begin, students delve into the rich bilingual libraries that nurture the love for reading and developing skills for a new language. Each classroom library offers a variety of Latine literature that invites students to not only fulfill their enjoyment, but also to understand our heritage and connect within the richness of our community. Some student favorites are *'Tía Isa Wants a Car'* and *'My Papi Has a Moto'*. Equally important, the lower grades always find ways to bring that *chispa de alegría* into the classroom. Last year, one of our classes celebrated *El Mes de la Herencia Hispana* by voting for the best Latine song, which created spaces for students to show their best moves to the rhythms of Celia Cruz, Oscar d'León, Juan Luis Guerra and even a Mariachi band. Certainly, the *orgullo latino* brought smiles and boosted our learning that day.

In 1st grade, students explored the 'How To' unit, where they learned to write a book that gives detailed steps, through an aspect of their culture. Through a variety of fun hands-on activities, students experienced engaging ways to learn about other cultures and beliefs. The class learned the steps to crafting a piñata, a process that requires time, *flexibilidad y paciencia*. Students listened to stories and sang popular songs related to piñatas as they engaged in the writing process. Due to their background knowledge, some of them said 'Armando, you are missing a step…you need to tell the readers what goes inside the piñata!'. Every day they asked '*¿cuando la vamos a romper* [when are we going to break it]*?*'. By making a piñata and creating a rich writing piece about the process to make one, students were afforded a rich cultural experience that connected and/or strengthened student*s*' *bilingüismo, biliteracidad y multiculturalismo.*

Student-driven inquiry is another way in which students solidify their commitment and purpose as bilingual beings in our world. One of the projects that our 4th grade students complete is the *'Historia de mi lenguaje'* project. During this unit, students collaborate with family members to explore their entire linguistic repertoire and cultural history. First, students interview a family or community member with questions that will inform their project. Next, students synthesize what they learned by either creating a video, poster, song, visual representation or an essay, which they present to teach about their family's culture and language. Students are proud to share about their heritage, as many families also speak Indigenous languages, such as Náhuatl and Mazahua. Student pride, curiosity and appreciation for one another seem to blossom once we open and share these cultural treasures that our families have passed down to each one of us.

Celebrating Diversity through Joyful Moments

At Dos Puentes we love to celebrate our common goal of *bilingüismo, biliteracidad y multiculturalismo*. It's important to our community that our students take pride in the fact that they are a culturally diverse group of students who are learning in two languages and across many cultures. As a staff, we often seek ways to promote and celebrate this as a way to

Image 1.2 Fifth graders celebrating at their graduation school dance. Photo by Katherine Higuera-McCoy

counter students who gravitate toward English as they progress through the grades. We make special efforts to celebrate the continued progress of all students as Spanish learners – especially those who come from Spanish-speaking homes – as we remain conscious to avoid overly focusing on white students who are new to Spanish and often garner more praise for their bilingualism than their Latine peers. Some ways we celebrate our students' *bilingüismo y multiculturalismo* include *Locura por la lectura*, school dances such as *Manos Unidas* (Hands United), Bilingual Pride (Ode to Dos Puentes), Lunar New Year, International Night/Talent show, the science fair and potlucks (See Image 1.2).

Adriana Cando, a parent, shared how she valued International Night as a meaningful school celebration for her family. On one hand, she appreciated how the school principal connects with the attendees. 'I appreciate that Dr Hunt (the school principal), who is from the US, always speaks in Spanish at International Night. I think that it motivates the immigrant families to take more risks to speak English.' She also discussed how the event brings different cultures together in the school setting. 'So many people could connect. We would transmit our cultures to each other by asking questions such as, "Where is this dish from? What is it called?" People from many different countries would speak to each other without hesitation. We all found a way to communicate, and there was always familiarity and respect for each other's cultures.' This mother's reflection demonstrates just one way how our school lives its commitment to celebrating our community.

Singing and Dancing Together

The arts allow the Dos Puentes *comunidad* to celebrate our diversity by holding joyful community gatherings aimed at allowing children to celebrate their love of music together. School staff and families come together multiple times to make these special events memorable. The first school dance was held in 2018 to raise funds for a 4th grade trip to visit a nature center in upstate New York. Since then, we have held multiple online and in-person dances. *Manos Unidas* was a virtual celebration during the worst of the COVID pandemic that brought us together to raise money for families in need, as well as a virtual Halloween Costume Party and a Lunar New Year dance, which was a thematic dance party filled with instructional moments and activities.

Since our first school dance, we have come to realize the importance of creating joyful musical spaces for children that include them in the process. While organizing and curating our school dances, we make consistent efforts to incorporate a diverse selection of music that represents the various cultures in our school. Sharing music in a public space is a powerful way of building pride and empathy for one another while creating positive associations with one's school experience. At this point, we have some songs in Spanish that have become unofficial anthems of Dos Puentes, such as '*Vivir Mi Vida*' by Marc Anthony and '*Madre Tierra (Oye)*' by Chayanne. We purposefully highlight the multilingual nature of the music that we love, which has brought us all closer and become part of the identity of Dos Puentes.

Locura por la lectura en el mes de marzo/March Reading Madness

At Dos Puentes, March is the month where we take extra care to reinvigorate reading skills in both English and Spanish through a grand celebration called *Locura por la lectura*. At the start of the month, the school gathers together in the auditorium for an assembly to get everyone excited about reading, especially in Spanish as over time students tend to favor English due to its position as the language of power. At this point in the year, most students have already grown significantly as readers, but they might need a push to reconnect with their goals as Spanish readers.

Teachers Ms Madrigal and Mr Horowitz build excitement about reading and encourage students to make aggressive reading goals for the month of March. We remind students to focus on their objective, especially in their new language, and encourage them to implement the reading behaviors necessary to ascertain them. Each class measures the minutes or pages that they have read in each language to receive prizes. Through music and drama, we inspire the students to chant, sing and scream about becoming a stronger bilingual reader. I (Jason) wrote a song in Spanish to help us spread the message, called '*¡Yo, Yo, Yo, Leo!*' (I, I, I, read!). During

¡Yo, yo, yo, leo!

Preparándome,
Pongo mis lentes,
Yo soy,
Inteligente,
CON los ojos,
CON la mente,
Lánzate,
A leer con Dos Puentes,

Lánzate, a leer con
Dos Puentes (4x)

Yo yo yo, leo (4x)

En mi clase, leo,
Con mis amigos, leo,
En mi casa, leo,
¡Pasa lo que pasa, leo!

Yo yo yo, leo (4x)

A mi me gusta leer, (hey!)
Subir al otro nivel, (hey!)
A mi me gusta leer, (hey!)
Subir al otro nivel. (hey!)

Yo yo yo, leo (4x)

Image 1.3 Lyrics for the March Reading Madness song, '*Yo, yo, yo, leo.*'

this month, students of all ages can be heard singing the lyrics around the school (See Image 1.3). In 1st grade students fell in love with the fun and exciting folk tale of '*La Tortilla Corredora*' by Laura Herrera. The fun elements such as the onomatopoeias make students think of faraway landscapes, foods, animals and other memories from their family's countries of origin. We all engage in a melody of rhymes and giggles that turns this and other books into captivating moments that bridge home.

One parent described the challenge as a didactic and non-traditional approach to motivate their child to read books in Spanish. They said, 'My child would come home from school and say, "Today we are going to read because we have to win!"'. While highlighting the importance of succeeding in the reading competition, we use this time to reinvigorate the pride that we share collectively as bilingual readers.

Conclusion

Dos Puentes is the place where our students, families, and staff work together to develop an inspiring learning space that invites them to flourish and celebrate their cultural and linguistic diversity, while highlighting the importance of learning in Spanish to push back against the dominance of English. Beginning in kindergarten, literacy has an important role in establishing the foundation for students to deeply explore *bilingüismo, biliteracidad* y *multiculturalismo*. Throughout the years, we all take part in celebrations that make our hallways and classrooms vibrant with our many ways of languaging. Through traditions that involve teamwork, music, dance, artwork and food, we seek to enrich our curriculum and create powerful moments of joy that bring our goals of developing biliteracy to fruition. As one parent reminded us so eloquently, 'Our kids acquire English from one day to the next, but *manteniendo su lengua es más difícil (*maintaining their Spanish is more difficult). Surely they will still speak it, but reading and writing will become more of a challenge as they get older. In this aspect, I hope that Dos Puentes never changes the way that it continues to support the development of bilingualism and biliteracy for all students'. Without a doubt, we hope to continue manifesting a trusted *espacio para el bilingüismo*, where everyone can build upon the foundations of our diverse community in responsive, creative, and joyful ways.

Researcher Commentary

Cecilia M. Espinosa

Lehman College, CUNY

> 'We need humanizing pedagogies that center the genius, justice, joy, love, and humanity of our children' (Muhammad, 2023: 21).

From a humanizing pedagogy stance, teachers, students, community members, security guards, office, cafeteria, custodial personnel, families and administrators should receive ample invitations to enter joyfully as engaged co-participants and co-creators of a dynamic and inclusive learning space. Dos Puentes is without a doubt, such a school, where bilingual, brown and Black Latine, and Indigenous children do more than endure, they thrive (Love, 2019). This is clearly an intentionally created space where learning and teaching are joyful acts from the instant its doors open, throughout the school day, and all the way to the after-hours.

Context

At Dos Puentes, the educators attend with care to the classroom environment, by ensuring the languages of children and their families are reflected, can affirm and can serve as support to the learners. These educators understand the importance of disrupting monolingual spaces (including within a dual language setting) by placing 'the language practices of the community at the center of instruction, rather than the named languages' (Sánchez *et al*., 2022: 152). Dos Puentes is a Spanish-English dual language school that intentionally creates spaces of visibility for all the languages the children bring, for example, Nahualtl and Mazahua.

In this school, teachers also attend carefully to the diversity of their classroom libraries. They do it by critically interrogating their book collections, ensuring these offer mirrors to the diverse identities, interests, needs and lived experiences of their diverse bilingual students (Espinosa & Ascenzi-Moreno, 2021). The teachers at Dos Puentes are committed to, '*formar a los alumnos como lectores letrados y no simplemente alfabetizados....'* (Garrido, 2014: 30). Garrido is speaking about the importance of carving out spaces where readers choose to read and can critically analyze and discuss texts. Students develop their literate voices when it centers on their lived experiences (España & Herrera, 2020).

Discussion

In this school setting, there is space to pose questions and engage in curriculum inquiries about their families' and communities' languaging practices. The curriculum Dos Puentes has imagined is one that normalizes how families and communities language (Sánchez & García, 2022). They accomplish this by aligning their work with inquiry studies that lead them to critically learn about, examine and understand their own languaging capacities, as well as those of others in the community and the larger world. This is a learning space that values multimodal learning, one that expands what is traditionally considered curriculum in most conventional school texts. In this setting 'out-of-school literacies' serve 'as rich resources for school-based literacies' (Brown & Hao, 2022: 305).

Dos Puentes is a school that recognizes that for all their bi-multilingual students to succeed, they must celebrate and build on 'the multiple meaning-making potential of [the] children, as they extend these practices to encompass those [traditionally more] valued in schools' (García & Otheguy, 2017: 59). At Dos Puentes, educators hold a broad and complex vision of language and learning. It encompasses the semiotic aspects of language (gestures, visuals, sounds). These educators recognize that for a child to learn with more depth and complexity and to more fully express what they mean, the school's conceptualization of language learning must go beyond the written and the oral forms.

Dos Puentes resists the idea that learning in linguistically racialized communities can only happen with dittoes and drills done with paper and pencil. Instead, the school acknowledges that there are other important meaning-making possibilities and that many of these come from the families and the community. This is a reason why at Dos Puentes learning also happens through the integration of joyful music, drama, dance and cultural artifacts. These additional semiotic ways of constructing meaning affirm, expand, nurture, celebrate and strengthen this bilingual learning community while helping its members to reimagine it. Educators at Dos Puentes embrace and practice what Wynter-Hoyte *et al.* (2022) call Revolutionary Love; they do it by, 'recognizing the innate brilliance, potential, and cultural richness of their Black and Latine students' (2022: 20).

In this school setting families are collaborators in the child's education. The educators at Dos Puentes know that 'to create a strong partnership between schools and families, [they] must work from a foundation of mutual respect...The goal is to create schools that are central to the larger community', as researcher López-Robertson (2021: 121), argues. At Dos Puentes families 'know they matter. They also know that their way of making meaning matters' (2021: 122). This stance is central to the school's life.

References

Brown, S. and Hao, L. (2022) *Multimodal Literacies in Young Emergent Bilinguals: Beyond Print-Centric Practices*. Multilingual Matters.

España, C. and Herrera, L. (2020) *En Comunidad: Lessons for Centering the Voices and Experiences of Bilingual Latinx Students*. Heinemann.

Espinosa, C.M. and Ascenzi-Moreno, L. (2021) *Rooted in Strength: Using Translanguaging to Grow Multilingual Readers and Writers*. Scholastic.

García, O. and Otheguy, R. (2017) Interrogating the language gap of young bilingual and bidialectal students. *International Multilingual Research Journal* 11 (1), 52–65. https://doi.org/10.1080/19313152.2016.1258590

Garrido, F. (2014) *El buen lector se hace, no nace: Reflexiones sobre la lectura y la escritura*. Paidós.

López-Robertson, J. (2021) *Celebrating Our Cuentos: Choosing and Using Latinx Literature in Elementary Classrooms*. Scholastic.

Love, B. (2019) *We Want to Do more than Survive: Abolitionist Teaching and the Pursuit of Educational Freedom*. Beacon Press.

Muhammad, G. (2023) *Unearthing Joy: A Guide to Culturally and Historically Responsive Rurriculum and Instruction*. Scholastic.

Sánchez, M.T. and García, O. (2022) *Transformative Translanguaging Espacios: Latinx Students and their Teachers Rompiendo Fronteras sin Miedo*. Multilingual Matters.

Sánchez, M.T., Espinet. I. and Hunt, V. (2022) Student inquiry into the language practices de sus communidades: Rompiendo fronteras in a dual language bilingual school. In M.T. Sánchez and O. García (eds) *Transformative Translanguaging Espacios: Latinx Students and their Teachers Rompiendo Fronteras Sin Miedo* (pp. 134–155). Multilingual Matters.

Wynter-Hoyte, K., Braden, E., Myers, M., Rodriguez, S. and Thornton, N. (2022) *Revolutionary Love: Creating a Culturally Inclusive Literacy Classroom*. Scholastic.

2 Translanguaging: Moving Beyond *"los dos" Lenguajes*

Diane Figueroa and Karina Malik

Dos Puentes Teachers

As bilingual Latinx teachers in early/childhood education who grew up navigating two different worlds, cultures and languages between our home and school environment, we understand how linguistic school practices can be exclusionary. Our own lived experiences have taught us about the importance of inviting our students to communicate in varied ways, regardless of language rules and structures. Welcoming students to communicate without linguistic barriers in the classroom plays a critical role in our students' sense of belonging in the classroom and the larger school community. When we restrict our students' communication to one language or variety, we deny parts of their identity. Throughout this chapter, we will share our experiences guided by the following question: How do we welcome childrens' whole selves into the classroom to center their varied identities and their complete linguistic repertoire?

To answer this question, we will refer to some of our classroom practices grounded in translanguaging. Translanguaging is an act where multilingual people access different features of their language repertoire to maximize communication. It has more to do with communication than with language itself. Especially since students don't just come to school speaking either Spanish or English and even within a bilingual program, parts of their full linguistic repertoires can often be overlooked. As such, the ability to translanguage in our classrooms is a norm and a talent that has remained unrecognized or ignored by hegemonic practices. In order to disrupt the past and current patterns of communication and instructional approaches within dual language bilingual education programs we consistently affirm our abilities to translanguage inside and outside of the classroom environment. We also push and question our understanding of language as bilingual educators and a bilingual school.

Translanguaging Tensions in the Classroom

Within our school, translanguaging wasn't something that all teachers and administrators were initially on the same page about based on different experiences. Some strongly believed that only Spanish should be used in the Spanish classroom and only English should be used in the English classroom. This was especially because teachers felt the need to faithfully conserve and advocate for the space dedicated to the Spanish-speaking community that is represented through language advocacy within an English-dominated society. Others believed that we shouldn't have this rigidity around language and should move away from the practices that police how students and bilingual people language. Eventually, we realized that translanguaging not only broke down the barriers between English and Spanish but also promoted bilingualism in its truest form. It also created spaces for students to bring in other languages as well, embracing their full identities. We had students proudly sharing their Indigenous languages like Mixteco, Nahuatl and Zapotec, as each translanguaging lesson provided a safer space to share the complexity that exists in students' expression and identity.

In the early years of Dos Puentes, we all knew that we were committed to advocating for dual language practices in our classrooms and school environments (see the Introduction for more information about dual language bilingual education programming). However, it wasn't immediately clear to us that to uphold this commitment, we would also need to engage in the continuous study and exploration of language as a bilingual school. With the support of The City University of New York – New York State Initiative on Emergent Bilinguals (CUNY-NYSIEB) (see Chapter 16), an initiative that works to improve the education of emergent bilingual students, teachers were encouraged to actively understand the language practices and pedagogy across the grades by planning vertically to build on each grade's culturally and developmentally appropriate positioning of translanguaging in inquiry-based learning. Having dedicated time and space to understand how our students evolve linguistically was a powerful foundational understanding for our translanguaging work. As educators, we recognize that it is up to us to create restorative spaces that center the identities of our students through inclusive language practices, read-alouds, community walks and varied materials and experiences where our students' whole identities are affirmed.

Estudiando Translanguaging

Translanguaging began to enter the classroom as an exploration of students' language practices. The inquiry unit we describe created a learning space for understanding language as a fluid and ever-changing facet of students' intersectional identities. The essential question of this

3rd grade curriculum unit was 'Why does language matter?' and has served as the overarching big idea in students' investigation of the language across the different spaces: self, family, classroom community, surrounding community and world (see Image 2.1). For students to make such profound connections, the core of the investigation must begin with the student's identity, those roots are grounded at home and part of family knowledge. Once students are able to make connections using the roots of their language identity, the next layer to explore is the classroom community. These layers and different spaces in which these language practices exist allow students to examine their own communities and the larger world with firm ideas and wonderings about why language matters through different lenses.

¿Por qué importa el lenguaje?

Students took on the role of bilingual ethnographers who observed, studied and identified important questions about translanguaging. As researchers, students also took on the role of teachers and learners. The teaching and learning practices facilitated by 3rd grade teachers were centered on students' positionality as agents of their own learning throughout the unit and in their own linguistic and cultural learning trajectories at Dos Puentes and beyond.

El uso del lenguaje

Students began the exploration of translanguaging through the lens of the self. To begin this exploration, students examined 'When you code switch at work' a video from Pero Like, a bilingual and bicultural media outlet. The main character, Julissa Calderón, changes how she languages depending on the individual interactions she has at work. As students made observations, asked questions and shared their thinking, they made personal connections to their own lives. For example, David noted that Julissa's body language and tone changed as she spoke to different people, within and across the variations of Spanish and English. He said 'she is deciding who she feels comfortable with'. Another student, Carmen, also identified the types of Spanish being used, she said 'Es Dominicana porque le está voceando a su amigo, solo haces eso con tus amigos porque estás cómodo'. Carmen also noted, 'Si es verdad porque con la muchacha blanca, se pone seria y cambia a inglés, como que su manera de ser cambia'. In this initial activity, students are exploring how language shifts in spaces like the workplace, but also students are making connections across intersections of their lives.

To further examine translanguaging, students were asked to create a linguistic map of themselves. Each teacher modeled their own map. As a bilingual and bicultural teacher, it felt like I had to dig deep into my own

Image 2.1 A chart for students to explore the roles languages play in different aspects of their lives. Photo by Diane Figueroa

linguistic journey to then be able to model it to my students. As a language learner, I had to explore my own language identities that were never recognized or valued in my own learning experiences in US schools. Teachers had to study and reflect on their own journeys with language at home, work, school and society to demystify the misconception of language as correct or incorrect.

Language has power in all spaces, shapes, forms and variations. As teachers, we have the power to show that language is ever changing and co-constructed by its communities through this activity, which led students to question and affirm their linguistic experiences. For example, students claimed languages as their own, although being ambivalent in the beginning to do so as language learners with different proficiencies. Gabriel asked 'Can I add Spanish and Hebrew to my map, even though I am still learning to speak both languages?'. The teacher affirmed Gabriel's desire to add these languages to his map and asked him to think about how he moves within these different spaces and with whom he speaks across these languages.

As students began to identify their use of language across their lived experiences, many students used different colors to mark differences in language while others noted the people and communities that they communicate within each respective variation of the language. For instance, Joy highlighted that she uses Spanish at home and with friends at school, while she uses French with her mom, dad, younger people and even her dog. Students were then able to share their linguistic maps with each other in a gallery walk.

Family Language Inquiry

Seeking to understand that language is expansive and encompassing all variations and uses, the next lens of study consisted of the guidance of students' families. At Dos Puentes, family engagement is key to students' learning. During a Family Friday (see Chapter 9), teachers, parents and students are learning together about twice a month and in this instance, students have the opportunity to learn from parents to examine the use of language through family knowledge and history.

Prior to Family Friday, students prepared an interview sheet with questions to ask their family members about what languages they speak, how they learned the languages, why they learned them and who they communicate with. One student named Sarah and her mom Ana were in conversation about the languages the mom speaks when Sarah noted that English was not a language her mom learned as a child. Sarah then asked her mom, '*Mami, ¿, por qué aprendiste inglés más tarde?*'. To which the mom replied '*Tuve que, me mudé a Estados Unidos y necesitaba aprender para comunicarme*'. Ana then nodded and said '*por eso me tienes a mi para ayudarte y tu me ayudas con el español*'. The role of teacher and student is interchangeable for students, teachers and parents in this learning space, where parents and students explore why language matters and how it shapes our realities in an ever-changing world. Students and parents were then able to share the languages that are spoken, read and written. This allowed students to create a powerful sense of belonging and existence as they navigate different transnational spaces, as many students have attended schools in the United States, Latin America and beyond.

El lenguaje de nuestra comunidad

The role of the community was crucial in this investigation of language through a community walk to expand on family engagement (see Image 2.2). As we explored our perceptions of language in the community prior to the walk, students believed that Spanish and English were the dominant languages in the surrounding community. One student commented, 'This is Little Dominican Republic, people speak Spanish here and also English sometimes'. Students agreed, nodding and affirming with hand signals. Students even asked if they could ask community members questions and wrote those questions down on post-it notes to put on our 'What I KNOW, What I WANT to learn, and What I LEARNED' (KWL) chart. One student even asked, 'Does the language count if it's written on paper or a sign?'. The teacher told students they are investigators, affirming that language is valid in every form.

At the start of our community walk, students flocked to their first observation: a banner that hung on the fence of the school, which included several different languages such as English, Spanish, Korean, French and Arabic. A student named Angel said to another student Rafael, 'Does this mean that people at Dos Puentes can speak and read all of these languages?'. The other student responded non-verbally with a head shake and pointed to the Hebrew word to proudly highlight that his language was represented on the banner as well.

As the groups crossed Broadway with their teacher and parent chaperones, students were shocked to find that at their favorite spots, such as Dunkin Donuts and McDonalds, the workers spoke Bengali and Hindi. Also, while some street vendors spoke Spanish and English, others spoke Arabic and Indigenous languages from their countries. One student commented, 'Why do they know all these languages?' and the other student quickly said 'well, to communicate with us'.

Image 2.2 Students interviewing a local Russian-speaking shop owner, who also happens to be the father of twins who attend Dos Puentes. Photo by Diane Figueroa

Students reflected on the fact that many members of the Washington Heights community in which the school is located speak languages other than English and have migrated to the United States. While others living in the United States must also learn new languages to communicate with people in the community, moving away from messaging English is the only or primary language. Instead, students saw value across language practices. Exploring language allowed students to feel validated in their language practices and the linguistic decision-making that students make on a daily basis across home, school, community and the larger world.

Conclusion

Translanguaging recognizes the role of language and power in and outside of the classroom, allowing students in a Spanish-English bilingual school to see themselves and their surroundings beyond the lens of two languages. By becoming ethnographers, students come to understand how translanguaging empowers them to navigate the intersectional spaces in their lives. As hegemonic forces in society and schools affect how students view themselves, translanguaging provides a space in which students have the agency and power to reclaim linguistic identities and practices that push back on the messaging of white supremacy in the world that claims English as the most powerful language.

Researcher Commentary

Laura Ascenzi-Moreno

Brooklyn College, CUNY

The question of how teachers understand and integrate translanguaging theory and translanguaging pedagogy within dual language bilingual classrooms is critical. In this chapter, Diane Figueroa and Karina Malik chart how they understand translanguaging in relation to their own roles as teachers, curriculum designers, and members of a community and bilingual school. In doing so, they explain how translanguaging is not simply a pedagogical technique that is to be employed in the classroom, but it is also a lens through which educators can reflect about language, language learners and curriculum.

Context

As translanguaging theory and pedagogy has become increasingly popular across educator communities, the ways that it is taken up and put into practice is of critical importance. While scholars have found that translanguaging pedagogy holds the possibility to be transformative for leadership, pedagogies, and teachers' ideologies, there is a continued need to understand how these processes happen from the perspective of teachers (Espinosa & Ascenzi-Moreno, 2021; García & Kleyn, 2016). Furthermore, it is critical to the bilingual education community to understand how educators in the field grapple with the changing landscape of bilingual education as they integrate translanguaging theory and pedagogy into their professional and classroom practices (García *et al.*, 2017). Lastly, the connection between classroom practices and policies that guide programming and instruction needs is key to having cohesion across a school.

Discussion

Figueroa and Malik offer an insider view of how translanguaging theory and pedagogy took root across their teaching and reflective practices. Because Dos Puentes is distinguished for its commitment to dual language bilingual education and the community that it serves, the school's mission supports teachers' professional work to understand bilingualism as a resource for students, families and communities. Of particular note was how the Dos Puentes faculty engaged in a collaborative study of language practices across all the grades within the elementary school. This, in turn, spurred an awareness among teachers that they would need to, 'engage in the continuous study and exploration of language as a bilingual school'. This understanding that students' language practices are dynamic, emergent and evolving and that because of the nature of language, teachers need to be involved in a continual study of how students' language practices change is both critical and novel. This type of engagement in complex issues that ultimately affect what and how teachers approach the instruction of emergent bilinguals stands in contrast to how language is typically conceived in schools – as standardized, static and normative.

This realization that the school needs to embrace a dynamic vision of bilingualism and be committed to it is a departure from how language learners are usually viewed. Students labeled English Language Learners (in New York State) are regulated by static bureaucratic processes that define mandated services. While these legal processes are important, they also can make a complex process of understanding the changing needs of emergent bilinguals into simple procedures. Figueroa and Malik's chapter is a testimony to how teachers can exert their professional expertise school-wide when deciding on how programming and policies for emergent bilinguals can take shape within a local context.

Figueroa and Malik describe in detail how translanguaging theory and pedagogy was also a catalyst for shaping changes with curriculum. Again, their testimony is illustrative of the transformative nature of translanguaging when it is used not simply as a scaffold but as a lens on curriculum. They describe how students in their 3rd grade class engaged in a study of language use in their communities. Starting from the questions that students had about language in their communities and through social media, they engaged in an exploration of how language is used in their local neighborhood – Washington Heights, New York. They discovered that even though they live in the neighborhood and view it as predominantly a place where people speak Spanish, that in fact there are many people who speak many other languages. Their description is powerful for several reasons. First, it is clear that when students ask questions that stem from their genuine interests, that the pursuit is meaningful and can take unexpected turns. The shift from thinking about their neighborhood as exclusively comprised of Spanish speakers to one that has a rich multilingual population is an expansive one. As teachers, we want children to learn about both themselves and about the world around them. Through this project, it was clear that students learned about themselves in relation to their community and expanded how they conceived of their own community.

Secondly, with this unit of study, the teachers also engaged in expanding notions of curriculum. In many schools, teachers experience curriculum as top down and external to themselves and their students. Curricula purchased by schools are written externally and written to be implemented in a range of locations. However, this curriculum is site-specific and, thus, meaningful for the students and teachers engaged in it. In shaping the curriculum, the teachers are engaging in powerful work as curriculum developers as well as shaping what counts as disciplinary content. Generally, teachers are expected to divide their day into disciplinary blocks: reading, math, social studies, science and the like. Yet, in the project in which they explored language within the community, the teachers and students brought together disciplines that for a purpose that was not defined but open. In doing this, the teachers positioned themselves and their students as researchers of language, community and themselves.

In this chapter, 'Translanguaging: Moving Beyond *"los dos" Lenguajes*', the authors describe how moving in this translanguaging space, not only impacts school policy and programming, but also the opportunities that both teachers and students have for growth rooted in local contexts.

References

Espinosa, C. and Ascenzi-Moreno, L. (2021) *Rooted in Strength: Using Translanguaging to Grow Readers and Writers*. Scholastic.

García, O. and Kleyn, T. (2016) *Translanguaging with Multilingual Students: Learning from Classroom Moments*. Routledge.

García, O., Seltzer, K. and Johnson, S. (2017) *The Translanguaging Classroom: Leveraging Student Bilingualism for Learning*. Caslon.

3 Building Biliteracy through Educators, Resources and Curricula

Lara Ginsberg

Dos Puentes Teacher

The very first question in our teacher interview process at Dos Puentes asks candidates to discuss their language identities and their vision of bilingual education: 'Share about your own journey to learn the languages that you speak. Why do you want to work at a bilingual school?' Rebeca Madrigal, founding teacher, explains that for the hiring committee, this is the most important question. It is crucial for all of the adults in our school to not only be fluent in both English and Spanish, but to also have a reflective stance and deep connection to their own personal language histories, as well as the depth, complexity and equity focus that grounds the dual language model. To actively counter the English linguistic hegemony that is so prevalent in our society and to attempt to create a space where both languages can have equal importance, space and time is an act of rebellion. To do so, bilingualism, biliteracy, metalinguistic awareness, cultural competence and content knowledge are all critical ingredients. The complexity of teaching in this context should not be underestimated. That is why the staff at Dos Puentes is at the heart of our work.

The word that I hear the most used to describe our staff culture at Dos Puentes is *collaborative*. We believe strongly in our collective efficacy and trust each other's areas of expertise, professional knowledge and deep commitment to our students. As an institution, we have cultivated deep relational trust that is undertaken through a sense of joy in our shared work. Our classroom teachers, out-of-classroom specialists, administrators, paraprofessionals, interns and student teachers meet frequently to plan across languages and across classes. Although the planning process can look different, we are always thinking carefully about the kinds of texts and tasks that we are using, how they can bring in student voice and choice, the language opportunities being provided and how to provide scaffolds, modifications and extensions. These careful deliberations allow each child to be engaged and challenged. Very rarely would a teacher at Dos Puentes open to a page of scripted curriculum and deliver the lesson exactly as written, as these curricula were created either without them in mind or with them at the periphery. Through our collaborative work, we support each other's efforts to shift, modify, stretch and expand our curriculum to meet our students' needs as well as reflect and represent our diverse and vibrant population.

A critical goal that we have for our students when they graduate is both bilingualism and biliteracy. To us, that means that students will attain fluency in both receptive and productive language whether they are coming to school bilingual or learning English or Spanish as their new language. Additionally, students will read and write in both languages (and perhaps others depending on their linguistic practices outside of school) and be able to leverage cross-linguistic connections (such as identifying cognates), and will build metacognitive awareness as they expand their vocabulary, make language choices and translanguage across contexts. This is no easy feat, and as a result, bilingual/biliterate instruction is extremely complex, challenging and nuanced. What may work in a more monolingual setting may fail in this context, due to the complexity of language demands or the heterogeneity of the classroom. Because of the nuance of the work, we must also be extremely collaborative and open to feedback and to sharing both our challenges and our areas of expertise with other teachers. For all these reasons, it is crucial to have educators who are flexible, resourceful, creative and deeply committed to developing a strong understanding of the interplay between cognitive and linguistic demands. It is our job to translate the theory of what high-quality multilingual instruction looks like into practice, to iterate, and to openly and honestly share our successes, setbacks and curiosities.

Adapting Curriculum: ¡Bienvenida, Tía Lola!

Let's take one example from our 4th grade literacy curriculum. In the first writing and reading unit of the year, students dive into realistic fiction. The mentor text used by the Teachers College Reading and Writing Project Curriculum, which Dos Puentes uses but adapts, is *The Tiger Rising* by Kate Di Camillo. It's a beautiful book that students around this age tend to find highly engaging as it highlights complex issues like bullying, making new friendships, and loss, while also showcasing a variety of literary techniques. However, we wanted to choose a text that would more closely match the cultural, linguistic and academic needs of our student population, and provide what Rudine Sims Bishops (1990) describes as 'mirrors and windows' for the experiences of our students. So instead, we have chosen to use *How Tía Lola Came To* ~~Visit~~ *Stay* by Julia Alvarez (2002), which tells the story of a Dominican-American family's funny, poignant adventures when their charismatic, possibly magical Tía Lola

Image 3.1 Lara Ginsberg reads aloud *How Tía Lola Came To ~~Visit~~ Stay* by Julia Alvarez to her class. Photo by Gerardo Romo

comes to visit from the Dominican Republic. The main character Miguel navigates his parents' divorce, sibling rivalry and issues of identity as a second-generation member of his immigrant family.

How did we land on this particular text? There are many critical considerations when examining, restructuring, shifting and planning for our heterogeneous dual language bilingual classrooms. In the case of this book, we were looking for a high-quality, engaging piece of fiction that students would connect with and that could provide opportunities for grade-level analysis, inferencing and showcasing a variety of writing techniques. Specifically, the text is modeled as descriptive language, character growth and change. In addition to the content, we are always thinking about language. Because of our 50/50 language instruction model, we often look for novels that are available in both languages. However, simply identifying books that are available in both languages is not always sufficient. For example, many English books published in the US have been translated into Castilian Spanish, a variety that may be less accessible to the majority of our Spanish speakers in New York City. Additionally, for a variety of reasons, the lexile level does not always neatly match up across languages, meaning that a book that might be at an early 4th grade level in English could be at an end-of-year 5th grade level in Spanish.

The novel *How Tía Lola Came To ~~Visit~~ Stay* proved to be a great fit for our needs for many reasons. First, thinking from the perspective of language, this book is accessible for our students in both languages, while also providing ample opportunities for vocabulary development in English and Spanish. It is an excellent piece of literature and although the series was originally written in English, there is a high-quality translation to Spanish in a variety that's accessible to our students. The translanguaging within the book made for interesting discussions about how we use different languages in different spaces, and why. The book even includes an afterward, A Word About the Spanish/*Una palabra sobre el español*, which is a discussion and celebration of the author's choice to use include many Dominican or Caribbean words, such as *chichiguas* for kites; *guineo* for banana; and *guagua* for bus. Additionally, Julia Alvarez is a Dominican American author, and in this novel, she incorporates some elements of magic realism, which allows us to explore and celebrate a cultural element of fiction made popular by Latinx authors such as Gabriel García Márquez.

In terms of developmentally engaging content, the book also provides explorations of complex topics that elementary school students may experience such as divorce, bullying and new friendships. It also delves into stereotypes and the challenges of learning a new language, social issues that are also very relevant to our particular group of emergent bilingual students. Engagement is an important piece of the pedagogical puzzle, especially when hearing a read-aloud text in a new language, as it can greatly impact students' affective filters, which is the socioemotional state a young person is experiencing that can either block or encourage new language learning and production (Krashen, 1985). Fortunately, the characters in *Tía Lola* are realistic, heartwarming and hilarious! Every time we read it, there are chapters that get students laughing so hard, tears stream down their faces. Tía Lola, is, as one student described her, 'a mix between Mary Poppins y *una tía mía de la República Dominicana*'. The students really connect to these characters in a profound way, which excites them and motivates them to engage in this read aloud, even if it will be a challenge for them to attend to a new language. Because of the students' investment in the book that is rooted in topics and linguistic elements they connect with, we were able to use the text to stretch their literacy skills, such as by having students engage in a lively mock trial to arbitrate a fight between the siblings Juanita and Miguel, or to write creatively about the characters, imagining new adventures and experiences for Tía Lola.

Lastly, the text is a great example of what Rudine Sims Bishop refers to as a 'window' for many of our Dominican students and gives an opportunity for them to share their funds of knowledge about special foods, customs, traditions and even visiting the Dominican Republic. For example, there's a whole chapter about *la ñapa*, a Dominican term for 'a little more'. One of our students, Delfry, who had moved to New York from the Dominican Republic only a few months before the school year started, felt so proud to be able to explain to the whole class about *la ñapa* and how to ask for it when shopping at a market. Reading this book was so impactful for Delfry as he started his first full year of school in this country. In his end of the year reading reflection, Delfry wrote that '*Un libro [con el cuál] me conecta fue Tía Lola por qué se trata de inmigración porque yo soy inmigrante* [A book that connects me was Tía Lola because it's about immigration because I'm an immigrant]'. That is the magic of a thoughtful, intentional text, task, or piece of literature: it elevates students' own experiences and creates opportunities for *all* students to be experts, authors, explorers and learners. And it is just one example of how as bilingual teachers we work to consistently center the realities of our students as we identify resources and modify curriculum to better connect with the cultures, languages and backgrounds of our students.

Conclusion

The magic of creating a space in which bilingualism can blossom requires thoughtful and dynamic educators, as well as an intentional yet creative use of resources. Although we have done a lot of work as a school to build our students' biliteracy, our work as bilingual educators is just beginning. An important area of growth for our school as a whole, and a challenge shared by many bilingual schools or even schools with multilingual students in the United States is finding and bringing in authentic texts originally written and published in Spanish, especially those that can be culturally sustaining to our bilingual learners. This will serve to elevate the Spanish literary curriculum, and support us in uplifting all of our students' receptive and productive Spanish to an even higher level as they become bilingual and biliterate.

References

Alvarez, J. (2002) *How Tía Lola Came To* Visit *Stay*. Yearling.
Krashen, S.D. (1985) *The Input Hypothesis: Issues and Implications*. Longman.

Researcher Commentary

Carmen M. Martínez-Roldán

Teachers College, Columbia University

This chapter by teacher Lara Ginsberg offers a glimpse of some of the complexities, joys and challenges involved in developing a strong bilingual program. I want to comment on three themes that resonated with my work as a bilingual teacher educator from Ginsberg's *testimonios*: (1) the importance of bilingual teachers' development of political and ideological clarity, (2) a reminder of the transformative power of bilingual teaching when educators are treated as professionals, and most of all, (3) the joy of teaching.

Context

Ideological and political clarity

When teacher Lara Ginsberg shared the interview questions she was asked as part of her hiring process, it reminded me of what Bartolomé and Balderrama (2001) proposed as the need for teachers to develop political and ideological clarity. That is, as bilingual educators we must ask why are we bilingual teachers and who are our learners? While dual language programs may become a commodity for some communities (Cervantes-Soon, 2014; Palmer, 2010), the *testimonios* of teachers at Dos Puentes take us back to the critical roots of bilingual education as a social justice and equity-oriented program. Bilingual education aims to give students whose learning has been stifled by the hegemony of English-only ideologies, access to quality education and the chance for every student to develop bilingualism and biliteracy while learning subject content. Bilingual teachers at Dos Puentes are deeply committed to this goal, which involves often going against the grain of accepting curriculum materials, expectations, and assessments that do not center their students' strengths and needs. Such political and ideological clarity is the context for many pedagogical decisions made by bilingual teachers, such as developing culturally sustainable pedagogies (Paris, 2012).

Trust in educators

Developing culturally sustainable pedagogies requires time, collaboration and the support of the school administrators. The experience of teachers at Dos Puentes shows us what can happen when educators are trusted as professionals who make daily decisions based on what they are learning from and about their students. Teachers need time for creating professional learning communities in which they can engage in inquiry with other teachers about topics that matter to them, pedagogies they want to explore, and problems they want to solve (Jaar, 2017). The example of the thoughtful substitution of an expected mentor text for a culturally relevant text, such as *How Tía Lola Came To ~~Visit~~ Stay* (Alvarez, 2002) shows the many considerations bilingual teachers take into account when making changes to the curriculum, given the implications for the heterogenous linguistic and ethnic composition of their classrooms. Such decisions reflect culturally sustainable pedagogies that not only support students' academic learning, bilingualism and biliteracy but also cultivate a sense of belonging to school and to their particular communities. When students see characters that look like them or like their relatives in protagonist roles in the books they read, such as the characters of Tía Lola, Miguel and Juanita in Alvarez's novel, a sense of possibility and pride of who they are is nurtured. Teachers who are trusted and receive the support to come together to create curriculum with their students, develop a great sense of empowerment that inspire new efforts and motivate them to face whatever challenges come their way as bilingual teachers.

The Joy of teaching

Some of the challenges bilingual teachers face, include the lack of bilingual and culturally relevant materials, the imposition of standardized assessments and policies developed by others not familiar with their bilingual students. However, Dos Puentes has organized their bilingual program in a way that shows us how bilingual teaching and learning can be, as teacher Ginsberg highlights, sources of joy. I have witnessed this joy from teachers at Dos Puentes as they talk about a child who finally blossomed or finally engaged with certain types of books; as they talk about a parent that told them how happy their child is; as they share how they have found their voice as teachers; as they talk about how supported they feel by their Principal or their senior teachers; and as they engage in agentive moves. This joy energizes teachers and creates an environment in which teachers and children can flourish.

Discussion

Bilingual teacher Lara Ginsberg shows us that we should not underestimate the power of teachers to create transformative learning spaces through the small or big curricular decisions they are constantly making. When teachers come together to create transformative learning contexts, there are no insignificant efforts; each agentive act, as small as it seems, counts. In a sociopolitical context in which so many master narratives undermine the outstanding work done by teachers on a daily basis, telling our stories is a way of enacting a critical transformative activist stance (Martínez-Roldán, 2021; Stetsenko, 2017). The activism of all individuals involved in Dos Puentes school is part of the long trajectory of activism that has characterized bilingual education. I hope that their stories inspire the reader as they have inspired me. Let's join these efforts by sharing our counternarratives of what is possible in critical bilingual education.

References

Alvarez, J. (2002) *How Tía Lola Came To Visit Stay*. Yearling.
Bartolomé, L. and Balderrama, M.V. (2001) The need for educators with political and ideological clarity. In M. De La Luz Reyes and J.J. Halcón (eds) *The Best for Our Children: Critical Perspectives on Literacy for Latino Students* (pp. 48–64). Teachers College Press.
Bishop, R.S. (1990, March) Windows and mirrors: Children's books and parallel cultures. In *California State University Reading Conference: 14th Annual Conference Proceedings* (pp. 3–12). California State University.

Cervantes-Soon, C.G. (2014) A critical look at dual language immersion in the new Latin@ diaspora. *Bilingual Research Journal* 37 (1), 64–82.
Jaar, A. (2017) Professional development of dual language teachers: Learning communities as potential sites of teacher identity, agency, and advocacy. Doctoral Dissertation. Teachers College, Columbia University.
Martínez-Roldán, C.M. (ed.) (2021) *Latina Agency Through Narration in Education: Speaking up on Erasure, Identity, and Schooling*. Routledge.
Palmer, D. (2010) Race, power, and equity in a multiethnic urban elementary school with a dual-language 'strand' program. *Anthropology & Education Quarterly* 41 (1), 94–114.
Paris, D. (2012) Culturally sustaining pedagogy: A needed change in stance, terminology, and practice. *Educational Researcher* 41 (3). https://doi.org/10.3102/0013189X12441244
Stetsenko, A. (2017) *The Transformative Mind: Expanding Vygotsky's Approach to Development and Education*. Cambridge University Press.

4 Bilingual Activism *a Través de la Lectoescritura*

Ashley Busone-Rodríguez and Karen Mondol

Dos Puentes Teachers

Creating Activist Spaces

Being both bilingual and an activist is not simply a coincidence. By nature of who we are, bilinguals are either thrust into or already exist within a border between identities and cultures. We are at war with ourselves and the world, either fighting to maintain or *rescatar el lenguaje que* we inherited from our ancestors or fighting to create a world that would be accepting of our fellow bilinguals. Anzaldúa (1987: 76) writes, 'Wild tongues can't be tamed, they can only be cut out' and so it is true that bilinguals become activists almost as if by nature. We are *resistentes*, we are freedom fighters. Bilingualism and activism in the context of our elementary school is no different. We exist in Washington Heights, a neighborhood that finds itself very much in a border space; our students are people of borderlands. Some are immigrants or descendants of them. Some are Black and brown, biracial and white. Some are trans, most are bilingual and many are neurodivergent. It is because we exist within these borderlands that we need to create activist spaces.

Dos Puentes came to be because of movements like those led by the youth, families and educators of national and local civil rights organizations. We exist today within the context of bilingual education movements across the Americas. It is because of this legacy that we believe that creating activist spaces in our classrooms is not an option, but rather a necessity and a responsibility to our community. We work together to maintain the spaces that the bilingual activists of yesterday fought to create. The children in our community deserve what we think of as 'the base' and 'the space' to talk about, involve themselves in, and reflect on how they can relate to and change the issues they see in our community. The 'base' is the foundational knowledge and language to do so, and the 'space' is the freedom to try out new ideas and become activists in their community. Dos Puentes has worked to provide both.

As bilingual students and educators, we have a duty to learn about and stand up for what we believe in and for the rights of all people in our community: this is what it means to be an activist. Gabriel, our 5th grade student, offers a useful definition of an activist: 'I see myself as an activist by making my voice heard. I feel that just expressing myself and standing up for what I believe in is an example of an activist'. Gabriel has benefited from the base and the space to learn and talk about activism. He has gained knowledge through content such as read-alouds and other shared experiences, and he has benefited from explicit language instruction on this topic. Bilingual activism begins in kindergarten, when students are involved in learning about and creating public service announcements (PSAs) based on environmental concerns in our community. It is continued in 1st grade with in-depth explorations of identities and respect for differences. In 2nd grade, students learn about the history and diversity within New York City and how activists have played a part in this. In 3rd and 4th grade students study social issues and respond by stating their own opinions and convincing others to care about these matters. In 5th grade, the student council enthusiastically promotes school-wide events and community service projects in the name of activism. These curricular choices have been made based on our literacy curriculum from the Teachers College Reading and Writing Project (TCRWP), but augmented with the adaptations and additions from students and staff in our community to nurture social awareness.

Learning About Activism through a Historical Lens

Providing students with the base and the space to practice activism requires that we teach through a historical lens. Students study the Civil Rights Movement through the eyes of the people who experienced the hardships and victories endured during this era. By analyzing their bravery and struggle, students realized that through community efforts, civil rights activists used nonviolent tactics to advocate for positive change. The big focus of this unit is to empower bilingual activists to notice and challenge injustices centered on race and anti-blackness by sharing their opinions and knowledge. Through the use of articles, read-alouds, images, songs, primary sources and videos, students cultivate their understanding of historical activism. Some mentor texts we lean on to give students a sense of history and cultural literacy are *Ruth and The Green Book* (Ramsey, 2010) and *Sit-In How Four Friends Stood Up by Sitting Down* (Davis Pinkney, 2010). This literacy unit addresses the 5th grade standards of research to build and present knowledge and informational writing (see Image 4.1). Therefore, this approach is not a departure from the mandated curriculum but rather a more meaningful way to teach the required skills and concepts.

In cultivating the base and the space for our young bilingual activists, we believe in the importance of exposing them to other youth-led movements. Shoji, a 5th grade activist, was mesmerized by researching The Greensboro Sit-Ins and the Birmingham Children's Crusade of 1963. He was inspired by the young activists who courageously championed children's rights and helped solidify a sense of advocacy and agency among the new generations. Shoji reflected that, 'Even after all the horrible things done to them, they did not retaliate, they kept coming back, to fight for justice, and for what is right. Personally, I don't think I could have endured that much, and I probably would strike back, but not the students. The students were stronger, and more mature than their age, and I personally admire them for that'. In addition to books, students interpreted songs from the Civil Rights Movement. In response to Pete Seeger's classic song, 'We Shall Overcome', Adalyn expressed, 'It empowers people to keep going. We should all believe that things will get better, no matter what the case is. We should all have hope and be brave'. Through this research project, Shoji and Adalyn became more aware of the ways they can make a difference in our community and the resilience that is necessary to do so.

In this multicultural 5th grade class, we encourage cultural and social exchanges to foster understanding and empathy. Through this unit, students became more mindful about how they use their linguistic skills to express their ideas, learn from others and, eventually, develop a greater appreciation for the rich diversity in the world.

Image 4.1: Justin's bilingual project outlines the importance of the sit-ins. Photo by Karen Mondol

Becoming Activists

Students in our classrooms show us the issues that matter most to them. These issues are not only about 'other people' but about the students themselves. Recently, I (Ashley) was teaching a three-week literacy unit about social issues in my 3rd grade classroom. My colleagues and I crafted the unit by splitting the time into three mini topics to explore: (1) race, (2) gender identity and (3) immigration. At Dos Puentes, we treasure read-aloud time and students in all grades are accustomed to getting comfortable on the carpet together and listening to a story. We work hard to find authentic and 'Own Voices' texts – books that have been written by authors whose identities are represented in the story – and often represent our students' varied identities, too. The most powerful part of the read-aloud time is listening to students' reactions to what is being shared: *'¡Yo tengo una conexión!', '¡Mi familia es así!'* and 'That happened to us, too'. These reactions open activist spaces and allow us to dream together about how to express ourselves, how to connect with one another and how to change the world.

I began the week on gender identity by sharing a picture book called *Except When They Don't* by Laura Gehl (2020) to explore issues of the limited views of gender binary and gender stereotypes. In the book, Gehl writes, 'Girls sashay in sparkly shoes. Boys wear clothes of only blue. Boys cut bad guys down to size. Girls paint purple butterflies. Except when they don't' (2020: 4). Students immediately reacted to the text as I read it. Hands shot up and whispers could be heard across the carpet. 'I hate sparkles even though I'm a girl,' one student said. 'I wish I could take dance classes,' said another student who identifies as a boy. Students connected over the frustrations of people assuming their likes and dislikes based on their gender identities. They began to ask questions about the real implications of gender identities while I hurried to scribble all their brilliant ideas down on chart paper: Does gender impact your job as a grown up? Does it matter what you wear? Why do people do gender reveal parties? *¿Qué significa ser transgénero? ¿Uno puede ser de los dos géneros?*

Following this conversation, I led students through a brief history of gender-rights activism. We learned about the implications of the law on gender, families, and especially transgender people. One of the most important parts of this unit was being highly explicit with the vocabulary in both English and Spanish. We teach about the difference between biological sex and gender; we talk about words like 'non-binary', *'femenina'* and 'construct'. Students begin to grasp that there are many gender-based issues in our community and are left with the question, 'What do we do about it?'. After lessons like these, we often hold space for creative reflections with the following prompt: 'How will you share what you learned with others?'. Students choose between creative stations such as sign making, song writing, painting, collage, poetry and essay writing to create their responses and then we have a time of sharing (see Image 4.2). If students feel comfortable

Image 4.2 Students responded to the lessons on gender identity and justice through art. A student holds a handmade sign that reads: 'Gender doesn't matter' with signs for 'boy', 'girl', 'neither or both'. Photo by Ashley Busone-Rodríguez

and interested, they take their work home to share with their families. If they prefer, we present the work in the hallway for the rest of the school to see. This has become a school-wide practice as students revisit these themes each year and continue to grow as activists.

Of course, there are challenging moments that come with discussing difficult topics and activism in our classrooms. Recently, we received a note from a parent who had concerns about their child learning about the gender spectrum. They requested that I stop teaching this curriculum. I reassured the parent, with the support of my administration, that their child has been learning about and alongside non-binary people for many years at our school. I reiterated that we do our best to choose developmentally appropriate texts and terms to share with children and that we are always open to answering questions from children and families. As I see it, teaching about and practicing gender inclusivity (like many other forms of activism) is non-negotiable and while I can appreciate this parent's hesitancy to expose their child to new and complex concepts, I refuse to modify our curriculum and be complicit in the erasure of the gender non-conforming community. The identities of my non-binary students are valid and they deserve space and time in our classroom.

Activism in Action at Dos Puentes

The activism of Dos Puentes students is deeply connected to their learning and also permeates beyond the formal learning spaces. The student council is a group of 5th graders that are elected by their peers. It has proven to serve as an enriching experience with lasting positive impact which inspires children to pursue their activist voice. For example, after learning about the Russian invasion of Ukraine in the Argument and Advocacy writing unit, the Student Council encouraged our community to help impacted Ukrainians. Students read articles, wrote essays, made posters and used their bilingual voices to share opinions and questions with

Image 4.3 Donations by our school community for impacted Ukrainians. Photo by Michelle Madera Taveras

their community. They then set forth a campaign to collect donations of food, first aid and clothes (see Image 4.3). Michelle Madera Taveras, staff advisor for the Council, proudly shared that, 'Through this student-led initiative, our students were empowered leaders within our community. They were very proud of the flyer they created for the collection, the announcements they made, the (bilingual) robocall recorded, and their weekly visits to each class for collection'. Students' spirit of empathy and generosity inspired inquiry and activism around this world event.

Conclusion

Dos Puentes students are a product of the base of many years of intentional curriculum development and opportunities to learn about bilingual activism. We are proud of the ways that our staff works together to give space to students to become activists. The result is a group of students who have and exercise their own bilingual activist voices. One 5th grader, Robin, told us, 'Lo que me enseñó es que todos somos líderes y todos podemos hablar, tenemos una voz por una razón [What this taught me is that we are all leaders, and that we all have a voice for a reason]'.

References

Anzaldúa, G. (1987) *Borderlands/la Frontera: The New Mestiza*. Spinsters/Aunt Lute.
Davis Pinkney, A. and Pinkney, B. (2010) *Sit-In: How Four Friends Stood Up by Sitting Down*. Little Brown Books for Young Readers.
Gehl, L. and Heinsz, J. (2020) *Except When they Don't*. Scholastic Inc.
Ramsey, C. (2010) *Ruth and the Green Book*. Carolrhoda Books.
Seeger, P. (1963) We shall overcome [Song]. Columbia Records.

Researcher Commentary

Luz Yadira Herrera

California State University, Dominguez Hills

Bilingual education has never been neutral. In their critical review of bilingual education in the United States, Flores and García (2017) remind us of the trajectory of bilingual education beginning from its grassroots origins with the intention of sustaining cultural and linguistic pride to the commodification of bilingual education. They also remind us that bilingual education has been contested in varying contexts with the purpose of establishing English-only policies in schools, including the passage of legislation at the state level that dismantled bilingual education programs (i.e. CA Prop 227 in 1998, which was eventually reversed in 2016), to its subsequent rebranding as 'dual immersion' or 'dual language' in an effort to push an enrichment model of education to appeal to white, middle-class families. Bilingual education has always been political (for the gentrification of bilingual education, see Valdez *et al.*, 2016). Contextualizing bilingual education in this way is important given how Ashley Busone-Rodríguez and Karen Mondol describe how in serving a borderlands community at Dos Puentes, nurturing activism among its students was critical. Moreover, the authors show us a glimpse into the possibilities of an intentional curriculum design with the community and criticality at its center.

Context

Palmer *et al.* (2019) propose that in addition to bilingualism, biliteracy and biculturalism as fundamental goals for bilingual education, critical consciousness must be central and established as its fourth pillar.

Rooted in Paulo Freire's (1970) concientização, critical consciousness is our ability to *read the world,* that is to understand systems of oppression and power as well as our role in challenging and correcting inequities (as cited in Palmer *et al.*, 2019: 123). Moreover, this awakening is not just for students, but also for teachers, leaders, caregivers, and community partners. The elements in critical consciousness include the interrogation of power, historicizing schools, critical listening, and engaging with discomfort. Together, these elements provide opportunities for learning about the ways power dynamics are continuously at play, for instance, noting in two-way bilingual education contexts how schools treat white versus Latinx families, and ensuring equitable access (Palmer *et al.*, 2019). Historicizing schools means creating an awareness of the political struggle for bilingual education and tracing this to the long history of oppression of marginalized people. Critical listening is about interrupting those that dominate the discourse inside and outside classroom spaces to ensure that power is equitably shared. Finally, engaging with discomfort invites families to recognize and share the burdens which Palmer *et al.* argue can move people to action toward equity and justice.

In thinking of curriculum design that is rooted in critical pedagogy and consciousness, España and Herrera (2020) propose a social justice centered approach to teaching bilingual children they call *temas, textos, and translanguaging.* That is, designing teaching and learning experiences around *temas* or themes that are culturally and linguistically sustaining (Paris, 2012) to the students that we teach, *textos* that include multimodal texts and support the learning of these topics while affirming our students' identities, cultures and language practices. Finally, educators must create intentional *translanguaging* spaces in the classroom by inviting students to use their entire linguistic repertoire to engage with the content, make connections, and make meaning. This approach offers a way to center the voices and experiences of bilingual children, fostering activist spaces in the classroom, like Dos Puentes has done.

Discussion

Dos Puentes has created a 'base' for its students by generating opportunities to reflect on issues that the community is grappling with and supporting their students as they are coming into consciousness about issues that surround them. This is being done while simultaneously nurturing a 'space' for students to have the freedom to strategize a course of action in response to the issues they care about. This, however, cannot be achieved without developing a school curriculum that focuses on historizing and contextualizing youth-led movements, social justice issues at both the macro and micro level, and creating opportunities for students to learn about what justice looks and feels like. The intentionality in their curriculum design that sustains the base and the space not only reflect a critical consciousness, but also a pedagogical approach rooted in social justice, much aligned to España and Herrera's (2020) *temas, textos, and translanguaging* approach. Dos Puentes's curriculum centers culturally sustaining topics like the Greensboro Sit-Ins, along with their use of multimodal texts to learn about this youth-led movement through 'Own Voices' literature, students' research and music. Moreover, the teachers created opportunities for students to engage with the content using all of their linguistic repertoire as revealed by Justin's bilingual tri-fold poster on the sit-ins. As Palmer *et al.* (2019) argue, bilingualism, biliteracy and biculturalism is only strengthened when critical consciousness is a central focus in bilingual education.

References

España, C. and Herrera, L.Y. (2020) *En Comunidad: Lessons for Centering the Voices and Experiences of Bilingual Latinx Students*. Heinemann.

Flores, N. and García, O. (2017) A critical review of bilingual education in the United States: From basements and pride to boutiques and profit. *Annual Review of Applied Linguistics* 37, 14–29. https://doi.org/10.1017/S0267190517000162

Palmer, D.K., Cervantes-Soon, C., Dorner, L. and Heiman, D. (2019) Bilingualism, biliteracy, biculturalism, and critical consciousness for all: Proposing a fourth fundamental goal for two-way dual language education. *Theory Into Practice* 58 (2), 121–133. https://doi.org/10.1080/00405841.2019.1569376

Paris, D. (2012) Culturally sustaining pedagogy: A needed change in stance, terminology, and practice. *Educational Researcher* 41 (3), 93–97. https://doi.org/10.3102/0013189X12441244

Valdez, V.E., Freire, J. and Delavan, G. (2016) The gentrification of dual language education. *The Urban Review* 48 (4), 601–627. https://doi.org/10.1007/s11256-016-0370-0

5 Critical Collaboration to Support the Bilingualism and Biliteracy of Children with Disabilities

Sabrina Poms and Teresita Prieto

Dos Puentes Teachers

At Dos Puentes, our team of multilingual, critical and special educators considers children's multiple identities, positionalities, languages and personal experiences in order to make informed decisions about their academic and social needs. This work cannot be done adequately in professional isolation or when siloing students in boxes and categories that only recognize their disability or one aspect of their language practices or identity. Instead, we engage in critical collaboration, involving co-planning between teachers in Integrated Co-Teaching (ICT) classrooms across the grade, and between special education teachers across the school. We use the framework of Universal Design for Learning (UDL) to meet students' diverse needs in an integrated setting. In this chapter, we will discuss the ways in which ICT teacher teams collaborate to foster bilingualism and biliteracy in students with disabilities. Then we walk you through a day in one of our ICT classrooms at Dos Puentes.

Our Integrated Co-Teaching Bilingual Program

At Dos Puentes, we believe that children with disabilities can learn multilingually. Each grade has a bilingual ICT class that provides students with Individualized Education Programs (IEPs) the opportunity to learn alongside students without IEPs, with support from both a general education and a special education teacher. Our ICT program is unique in that *both* the general and special education teachers hold bilingual licenses in order to follow our school-wide language allocation policy of alternating the language of instruction between Spanish and English each day. While our goal of developing students' biliteracy in Spanish and English applies to all students, it also meets the mandate to provide instruction for students with disabilities whose home language is Spanish and whose IEP delineates that they receive instruction in their home language. Our specialized program gives access to bilingual instruction for emergent bilingual students with IEPs who would otherwise be in a monolingual ICT setting. Our approach provides opportunities for these students to learn in their home language, make cross-linguistic and cross-cultural connections, and learn a new language with two teachers who specialize in bilingual instruction and language learning.

Our bilingual ICT program is supported by bilingual service providers, including counselors, a social worker, speech-language therapists, an occupational therapist and one-to-one paraprofessionals, many of whom come from the same communities as our students. The next section of this chapter brings you into the people and activities that make up the ICT program at Dos Puentes.

Meet a Bilingual ICT Team

Sabrina and Carmen are co-teaching for the first time in a 2nd grade bilingual ICT classroom. From the start, they pour a great deal of energy and time into nurturing their partnership in and out of the classroom, knowing that this investment will lead to a more functional, loving and supportive classroom for their students. They often describe the partnership as a marriage, recognizing the immense level of trust, negotiation and care that go into successful team teaching. Like other teacher teams at Dos Puentes, Carmen and Sabrina come from different cultural and linguistic backgrounds. They find that a sustained focus on building trust increases in the small moments they spend together, perhaps while sitting together analyzing student work, recounting small group discussions, calling parents, filling out referral or assessment forms, creating differentiated materials or sharing the general joys and challenges of the day.

In contrast to other models of special education, Carmen and Sabrina believe in meaningfully integrating all students and push back against classrooms that are integrated only by name, where everyone is in one classroom but the special education teacher *only* works with students with IEPs, in a separate part of the classroom, while the general education teacher works with the rest of the class. They are continuously working to define their roles, equitably divide the labor and ensure proper implementation of specially designed instruction. They recognize that they must develop their skills in different areas to complement each other as a team. Carmen works closely with her general education colleagues across the grade to hone her content knowledge, while Sabrina collaborates with other special education teachers to continuously reflect on pedagogical tools and frameworks that reduce barriers to the general education curriculum. They view their different roles as resources brought together for co-planning and co-teaching, instead of scripts that dictate who and what they can and cannot teach in their classroom.

Co-Planning with a Universal Design for Learning Framework

After sharing the day's highlights, Sabrina and Carmen analyze recently collected pieces of literacy data in both English and Spanish that includes phonemic awareness skills, phonetic reading and writing, reading fluency and comprehension skills. They use a critical, multicultural lens to consider the variety of experiences, skills and linguistic repertoires students bring to the classroom while previewing the objectives and lessons from the upcoming reading and writing units. With those overall objectives in mind, as well as individual IEP goals, the teachers design multi-modal and collaborative literacy centers using the educational framework known as Universal Design for Learning (UDL). The framework of UDL shifts the paradigm away from identifying deficits within students to recognizing barriers within the environment. UDL proposes that teachers design lessons that are accessible and adjustable from the start, instead of retrofitting lessons with adaptations and interventions after the fact.

Accordingly, Carmen and Sabrina create literacy centers to target specific skills to all children while providing varied ways of presenting the information, multiple ways for students to show what they know and opportunities to choose between a range of highly engaging activities. In this way, one lesson contains many different entry points for all students who rotate through both independent centers and those guided by either of the teachers, instead of only providing small group instruction as a tool for remediation.

The student groups and activities are designed around specific skills and modified when goals are met. Additionally, language dominance is an important aspect of making groups. For example, a few newly arrived students from the Dominican Republic are placed in a temporary grouping focused on Spanish literacy to build on their linguistic assets, while other children are grouped differently depending on the language of the day. Sabrina, the special education teacher, plans to target and monitor the progress of specific IEP goals within the centers' rotations without taking students away from the rest of the class. Carmen and Sabrina's UDL-based planning provides a more meaningful integration of students with IEPs than conventional groupings and models of remediation.

A Morning in an ICT Classroom

A typical day in a bilingual ICT classroom starts much like in any other classroom. A buzz fills the room as children greet each other, gather in little groups to gawk at the day's schedule, sneak a peek at the morning message and tell their teachers about lost teeth or anticipated playdates, all while tripping over scarves and lunch boxes that haven't made it into the closet yet. Teachers and paraprofessionals greet children and give reminders in the language of the day. Once the initial commotion tapers off, children settle into their morning work before gathering on the rug to start their morning meeting.

A morning meeting sets the tone for the day and serves many purposes for all children. The meeting itself follows a predictable sequence in either language. In this 2nd grade ICT classroom, both teachers go over the schedule of the day and highlight any anticipated changes. This practice benefits all children, as it specifically addresses the needs of those with challenges transitioning or who have difficulties with executive functioning skills. After discussing the schedule, children participate in shared activities and conversations that build community, foster respect for one another and give opportunities to practice the language of the day. The teachers want all children to feel safe and respected in the classroom while practicing social and empathetic skills. The skills practiced in the morning meeting make other collaborative academic activities successful.

Next, students stand up for a short movement break, check the schedule and get ready for literacy centers. A visual guide for the center rotations is displayed (see Image 5.1) as well as a visual timer. Students get the materials they will need for their rotations and quickly get started at their first center.

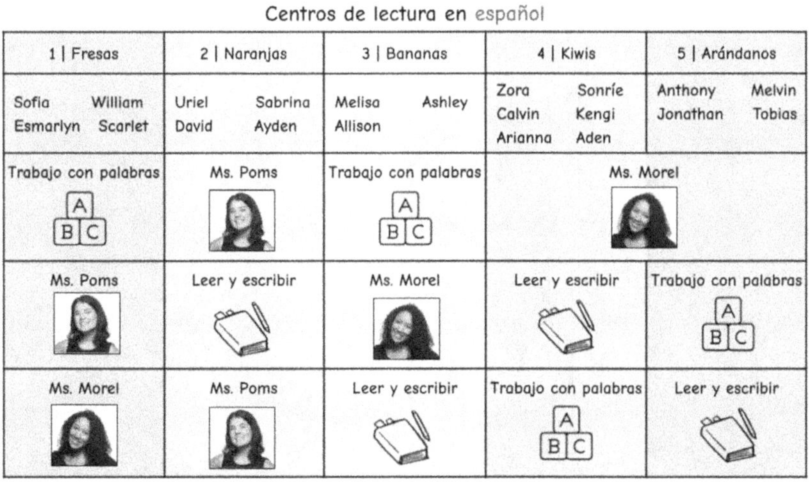

Centros de lectura en *español*

1 | Fresas	2 | Naranjas	3 | Bananas	4 | Kiwis	5 | Arándanos
Sofia William Esmarlyn Scarlet	Uriel Sabrina David Ayden	Melisa Ashley Allison	Zora Sonríe Calvin Kengi Arianna Aden	Anthony Melvin Jonathan Tobias
Trabajo con palabras [A][B][C]	Ms. Poms	Trabajo con palabras [A][B][C]	Ms. Morel	
Ms. Poms	Leer y escribir	Ms. Morel	Leer y escribir	Trabajo con palabras [A][B][C]
Ms. Morel	Ms. Poms	Leer y escribir	Trabajo con palabras [A][B][C]	Leer y escribir

Image 5.1 An example of the literacy centers rotation chart shown to children during the period. Photo by Sabrina Poms

Small Group Time: Specially Designed Instruction

At one of the teacher-guided centers, Sabrina prepares an activity in which students use the voice recorder app on a Chromebook or iPad to assist in the process of accurately transferring letter and syllable knowledge into their writing. She developed this specialized writing protocol during a series of additional planning periods in which special education teachers from various grades, including 1st grade teacher Teresita, met to discuss student work samples and assessment data. During that time, Sabrina shared about a group of four students, including three with IEPs for speech and language impairment, who all had difficulties with attention and working memory. The teachers were puzzled by the children's ability to name all of the letters and sounds when reading, but their inability to transfer this knowledge into their writing. This resulted in students writing random letters that did not correspond with what they wanted to say, or not writing at all. Together, the teachers

Image 5.2 Uriel writes independently with the voice recording app. Photo by Sabrina Poms

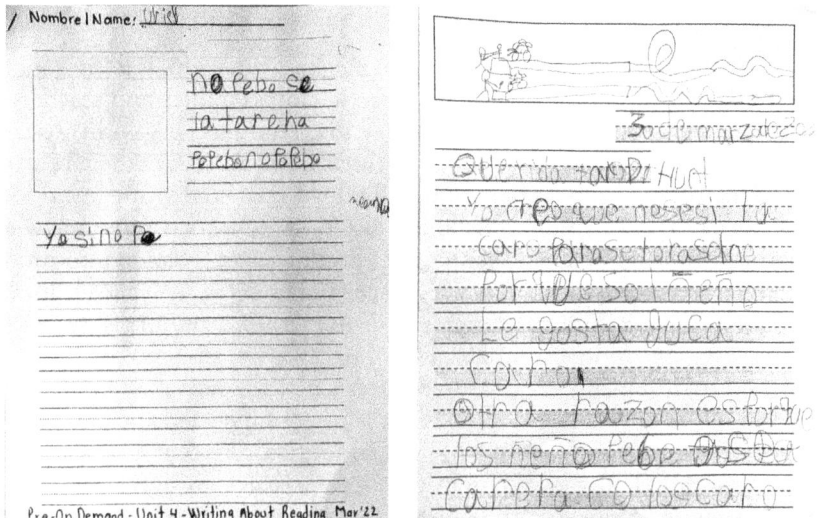

Image 5.3 & Image 5.4 Uriel's writing before (left) and after (right) the writing intervention was implemented. Photos by Sabrina Poms

closely analyzed the steps of the writing process through the lens of a bilingual student with these specific challenges and pinpointed where they could intervene. The team hypothesized that lessening the cognitive load of remembering a whole sentence through the use of a voice recording app could leave more room for accurately recording the letter sounds of each word.

Accordingly, the students at Sabrina's center began by reviewing the detailed writing protocol in their folders, then took out their laptops with the built-in voice recorder app ready. After learning to operate the voice recording app independently, the four students began to write more fluidly, more confidently, and with more motivation (see Images 5.3 & 5.4).

The students play back their sentences easily up to 10 times as they write. They are able to focus on segmenting each sound at the word level instead of getting stuck on retaining the whole sentence. They more fully utilize visual tools such as syllable charts or sight word lists because they focus on one word at a time. Importantly, their level of engagement and independence has increased as before they relied on the teacher to repeat the word. A few students still need assistance with initial brainstorming and forming a complete sentence before recording, but the longer they use the voice recorder, the less they rely on this support. One student comes up to Sabrina at the end of the center saying, '¡Mira cuánto escribí! ¡Lo hice sólo!'. This intervention gave bilingual students with disabilities ownership over their work and a high level of engagement. The tool created multiple access points and allowed for fading support over time.

Conclusion

The work involved in teaching bilingual students with disabilities can be complex, but also very impactful for students, families and teachers. Through the close collaboration between ICT co-teachers and vertical teams over the years, we have seen that intentional practices that consider the interaction of students' disabilities, linguistic repertoires and identities allow students to thrive in our bilingual special education program. We have seen that bilingual students with disabilities can blossom in integrated settings with their peers while receiving ongoing special education supports. When ICT teams design supportive experiences for all students to listen to one another and learn from each other, respectful and safe learning environments are nurtured. Over time, we have also discovered that this work only happens when ICT teams are supported and balanced. As ICT teams change from year to year, it is critical to create spaces within our school for these new relationships or 'marriages' to settle, trust one another, build cross-cultural connections, and understand their roles as special and general education teachers, in order to successfully teach our bilingual students with and without IEPs.

Researcher Commentary

María Cioè-Peña
University of Pennsylvania

This chapter highlights the critical value/impact of well-supported, collaborative teaching partnerships. It is also a reminder of the need for intersectional policies, practices and pedagogies that consider the multiplicity of a child, particularly those classified as emergent bi/multilinguals with dis/abilities (EBwDs).

Context

Required by No Child Left Behind (NCLB), the disaggregation of student data across eight categories – racial/ethnic and socioeconomic categorizations along with 'English Learner' (EL) and 'Student with Disabilities' (SWD) classifications – allowed educators and policymakers to develop deeper understandings of *de facto* school segregation. Schools today encounter profound levels of racial and intellectual segregation; Special Education (SpEd) is riddled with problems of disproportionality and overrepresentation of racialized learners (Cartledge *et al.*, 2016); and bilingual education (BilEd) is navigating the gentrification of dual language programs (Valdez *et al.*, 2016). Thus, BilEd and SpEd continue to serve as hypersegregated educational spaces (Elder *et al.*, 2019; Sung, 2018). One reason for these ongoing issues with racial and intellectual segregation are the categories themselves and how they are used. Although classifications are meant to determine services a student is entitled to, they often result in the positioning of students through deficit-oriented perspectives that focus on their needs without accounting for strengths. Similarly, the manifestation of reductionist demographic markers – stemming from learner classifications like low-income, EL, and/or SWD – rarely account for the experiences of students whose lives are impacted by multiple systems of oppression at once like capitalism, xenophobia and ableism. As a result, students' experiences are directed by their perceived schooling needs which are often placed on a hierarchy where either language- or disability-related needs triumph but rarely both.

Part of the reason the holistic educational needs of EBwDs often go unmet is because this dichotomous understanding of disability-related need OR language-related need persists due to siloed educational policies and programs. Currently, SpEd policies are governed by the Individual with Disabilities Education Act (IDEA). Language related needs, on the other hand, are governed by policies focused primarily on English acquisition. These policies stem from Every Student Succeeds Act (ESSA), the federal K-12 education law of the United States. IDEA was established to address the educational inequities that people with dis/abilities have experienced (Fleischer & Zames, 2012). However, while IDEA asserts the need for bilingual assessments to determine eligibility for SpEd services, it does not address the specific pedagogical needs of multilingual children (Cioè-Peña, 2017b). On the other hand, language educators carry their own history of oppression in which racialized people's languages and ways of languaging are used as indicators of an inherent inferiority regarding intellectual capacity and social value (Schissel, 2019). As a result, language advocates have engaged in a campaign to elevate bilingualism from an indicator of needs to bilingualism as an academic, sociocultural and economic resource.

The commodification of bilingualism unfortunately resulted in erroneous conceptualizations of who could be bilingual and who could not (Cioè-Peña, 2017a). Subsequently, narratives of superiority were used to establish the ideal BilEd student as a user of standard practices, who can perform orally, and who will be able to maximize the sociocultural and economic value of bilingualism (Cioè-Peña, 2017a/b). Therefore, while BilEd programs focused on multilingual maintenance grew and inclusive education programs for SWDs expanded, we did not see the simultaneous development of bilingual inclusive education settings as the program in this chapter highlights.

Discussion

Sabrina Poms and Teresita Prieto's description of the collaborative, supportive and professional learning community that is central to Dos Puentes's identity and success left me feeling incredibly hopeful. While I lament the fact that during my tenure as a bilingual SpEd teacher in the

2000s, I did not have access to the kinds of institutional supports and encouragement available to teachers at Dos Puentes, I feel encouraged knowing that not only do programs, classrooms and schools like this exist now, they are also successful! The attention to and investment in the academic *and* linguistic growth of multiply-marginalized learners that Dos Puentes provides can serve as a model of liberatory and justice-oriented praxis that includes all learners, all day, in all ways. Furthermore, this chapter is a reminder that we do not have to wait for intersectional policies; we can instead manifest truly inclusive programs and practices that support and celebrate our students as whole beings with ties to communities, cultures and languages that defy the neat categories that labels like EL and SWD strive for. Poms and Prieto show us that what is needed, first and foremost, is a desire to see children as whole beings, and, just as importantly, to support co-teachers in developing meaningful relationships where they co-lead, co-teach and co-learn in ways that allow all classroom members to find success.

References

Cartledge, G., Kea, C.D., Watson, M. and Oif, A. (2016) Special education disproportionality: A review of response to intervention and culturally relevant pedagogy. *Multiple Voices for Ethnically Diverse Exceptional Learners* 16 (1), 29–49.

Cioè-Peña, M. (2017a) Disability, bilingualism and what it means to be normal. *Journal of Bilingual Education Research & Instruction* 19 (1), 138–160.

Cioè-Peña, M. (2017b) Who is excluded from inclusion? Points of union and division in bilingual and special education. *Theory, Research, and Action in Urban Education* V (1). https://blmtraue.commons.gc.cuny.edu/2017/02/24/who-is-excluded-from-inclusion- points-of-union-and-division-in-bilingual-and-special-education

Elder, T.E., Figlio, D.N., Imberman, S.A. and Persico, C.L. (2019) *School Segregation and Racial Gaps in SpEd Identification* (Working Paper No. 25829; Working Paper Series). National Bureau of Economic Research. https://doi.org/10.3386/w25829

Fleischer, D.Z. and Zames, F. (2012) *The Disability Rights Movement: From Charity to Confrontation*. Temple University Press.

Schissel, J.L. (2019) *Social Consequences of Testing for Language-minoritized Bilinguals in the United States*. Multilingual Matters.

Sung, K.K. (2018) Raciolinguistic ideology of antiblackness: Bilingual education, tracking, and the multiracial imaginary in urban schools. *International Journal of Qualitative Studies in Education* 31 (8), 667–683.

Valdez, V.E., Freire, J.A. and Delavan, M.G. (2016) The gentrification of dual language education. *Urban Review: Issues and Ideas in Public Education* 48 (4), 601–627.

Pillar 2 Introduction

Las Familias son Partners, Leaders and Advocates

Consuelo Villegas, Yesenia J. Moreno and Tatyana Kleyn

Dos Puentes Founding Parent Coordinator, Teacher and Co-Founder

A family is a child's first teacher, and their home is their first school. At home children begin to understand cultural norms and traditions, communicate in the language(s) of their family and begin to navigate the world. When children reach school age, it is an opportunity for this learning trajectory to continue, ideally as seamlessly as possible. But this can only happen when families are fully welcomed into a school and given the opportunity to play a central role in their children's education as they become part of a larger school community. Within a bilingual school, the bridge between home and school is fortified as the home languages and cultures of families are valued and centered in teaching and learning.

As the pillars of Dos Puentes were planned, we knew the education of students could not be separated from their family and home. The *familia* pillar focuses on forming and maintaining strong home-school partnerships to support the academic and socioemotional development of every child. This is done by building a community that links home and school and values each, individually and collectively when it comes to students' learning, languaging and overall development. The *familia* pillar considers issues of power, and works to elevate the voices of families from racially minoritized, immigrant and low-income homes. These are often the people who tend to be overshadowed by those with louder and more privileged voices (Chávez-Reyes, 2010). The home-school partnerships must build from, and be responsive to and inclusive of, the realities of students' home lives and the funds of knowledge that they bring to school (Moll *et al.*, 1992). Such a community requires strong two-way structures that are taught, maintained and revisited to ensure families have full access to student learning, school activities and resources for schooling and beyond.

Traditional family involvement, also referred to as a 'bake sale' model, centers families' participation in fundraising and helping with various school activities (Warren *et al.*, 2009). This contrasts family engagement where the focus is on 'partnership, collaboration, and shared decision making among schools, families, and communities' (Lowenhaupt, 2014: 3). Warren *et al.* (2009) connect this to relational power that is shared by families and schools as they 'look to their shared interest in advancing the education and wellbeing of children to help them work through inevitable differences and conflicts' (2009: 2213). In practice this means school initiatives and committees that impact larger school policies, curricula and programs that include the voices and views of diverse families.

At Dos Puentes this engagement is seen through the lens of *las familias* as partners, leaders and advocates. This requires that the strengths, voices and concerns of families across different groups surface, and that decisions be made collectively. Occasionally this requires difficult conversations as conflicting ideas emerge, especially when families come from different cultural, linguistic and socioeconomic groups that are not equally positioned within a society where whiteness is centered (even when white people are not a numerical majority) and racism and linguicism persist. But finding the space to hear various viewpoints while highlighting the voices of the most vulnerable is a way to ensure families become active participants in their child's education and school *comunidad*.

We focus on families rather than just parents, as children have many important adults in their lives. Affirming and including diverse families ensures all those people are part of the bonds that are made between home and school. Factors such as family structures, migration and the (in)ability to cross borders, work responsibilities, extended hours and even incarceration all challenge the idea of a nuclear family unit. Families include grandparents, *tías y tíos*, siblings, *primos*, *madrastras*, *padrastros*, caregivers, neighbors and all those who play a significant role in a child's daily life. For many of our immigrant-origin families it is common for multiple generations to live together and share caregiving responsibilities. Students become a reflection of their unique and broadly defined family unit and for this reason, partnering with families – in the broadest sense of the word – in a student's education is vital for their academic, linguistic and psychosocial growth as school and home are bridged. Pillar 2 is supported by our parent coordinator and a range of structures and tools that enable families to be partners who provide input and share leadership for the benefit of their children and our collective community.

An Advocate for *Familias*

The New York City Public Schools require all schools to hire a parent coordinator. This multifaceted position includes supporting families, serving as the liaison between home and school, addressing questions and concerns and working with the Parent Association (PA). However, we also feel the title is limiting for the reasons we explained above regarding how parents are often not the only adults intricately involved in the education of children, especially in NYC. While the title is parent coordinator, Consuelo Villegas works with all family members and goes above and beyond the position description. Her role is critically important because 'traditional forms of family engagement may fall short in so far as those practices encourage families to engage with schools, rather than schools to engage with families' (Lowenhaupt, 2014: 22). Consuelo makes the effort to build linkages from the schools with families right from the start. She is often considered the heart of the school, as she welcomes every family and attends to an abundance of needs. The care, love and advocacy that she demonstrates daily builds trust and ensures families from all different backgrounds are seen and heard.

Perspectives from a 'Parent' Coordinator

As the Parent Coordinator at Dos Puentes, I (Consuelo) make it a priority to get to know each of our families. Through our interactions I aim to build a sense of *confianza* and compassion. I work with families individually from the moment they consider enrolling their child until I see that child graduate from 5th grade. Each family is unique. Once I have made a connection with them, I am able to address concerns they may have or provide clarification. In the decade that I have been in this position, I see how many families are anxious to learn how to best support their children and to build trusting relationships. My purpose is to offer them the tools necessary to advocate for their child and family. These tools can include workshops on literacy in general, or in Spanish or English specifically, access to online messaging systems, support in creating an email account or providing enrichment programs for their children. But my work also goes beyond the school doors. I have had conversations about ill family members, marital troubles, postpartum depression, food insecurities, illiteracy, domestic abuse and deportation. These issues span cultures, languages and economic levels. The most important aspect of this work is to remember that each family is different, yet they are all seeking the best avenues to support their children.

Las Familias son Partners, Leaders and Advocates at Dos Puentes

In order to truly enact our second pillar, we have to go beyond parent participation and engagement to encourage families to guide the work and approach of Dos Puentes. This is never an easy shift, and it is particularly important and challenging in a bilingual school where some of the families come from oppressed communities who are directly impacted by racist and xenophobic policies that aim to silence their voices and overlook their strengths and needs. To counter this positioning of minoritized families, Dos Puentes tries to be intentional in creating spaces for marginalized families in our school and have them serve in leadership roles whenever possible. Below we outline examples of school structures where families serve as partners, leaders and advocates. Then, the following six chapters within this pillar take us into the deliberate, powerful and sometimes messy ways families are active members of our school community.

Las Familias as Partners

Without the partnership of our families, we would not be able to provide a holistic education that is culturally and linguistically relevant and sustaining for our students. The home-school partnership begins before any kindergartener or new student enters the school building on the first day of classes. The home visit is a hallmark tradition at Dos Puentes. The purpose of the home visit is to get to know the families and gain insight into the lives of our students. Two staff members embark on a scheduled visit to discover the skills and resources that each family can bring to the school community and glean their necessities. This is an opportunity for the family and child to meet school staff and have a familiar face greet them on the first day of school. The home visit also serves to share information about public schooling in the US and NYC if families come from a different country or if it is their first time in the school system.

Another hallmark tradition at Dos Puentes is Family Fridays. This is the day families look forward to the most, as they visit their child's classroom while they can meet other parents, their children's classmates and learn firsthand how the teacher interacts with the class. Depending on the grade, family members partner with their children and their peers (as not everyone can have a family member attend) to engage in activities that range from projects to skill building to educational games. Family Fridays are a powerful way to bring in the linguistic and cultural backgrounds of families and delve deeper into their history, identities and connections.

The work of the school could not happen without the support of families. At Dos Puentes grade-level parents serve as the liaison between the parent coordinator, classroom teachers and families. They use personal connections to increase the participation of families who typically feel excluded from formal school structures arising from deficient views of Latinx families where they are falsely positioned as having little to offer due to their linguistic, economic or formal education backgrounds (Song, 2019). Grade-level parents attend monthly meetings to discuss and promote upcoming classroom and school-wide activities such as movie nights, the annual auction and family picnics.

Families are also partners in dialogue via monthly principal chats with Dr Hunt. The chats are an important space for the exchange of ideas between families and the principal, who listens to their concerns or solutions as they engage in a dialogue to better the experience of the school community. The chats occur bilingually with everything stated in Spanish and then translated into English to ensure Spanish-speaking families feel included. During the chats families learn about school activities and initiatives from the NYC Public Schools as they also ask questions and provide their input. For example, families have been concerned about dismissal procedures, field trips, state exams and the school uniform policy.

Dos Puentes offers a range of events to bridge families from different backgrounds. International Night, potlucks and movie nights all help to foster a sense of community. International Night is a big event where families and students showcase their talents. This is where we see the richness each family brings via music, poetry, traditional dances, opera, theater, magic tricks, ballet and more. During the pandemic, the event was held online as relatives from all over the world joined to watch and even participate in this annual event where families and teachers partner in the holistic education and celebration of their children.

These are just some of the ways we partner with families in the education of their children so that they see themselves as central members of our Dos Puentes community. But we also want our families to take the next step as leaders and decision makers in our school.

Las Familias as Leaders

Families are the leaders of their children's education in the early years of their lives and at Dos Puentes we support families to continue their roles as leaders within the school. The idea of taking on leadership roles is not always a familiar one, especially for families who come from countries where educational expertise is solely placed in the hands of educators. We have observed that some Spanish-speaking families feel intimidated and reluctant to get involved, even in a fully bilingual school. Along those lines Chávez-Moreno (2019: 113) reminds us that 'white supremacy affects language-restrictive contexts *and* bilingual education settings, such as racially diverse dual-language and even all-Latinx programs'. Keeping this in mind, we work with minoritized families to remind them they are experts who know their children, their backgrounds and needs. And as a result, they have much to contribute as co-leaders in our school best.

The formal leadership roles at Dos Puentes include being part of the Parent Association, School Leadership Team and the Parent Advisory Committee (PAC Title 1). As members of these committees, families play a direct role in the decisions and approaches of the school. Their participation is not only beneficial to their children's education, but they can also educate themselves as they contribute to the academic, social and emotional experiences of all the students in the school.

A Parent Association (PA) is a typical structure in most K-12 schools within the US. However, the PA at Dos Puentes takes on a unique configuration to integrate the bilingual approach of the school, as well as the hesitancy of certain family members to take on leadership roles due to language, immigration status and/or limited formal education. The PA is composed of eight members for the following four positions: president, vice-president, treasurer and secretary. Each position has two members, one who is dominant in Spanish and the second in English or bilingual. One member is in the official role and the second is in training to better understand the role to build up confidence to serve officially the following year. Given the composition of the PA, meetings involve the dynamic use of Spanish and English via translanguaging, which includes translation as well.

The School Leadership Team (SLT) is a mandated committee that is required of all NYC Public Schools. It consists of the school principal, the PA president, the school's teacher-union representative, the PAC Title I (Parent Advisory Committee) representative and other elected educators and family members. The PAC representative makes recommendations about how to spend federal Title I funds, which schools receive based on the percentage of low-economic households. The SLT is charged with developing educational policy through the creation of a Comprehensive Education Plan (CEP). The SLT then conducts a yearly evaluation of the school's academic programs. As a bilingual school, our SLT has identified goals that are created via consensus-based priorities. Most recently those goals focus on content area learning, special education, prioritizing *el español* and the goal most closely connected to *las familias* pillar: ensuring that Spanish-speaking families have a voice in the school community.

A less formal, but equally important way that families lead is through a language exchange program. English- and Spanish-speaking families requested space and time to get to know each other. This appeal resulted in '*intercambio de idioma*' or 'language exchange' where family members from primarily Spanish- and English-speaking backgrounds come together to integrate our school community and practice their new languages. These exchanges help us to build trusting relationships across groups who sometimes have divergent world views and allow families to be leaders and teachers of their home language and affiliated cultures. The families meet once or twice a month, with a coffee in hand, to engage in conversation in a new language, and sometimes they take *paseos* to try out nearby restaurants or visit local museums.

Families have also taken on leadership roles in different aspects of our school life. They have given school tours to prospective families in Spanish, English and bilingually because they believe in our school and want to share the wonderful things that are happening there (more recently this has been within a context where local charter schools have made recruiting students a much more competitive endeavor, even within a public community school like Dos Puentes). During the COVID-19 pandemic, families noticed that a segment of our school community was struggling to meet their basic needs and moved into action, identifying grants and raising funds that led to $12,000 for distribution to those who needed it most.

While not all families come to us with a vision of being a leader at Dos Puentes, we encourage and support them to take on these roles to see the power they can have in their children's education and within the school community.

Las Familias as Advocates

The field of bilingual education is foregrounded through advocacy. In the US it was a Chinese immigrant family who sued the San Francisco school district because their child was provided with instruction, curriculum and resources only in English and without modifications. As such they were unable to understand the content and progress academically. This led to the federal Lau v. Nichols (1974) ruling that required all students with the 'English Language Learner' designation across the country to have access to bilingual education or English as a new/second/additional language support. In NYC it was the Puerto Rican community who fought for the ASPIRA Consent Decree, also passed in 1974, that fortified the rights of students to access bilingual and English as New Language (ENL, as is the official terminology in NYS) programming (ASPIRA, 1974). While these federal and local policies are important, they still do not ensure an equitable and linguistically relevant education for racially minoritized students, even within bilingual programs. This means that advocacy for the human, educational and linguistic rights of students is still required. And immigrant-origin families are especially well positioned to fight for the rights of their children – as evidenced in the landmark Lau v. Nichols case – despite sometimes feeling they do not have the right to make demands upon teachers, administrators, schools and even larger policymaking bodies.

At Dos Puentes advocacy occurs on many levels. The administrators advocate for funding for their increasing population of multilingual learners. Teachers advocate for curriculum and resources that allow them to teach content in Spanish in authentic and connected ways. Families advocate for uniform programs that create a more equitable situation for students from varying socioeconomic statuses, free afterschool programs and book fairs to ensure students have access to bilingual and Spanish literature.

While some families feel empowered to advocate when issues arise on an individual level for their child or collectively, this is not the case for

Image P2.1 The Rincon Hispano *grupo* following a meeting with Parent Coordinator Consuelo Villegas (center). Photo by Maria Martinez

everyone. As the parent coordinator I (Consuelo) created Rincón Hispano in 2021 specifically for Spanish-dominant parents who are in the early stages of speaking English (see Image P2.1). Some families expressed to me, in confidence, that they were scared to come out and speak publicly and needed a safe space to share their concerns and aspirations. I also observed their reluctance to speak out in larger events, even though the meetings were held bilingually and often with Spanish as the primary language. This signifies that the empowerment of families goes beyond linguistic access and branches out into a fear of being seen and heard. Rincón Hispano serves as an entryway for families who are in danger of fading into the background to build their confidence to speak up, express their concerns and bring forward new ideas to improve our school.

Rincón Hispano meets monthly to build the leadership skills of our families to position them to advocate for their children. I love to hear their voices and see the representation from diverse countries, Indigenous backgrounds, immigration statuses and levels of formal education. Some meetings function as workshops about navigating the school system, with a focus on understanding special education services and rights and accessing city-wide programs. Other meetings are led by classroom teachers to orient families to the literacy and math instruction, as well as how to use technology as a tool at home. Rincón Hispano also provides the space for families to teach each other or share resources. Families may share how they approach math from their country of origin and compare it to the math problem sets their children bring home for homework. Rincón Hispano participants also help integrate cultural holidays into the school community. For example, families may showcase *parrandas*, a Puerto Rican musical tradition during the holidays across the classrooms. Families make connections to their own cultural traditions and find ways to integrate them within the school.

We have found focusing on empowering Spanish-dominant families is imperative to building an inclusive school community. When we support those who are the most vulnerable, we ultimately bring everyone up together. Rincón Hispano participants are slowly starting to make their voices heard at Dos Puentes as more family members volunteer to take on leadership roles by becoming members of the SLT or grade-level parent representatives.

Our families ultimately are concerned for the wellbeing of their children and want them to be in an environment that allows them to learn bilingually. To that end, they advocate for numerous programs and initiatives within the school. After an alarming increase in needles from drug users in the area, concerned families partnered with the Corner Project, a community-based organization, to help clean areas around the school prior to the start of each day (see Chapter 20). Our school garden has been maintained primarily by families who take it upon themselves to collaborate with teachers. It is a space where everything is labeled bilingually and the activities held there are tied to the curriculum. Classes visit the garden to plant and eventually prepare and eat the vegetables grown there, or simply to enjoy a relaxing read aloud surrounded by the vegetation (a rarity in NYC).

Advocacy is never easy, but it is critical for bilingual schools to have staunch advocates in their families to push for the rights of their children to learn bilingually, and do so in a safe environment where they have access to instruction and resources that are connected to their linguistic and cultural backgrounds. And given the uneven terrain in the power and resources of families within diverse dual language bilingual programs, where gentrification gives unwarranted privilege to those who are white and/or speak English, it is up to schools to support families in finding their voices and power to advocate for changes to classroom practices, school programs and state and federal policies.

Section Overview

This section is made up of six chapters that show the myriad ways the *familia* pillar comes to life at Dos Puentes. In Chapter 6, 'Families as Educators, Leaders and Advocates', founding teacher Stephanie Ubiera and parents Adriana Cando and Ained Casado take us into how families and educators collaborate in various roles for the betterment of their children and the school community. In Chapter 7, 'Bridging Home and School', teacher and parent team Sacha Mercier and Amy Withers walk us through a trademark of Dos Puentes, the home visit, as well as student-led conferences and Individualized Educational Plan (IEP) meetings. In Chapter 8, 'Family Diversity as a Strength and a Challenge', community advocate and parent Annette Fernandez brings to light the ways a diverse school community like Dos Puentes simultaneously thrives and struggles to work together among the racial, ethnic, socioeconomic and migration differences that exist within a gentrifying community. In Chapter 9, 'Building *Comunidad*', parent Elga Castro Ramos takes us into the quintessential Family Friday experience and shows us the inner workings of the Parent Association. In Chapter 10, 'Socioemotional Learning and Support', teachers Irving Mota and Kimberly Bautista share how they address students' socioemotional struggles they carry between home and school through an approach developed by Arlène Casimir called Holding Space. Finally, in Chapter 11, 'Remote Learning through a Pandemic', parent Aaron Sidlo reflects on the experiences families of different backgrounds faced when Dos Puentes – and schools across the nation – shifted to online instruction during the COVID-19 pandemic.

Building an inclusive school community cultivates a meaningful education for each child and subsequently their family. Although it takes a concerted effort, everyone benefits from the engagement of socioeconomically, linguistically and culturally diverse families. But this requires going beyond volunteering at bake sales or raising funds to the full participation of *familias* as partners, leaders and advocates.

References

ASPIRA of New York Incorporated *et al.* v Board of Education of the City of New York, *et al.* 1974. 72 Civ. 4002 S.D.N.Y. (MEF). Consent Decree, August 29.

Chávez-Moreno, L.C. (2019) Researching Latinxs, racism, and white supremacy in bilingual education: A literature review. *Critical Inquiry in Language Studies* 17 (2), 101–120.

Chávez-Reyes, C. (2010) Inclusive approaches to parent engagement for young English language learners and their families. *Yearbook of the National Society for the Study of Education* 109, 474–504.

Lau v. Nichols (414 U.S. 563, 1974)

Lowenhaupt, R. (2014) School access and participation: Family engagement practices in the new Latino diaspora. *Education and Urban Society* 46 (5), 522–547.

Moll, L., Amanti, C., Neff, D. and Gonzalez, N. (1992) Funds of knowledge for teaching: Using a qualitative approach to connect homes and classrooms. *Theory Into Practice* 31, 132–141.

Song, K. (2019) Immigrant parents' ideological positioning on bilingualism. *Theory Into Practice* 58 (3), 254–262.

Warren, M., Hoong, S., Leung Rubin, C. and Sychitkokhong Uy, P. (2009) Beyond the bake sale: A community-based relational approach to parent engagement in schools. *Teachers College Record* 111 (9), 2209–2254.

6 Families as Educators, Leaders and Advocates

Stephanie Ubiera, Adriana Cando and Ained Casado

Dos Puentes Founding Teacher and Mothers
Translated by Angela Paredes Montero

Dos Puentes Elementary was a leap of faith that set the foundation for the collaboration between families and educators. There were so many questions to answer. What role will families play? What can the faculty provide for families and what can they provide to the school? Joining Dos Puentes was an easy choice for us, the educators, because we foresaw the possibilities in our shared vision. Meanwhile, parents were searching for a school to call home, where they felt welcomed and knew that not only their child, but they too were in the right place.

In this chapter, parents Adriana and Ained, alongside a founding teacher at Dos Puentes, Stephanie, respond to these questions and challenges. We address the force behind the collaborative relationship and what it meant for families to take their place as leaders, educators and advocates.

As *leaders*, our families were in the forefront of many of the decisions that impacted our school's direction. Their participation through various committees, events and learning opportunities made its mark and established a tradition of leadership that has become a cornerstone of our Dos Puentes community.

As *educators*, our families took on an active role in teaching and learning alongside their children. They were welcomed into the classroom to be partners in their child's learning and partake in the curriculum, in many instances by helping to shape it. They became empowered to ask about the curriculum and school structures to gain a deeper understanding in order to take on decision-making roles. This practice goes against traditional norms of public education where families are intended to participate in ways that are supportive (such as bake sales, fundraisers, class parties) rather than foundational.

Image 6.1 The family photo that was taken during the home visit, when Anthony (in the school t-shirt) entered Dos Puentes. From left to right: Father, Marco, Daughter, Katherine, and Adriana Cando. Photo by Adriana Cando

As *advocates*, our families have found their voices to make an impact on not only their children's education, but our school and community. Our Parent Coordinator, Consuelo Villegas, was pivotal from the front line for families as the first stop at Dos Puentes. Many of our immigrant families have sought out a new understanding of education within Dos Puentes. This chapter will explore the role of families in these three areas through the lens of immigrants who place their hopes and dreams for their children within the school.

Families as Educators

Our son started attending Dos Puentes in 1st grade. Our first connection with the school was during the home visit. It was an important and very special experience that motivated our family to take an active role in the school. The teachers came to our home and welcomed my son with a book bag and a t-shirt with the school logo (see Image 6.1). They also asked questions to get to know our family, and established a collaborative relationship. We treasure the photo of our home visit and appreciate the support we received in my son's educational journey. We felt a special connection with Dos Puentes because they were able to provide academic, social and emotional support and guidance.

As an immigrant parent (Adriana), my husband and I aspired to pass on our language *el español* to our children, and our priority was to find a bilingual school. Thank God our neighborhood had excellent schools and Dos Puentes was one of them. Since we spoke Spanish at home, my children were gradually immersed in their second language, English, at school. We wanted to keep our language, so we told our children '*de la puerta para afuera se puede hablar inglés y de puerta para adentro será en español* (outside this door you can speak English and inside this door it's Spanish)'. This rule worked because the children spoke English with their friends and Spanish with us.

Thanks to Dos Puentes my son is now bilingual. His teachers were fun and engaging and the school was the best place to learn a new language since they provided language and cultural development. It was a phenomenal experience. We supported our children at home by reading, singing, writing and speaking Spanish. One of the challenges we had was speaking *el Spanglish*, and the school continued to support us in this regard. The school encouraged parents to take English classes and organized events to involve us. For example, on Family Fridays, families brought objects that represented their cultures, such as a *pilón*, a mariachi hat, a faceless doll from the Dominican Republic and a dala horse from Sweden. We learned alongside our children about other cultures and were proud to see them share ours. It was a memorable experience.

Teachers and staff at any school play a vital role in supporting immigrant families with language barriers. It is important they are kind, attentive, friendly, available and responsive since immigrants can feel afraid and ashamed of not being able to express themselves and be understood. What makes Dos Puentes special is *la confianza* built between the school and the families. Family engagement in events like the Harvest Festival or International Night, despite language barriers, connects us, creates community within the school and breaks down barriers.

Immigrant parents should also join the Parent Association (PA), and the School Leadership Team (SLT), or become class representatives. Sometimes, we feel at a disadvantage in participating in these committees because of our limited educational background. However, in these roles, we have the opportunity to make school building decisions such as maintenance, heating, or cafeteria and playground renovations.

This community has opened many doors for immigrant parents, including those without advanced formal education. This allows us to join these committees or volunteer at school events to strengthen our sense of belonging to the school community. When we proudly share our roots, we contribute to creating a welcoming environment in the school community.

Families as Leaders

I (Ained) have always been a quiet and shy person, often following the crowd. In my adolescence I was never the person to propose an activity or initiate a friendship. When I came to the United States from the Dominican Republic I had to learn how to advocate for myself, in high school and later as an undergraduate university student. I understood the concept of being responsible for myself, but now I was a mother. That is when my world became my daughter's world, and I knew that whatever I needed to do from that moment on had to be better to ensure all she needed was provided for. My interest in being involved in Ximena's school started early on when she was in head start and continued in Dos Puentes. Always attending the family events, I wanted to see and learn how to best support her in this new journey through elementary school.

My participation in various school events made me feel like I was part of a larger family where everyone helps raise each other's children. Because Dos Puentes is a community-oriented school, I felt the need to help in any way possible. Being a leader within your family is a normal role for any parent since we are always guiding and teaching our children through the early stages of education and the development of socioemotional skills. Besides the love and affection we give our children, it is imperative to teach them the things that are important for us.

As a first-generation immigrant, I learned early in life about the importance of reusing and recycling items that many people nowadays might consider trash. With my inner sense of play and creativity, I taught my daughter how recycling was not only important for the environment, but that it could be fun! When my daughter was in 2nd grade, I had the opportunity to share my passion for creative recycling with a group of students who were part of the afterschool program that was then run by school staff and volunteers. That year volunteers were scarce, classes were limited, and many children needed after school care. Looking at the dilemma that the school was facing I volunteered my time to help. I gathered many ideas that were creative, fun, easy, and of course educational for a 6-8 week course. One of those activities was making paper plate analog clocks, where the students used their knowledge of these clocks and how they work to create their version using card stock, markers, paper plates, and whatever else they would like to use to create their masterpiece. I had the opportunity to see firsthand how the students helped each other in English and Spanish and shared their approaches to the activities. Students would line up to enter the classroom, and the first thing they asked was 'what are we making today?'. Every time I heard that question, I felt a sense of pride and happiness that these simple activities gave the students something interesting to look forward to every week. Although at the beginning I doubted myself and my ability to lead a creative class as a parent without educational training, with the support of Ms Consuelo and the parents, this became a successful endeavor that taught children the values upon which our school was founded. It also taught me about myself and allowed me to see myself as a leader in the school.

Families as Advocates

In school settings, advocacy can take many forms. In some cases, parents may advocate for their children's best interests or promote their culture without fear. In other cases, we advocate to protect the safety and rights of the most vulnerable members of society. The events following the 2016 presidential election proved to be such a moment.

The morning after the election, I (Stephanie) was worried and uncertain about the country's future and my own future as a first generation daughter of immigrants. US-born and immigrant parents shared the same feelings and fears. The school's immediate action was to protect our families and provide moral support and peace of mind, to the extent possible. We began by informing families about organizations that were also there to help. Meanwhile, teachers wondered: how will we teach in a world where everything will change? Teachers did not sleep, thinking they would wake up in a nightmare. Many cried thinking about the children and their families who they knew needed to be held tightly.

Ms Consuelo organized a parent meeting shortly after the election as Trump's attacks on immigrants escalated. He called them criminals, rapists and prostitutes. He wanted to leave children orphaned in government-run institutions that acted as detention centers without a care for the dire impact of family separation or psychological harm. A student's mother had tears in her eyes as she shared she did not know what would happen to her if she was detained or deported. She feared losing her child.

Ms Consuelo was a voice of hope for everyone. She coordinated meetings with paralegals so the parents could receive the guidance they were seeking. Each case was different, but the families empathized with each other and shared information about their rights. Paralegals were available for support and provided valuable information about what to do if families were detained or if Immigrations and Customs Enforcement (ICE) came to their homes. The support extended to those dealing with the courts and Homeland Security. Although the atmosphere was tense, we were becoming tighter. It was a true community effort where families emotionally supported each other as they coped with the dangerous political landscape.

This moment highlighted the critical role of advocacy to fortify our community. The importance of communication between families and educators is what drives us toward where we all want it to be. It pushes us to continue to create a school community that is responsive to our most vulnerable at Dos Puentes.

Conclusion

There are so many aspects of Dos Puentes that have made it what it is, but mainly it has been the partnership of its families and educators. Our families bring a rich diversity to every classroom that impacts nearly all aspects of school life from how teachers think about curriculum down to how they decorate their classrooms and work on crafting school policies. This *confianza* among these two parties has made it possible for parents to feel at home in their children's school. Families are a non-negotiable and vital part of the school community, one that does not make you check your identity, culture and traditions at the door, but embraces them and provides opportunities to teach others about them across languages.

Teachers and administrators alike have often begun a conversation with a parent saying, 'I think you would be great for...' or '*Estaba pensando en tí porque creo que puedes* (I was thinking of you because I think you could...)' because we see in them the potential to make our school even better through their voice, even if they appear quiet. As the outside societal and political landscape is ever changing, we want our families and educators to use their collective power to show our students that change is possible when our voices are united in our collective role as educators, leaders and advocates.

Researcher Commentary

Ivana Espinet

Kingsborough Community College, CUNY

Families' relationships with educational institutions and educators have often been framed in a context of asymmetrical social and political relations that present a deficient perspective (Poza *et al.*, 2014; Shannon, 2011). Bilingual and immigrant parents are often accused of not being involved enough in their children's education. Olivos *et al.* (2011) argue that schools need to engage in a dynamic and collaborative process between families and schools. In examining the possibilities of families' partnerships with teachers, Gonzáles *et al.* (2005) focused on the critical importance of leveraging families' funds of knowledge. This approach sees the importance of understanding the social, historical, political and economic contexts of students' households and communities as resources and of building a relationship of *confianza* to bring them into educational spaces.

Families' roles and relationships in educational institutions go beyond participating in parent-teacher conferences and organizing school sales, they can instead, be multifaceted: families advocate for changes in larger educational policies (Fabricant, 2010; Mediratta *et al.*, 2009); they take on leadership roles at school level (Ascenzi-Moreno & Flores, 2013; Menken 2017); and families collaborate with teachers within the instructional spaces of the classroom (Espinet & Le, 2020; Miller & Khatib, 2023).

García *et al.*, (2017) propose a stance that fosters collaboration between children, families, communities, and educators using the term *juntos* [together]. The *Juntos* stance is informed by the beliefs that students' families and communities are valuable sources of knowledge and must be involved in the education process; that students' language practices and cultural understandings encompass those they bring from home and communities, as well as those they take up in schools and classrooms; and that educational institutions need to be democratic spaces in which teachers and students co-create knowledge, challenge traditional hierarchies, and work toward a more just society.

Discussion

The chapter 'Families as Educators, Leaders and Advocates' presents an example of the power that families and educators have when working in school from a *juntos* stance. Parents Adriana Cando and Ained Casado and teacher Stephanie Ubiera describe how families and educators build long-term collaborative relationships, starting with the home visits in which teachers learn about the families' funds of knowledge and begin to build a relationship of *confianza*. They share how families' individual experiences and differences are connected to a collective common experience within the school community.

The chapter also shows how families can build a space to partner as educators and become leaders proposing and implementing rich curricular experiences that engage children in learning. The recycling project is an example of how the emphasis on relationship building between families and school staff enabled a parent to bring in her valuable knowledge and leadership skills to teach children.

Children and families' experiences in school are shaped by social, historical and political forces. In a politically hostile environment, schools can either contribute to their alienation and sense of isolation or they can be a beacon of hope. Families' advocacy is essential to shaping educational institutions and providing counter-narratives. In the chapter, the authors illustrate how in a societally adverse context, educators and parents partnered to offer practical and emotional support to families in the school community.

To counteract the traditional asymmetrical relationships between families and schools, the authors propose a blueprint for the development of families' roles in three areas: (1) as educators, at home with their own children, and in school, sharing their funds of knowledge with other families' children; (2) as leaders who can help shape the curricular and pedagogical framework for the school community, and (3) as advocates who can provide support within the school community and to fight for a more just society. The experiences shared in this chapter provide an insight into the need for educational institutions to foster democratic spaces in which teachers, families, and students co-create knowledge by understanding the role of families as collaborators. This model puts an emphasis on new forms of relationship building among families and between families, educators and school staff.

References

Ascenzi-Moreno, L. and Flores, N. (2013) A case study of bilingual policy and practices at the Cypress Hills Community School. In O. García, Z. Zakharia and B. Octu (eds) *Bilingual Community Education and Multilingualism: Beyond Heritage Languages in a Global City* (pp. 219–231). Multilingual Matters.

Espinet, I. and Lê, K. (2020) Hand in hand: Parent collaboration in the classroom context. In CUNY-NYSIEB (ed.) *Translanguaging and Transformative Teaching for Emergent Bilingual Students*. Routledge. https://doi.org/10.4324/9781003003670-20

Fabricant, M. (2010) *Organizing for Educational Justice: The Campaign for Public School Reform in the South Bronx*. University of Minnesota Press.

García, O., Johnson, S. and Seltzer, K. (2017) *The Translanguaging Classroom: Leveraging Student Bilingualism for Learning*. Caslon.

González, N., Moll, L.M. and Amanti, C. (eds) (2005) *Funds of Knowledge: Theorizing Practices in Households, Communities and Classrooms*. Erlbaum Press.

Mediratta, K., Shah, S. and McAlister, S. (2009) *Community Organizing for Stronger Schools: Strategies and Successes*. Harvard Education Press.

Menken, K. (2017) *Leadership in Dual Language Bilingual Education*. [A National Dual Language Forum White paper]. Center for Applied Linguistics. Retrieved from www.cal.org/ndlf/pdfs/publications/NDLF-White-PaperOctober-2017.pdf

Miller, G.E. and Khatib, S.M. (2023) Honoring diverse cultures through family literacy approaches that build family, school, and community partnerships. *The Reading Teacher* 76 (5), 586–593. https://doi.org/10.1002/trtr.2181

Olivos, E., Jiménez-Castellanos, O. and Ochoa, A. (2011) *Bicultural Parent Engagement: Advocacy and Empowerment*. Teachers College Press.

Poza, L., Brooks, M. and Valdés, G. (2014) Entre familia: Immigrant parents' strategies for involvement in children's schooling. *The School Community Journal* 24 (1), 119–148.

Shannon, S. (2011) Parents engagement and equity in a dual language program. In E.M. Olivos, O. Jiménez-Castellano and A.M. Ochoa (eds) *Bicultural Parent Engagement: Advocacy and Empowerment* (pp. 1–13). Teachers College Press.

7 Bridging Home and School

Sacha Mercier and Amy Withers

Dos Puentes Teacher and Parent

Families are a child's first teachers and their home is their first school building. For this reason, we believe that building a *puente* between home and school is crucial for a student's academic, social and emotional success. When teachers and schools make it a priority to forge a partnership with the families of their students from the very beginning, they are assuring that each child will be supported on all levels and from all sides. This becomes even more important when looking at a bilingual school where communication is foundational. Families who feel heard by their school are more likely to participate and be present in their child's education.

In this chapter we focus on three structures that bridge home and school at Dos Puentes, located in upper Manhattan in the majority-Dominican populated neighborhood of Washington Heights. One of the protocols we are most proud of is our home visits to students' homes prior to them starting school. These visits represent the first step we take to build a bridge with the home. Not only are the visits meant to welcome the families into the Dos Puentes community, but they also show families our commitment to forming a relationship with them. Another structure we have adopted are student-led conferences where students are the bridge between families and educators. Finally, we have worked to create structures that include family and student voices in the Individual Educational Plan (IEP) process.

Home Visits

As a new teacher, I (Sacha) remember when I was first introduced to the concept of home visits. I was told that I would accompany another teacher to visit the homes of some of the new students entering Dos Puentes. This sounded interesting and I was eager to see what these visits were all about. As one fellow teacher put it 'It was somewhat strange going into the home of someone I didn't know. But I loved getting to see the students at home with their family. It was a completely new experience for me'.

The process started with a call to the family to explain the purpose of the visit and to set up a date and time. Most of the students we visit are starting kindergarten, but some are starting in a different grade, either because they changed schools or moved to the area, sometimes from another country. Interestingly enough, the family I first visited lived in my neighborhood not far from my house.

When we showed up at the apartment complex, we rang the doorbell and were buzzed in. We were greeted at the door by the 1st-grade student, his brother and grandmother. This particular family consisted of the mother, her two sons and the grandparents from Puerto Rico, who played a large role in the children's lives. What is amazing is that every student's family is different. Some live with their parents, others with their grandparents, some with extended families and others with many brothers and sisters.

After settling in, we were offered a drink. We then sat down with the family and asked them a few questions to get to know them better. Students and their families are often a little shy at the beginning of the questions, but quickly open up and share with us when they see we are not that different from them. One thing that usually puts them at ease is the fact that all our staff is bilingual and the visits are done bilingually. This creates a sort of trust early on as families see they would be understood. On this visit we spoke mostly in Spanish and we interspersed English when needed.

We begin the conversation with each household with approximately 10 questions. First, we ask the student's name and why they have chosen this particular name for the child. I love this question because it often leads families to tell us stories about their lives, their ancestors and their roots. It also sends a message that we care about and are interested in their child. We learned that our student's name had been chosen by his father to honor his grandfather as his namesake. We learned a bit about the father and how he had the children every other weekend.

Next we ask who lives with the student. This is another way the school makes a deeper connection to the family. We are not only interested in knowing who they live with, but also getting a better understanding of that family's history, social connections and economic status. While some of our families are well off financially, many live in poverty. This glimpse into our students' homes gives us a perspective on and an understanding about each family. On another occasion, I remember visiting a student who lived in the same room with his mother, sister and brother. Knowing this allows Dos Puentes to offer families support and assistance without them having to ask for it.

After a few more questions, we turned the interview around and asked our family what questions they have or information they'd like to share with us. '*Queremos que nuestro nieto aprenda a hablar español bien para que podamos comunicarnos mejor. Nosotros no hablamos inglés*

(We would like for our grandson to learn Spanish well so that we can communicate with him better. We don't speak English).' Many families are drawn to Dos Puentes because they want their children to learn their family's home language. 'I want my son to like school and learn how to read and write.' Other parents are worried about their children's socialization, learning right from wrong and becoming a positive member of society. Not only was it incredibly insightful to learn about this family's worries and wants, but it also allowed me to make a connection with the student as I had also been in a similar situation as a child. I moved to this country when I was 12 from France and French was my first language. During six long years in a monolingual English school, I struggled not to lose my French as English quickly became my dominant language. I even found it difficult to communicate with my father in French.

Now it was time for us to give them their lime green Dos Puentes t-shirt and take a picture of the family. This picture, along with many others like it, are later posted in the main hallway of the school for every new student to feel welcome and a part of the school *comunidad* (see Image 7.1). We said our goodbyes and the visit ended.

I saw that same student again on the first day of school. We looked at each other and waved anxiously, or maybe eagerly. He seemed so nervous and I was as well on this first day, but that very first connection we had both made during our home visit helped us face the day. And it's

Image 7.1 A bulletin board in the hallway of Dos Puentes featuring the photos of families taken during the home visits. Photo by Sacha Mercier

the same for many students who have started at Dos Puentes. As one parent said, 'My five-year-old felt so special and was happy to know a familiar adult face for the first day of school! As a parent I was utterly floored by this. It builds connection with families right away and instills a sense of trust'.

Student Voice: Student-Led Conferences

An important aspect in bridging school and home is student voice. Families and teachers at Dos Puentes have many opportunities to hear directly from students throughout the year about their goals, progress and reflections on their learning. I (Amy) recall a time we attended our oldest child's student-led conference (SLC) when they were in the 5th grade. SLCs are a different approach to traditional parent-teacher conferences that are led by educators and often devoid of students. On this day we sat together – our child, their father and myself – on a couch in the classroom as our child showed us pieces of work they were most proud of. The artifacts they shared included group projects; a reading grid that reflected their Spanish and English reading habits and levels; their latest writing publication with their goals for the upcoming unit; math checkpoints and end of unit assessments; and a reflection of their behavior and socioemotional coping strategies (for example, see Image 7.2). They spoke of difficulties that they had and how they overcame them, and what their goals were for the year – not only in academics but

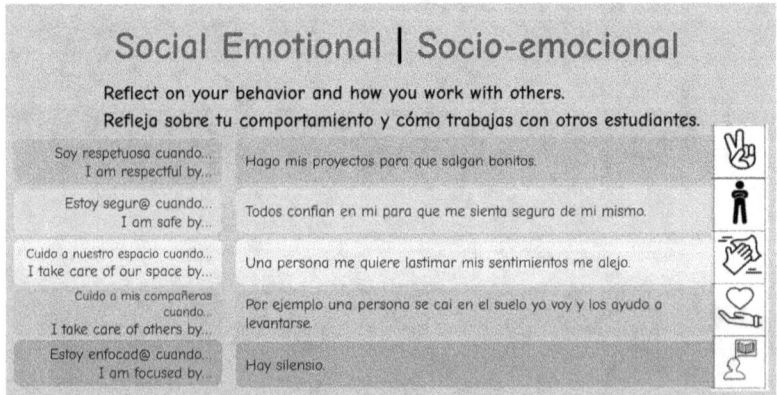

Image 7.2 A slide from a 3rd grader's presentation at a student-led conference. To prepare for the conference, students respond to the prompt (top left). They reflect on their own strengths in regards to working with others and being part of the learning community. Then, they come up with examples (listed in the column of bubbles on the right) of how they embody each of the aspects of the prompt. The chart provides a starting point for a conversation with families around the social-emotional aspects of their young person's school life.

also in their relationships within the larger classroom and school community. We took our time looking through their work and having conversations about their life in school. As we talked with our child, each teacher would stop by to see if we had any questions for them or anything else we would like to discuss.

The student-led conference structure at Dos Puentes was a pivotal change for our family in terms of gaining a deeper understanding of our child as a learner in a bilingual school. This structure also illustrates the importance at Dos Puentes of placing each child at the center of their learning. Felix, a 2nd grade student, reflecting on his experience with SLCs said, 'At first I was nervous to show my work to my parents. I was used to only my teachers seeing my work! But once we had the conference, I felt proud'. A father shared, '*Me gusta que sean los propios estudiantes quienes hablan de su trabajo en las conferencias. Es una buena forma de saber qué están aprendiendo y al mismo tiempo conocer el lugar, vivir la experiencia y conocer todo el entorno en el que día a día se desarrolla. Es de un gran valor para mi* (I like that it's the students who talk about their work at the conferences. It's a great way to know what they are learning and at the same time get to know the place, live the experience they are having and learn about the daily environment in which they grow. It's a great value for me)'. This father reflected that being in the same space that your child inhabits each day was meaningful, and felt the structure centered around his child as the owner of his own learning highlights the power of SLC.

Building and Strengthening Bridges: Developing Individual Educational Plans (IEPs)

Communication between the school and home is critical to make sure that everyone is informed and learning from one another. 'Initiating conversations is so important', shares Michelle Madera Taveras, a special education teacher at Dos Puentes. As a parent, I would often hear directly from teachers within the first few weeks of school about how my children were doing. In the 1st grade, this two-way communication helped my son's teacher and I establish daily communication between school and home that would best support my son. We worked together proactively at the beginning of the year and this remains one of my son's favorite years (and favorite teachers) of his elementary life.

The IEP process for students with disabilities can feel overwhelming for many families. Yet, this document is fundamental to ensure that each student receives the appropriate support for their learning. Establishing open communication is especially important when it comes time to explore evaluation and potential IEP planning for a student. Conversations around IEPs and a student's learning needs can be sensitive and anxiety-producing – for all involved! By establishing an open line of communication from the beginning of the year, and by focusing on the ways in which a student is thriving, the stress can be reduced and conversations can be more transparent and focused on using a student's strengths to support their needs.

In the case of my own child with an IEP, I (Amy) always felt like a partner during the IEP meetings. I felt free to ask questions, and advocate for my child. As Oli grew older, they began participating in the IEP meeting where they spoke directly about their lived experience as a student, advocated for their own needs, asked their own questions, and helped determine their goals and supports. When Oli moved on to middle school, they continued to confidently advocate for themselves via use of manipulatives during math and assistive technology to meet their goals. Equally importantly, I found that when teachers and other staff spoke about my children, they really knew and understood them as individuals. This has always been extremely important to me, that the schools my children attend understand who my child is.

Having said all of this, the IEP process is not perfect at any school, and Dos Puentes is always working to make it better. It is difficult to get translated copies of IEPs (the process takes months), for example. The IEP document can be long, complicated and difficult to parse out. Teachers at Dos Puentes have tried different ways to make the IEP document friendlier: highlighting parts of the IEP (such as student goals) that are especially relevant for families, or writing summaries of the IEP in Spanish. There can be cultural barriers to families participating in the IEP process as well. For example, a family might say to a teacher, '*Como usted diga, maestra. Usted es la profesional* (Whatever you say, teacher. You are the professional)'. However, families are true experts on their children! And so their voices are critical to establishing goals and deciding on accommodations. Going forward, Dos Puentes teachers and staff are hoping to establish pre-IEP meetings with families as a way to answer any questions, encourage their advocacy and provide coaching on what questions they may want to ask during the actual IEP meeting. The School Leadership Team (composed of an equal number of parents and school staff) has also established a subcommittee on Special Education to continue working to improve the IEP process with the goal of being more inclusive and respectful of families.

Conclusion

Building bridges between home and school is no small job in any school. It requires a lot of time, effort and intentionality. In a dual language bilingual school like Dos Puentes, we take this very seriously, it is in our name after all! Starting with the strengths of families, students and educators, we continually work to build and strengthen cultural, linguistic and academic bridges in service of our children.

Researcher Commentary

Carmina Makar

The City College of New York, CUNY

This case study highlights three practices that are unique to Dos Puentes: home visits, student-led conferences and inclusive participation in the Individualized Education Plan (IEP) process. These are but three pieces of the ecosystem of Dos Puentes, and they work in tandem with the larger vision of the school as they seek to build an active multilingual community.

Context

The practices Sacha Mercier and Amy Withers describe showcase the efforts to build bridges between the school and the community, making them central to the learning process. There is a paucity of research at the intersection of family engagement, on which much has been written (Ferlazzo, 2011), and the development of bilingual school-home communities. This case study contributes to this strand of the literature by highlighting how establishing authentic connections with multilingual families prompts the development of bilingual communities of practice.

Over two decades ago, Jean Lave and Etienne Wenger (1991) developed a model of situated learning in *communities of practice*, in which they argue learning happens when members are involved in a set of relationships over time and around things that matter to people. That is, transformation and learning occur based on significant community practices. When teachers conduct home visits, when families participate dynamically in the life of Dos Puentes, their roles come together effectively as a community of practice. However, in this particular case, we also observe teachers using language as a vehicle to make connections, to provide access to families, to participate fully in their students' community. Thus, Dos Puentes engages in these efforts and becomes a *bilingual community of practice*, in which language, identity and social justice contextualize the work of teachers and families as they strive to support their children.

Historically, school-community partnerships have been viewed as an effective way to support students and their families. However, these efforts have often been embedded in a deficit paradigm in which families are often seen to be lacking and schools are understood to be in place to compensate for a perceived deficit (Flores, 2005).

Historically, schools served the function of a community regulator '...where community members could hear lectures, debate about civic issues, and use the facility for recreation at night, on weekends, and during school breaks' (Stefanski *et al.*, 2016: 135). The different ways communities engaged with schools began to evolve and the first ways of understanding participation emerged, providing our first definitions of 'parental involvement' (Ferlazzo, 2011). These definitions restricted the notion of family and limited the ways of understanding participation in school. Recent trends in the literature have moved away from parental involvement toward the broader, more inclusive notion of family engagement (Harvard Family Research Project, 2021). Ferlazzo (2011, as cited in Stefanskis *et al.*, 2016: 138) explained that a school striving for involvement 'leads with its mouth – identifying projects, needs, and goals and then telling parents how they can contribute' while a school aiming for engagement 'lead[s] with its ears – listening to what parents think, dream, and worry about....not to serve clients but to gain partners'.

Discussion

Dos Puentes engages in these three pedagogical strategies in deliberate and systematic ways. These practices thus reveal a dynamic understanding of family engagement. Instead of viewing family engagement as an accessory to learning and community, Dos Puentes, through its home visits and intentional paradigm of involvement, is building an authentic bilingual community of practice in which students and their families are viewed as central in the learning process and critical to the development of the community and spirit of the school. There is clear understanding on behalf of the teachers of why these bridges matter. Practices such as learning more about a student's name or drawing from their family's background reflect an asset-based orientation to bilingualism and community. This case clearly outlines the need to go beyond parental involvement and engagement, towards a paradigm that understands these practices as fundamental building blocks with the student at the center of the process.

Table 7.1 Conceptualizing the role of families in bilingual communities

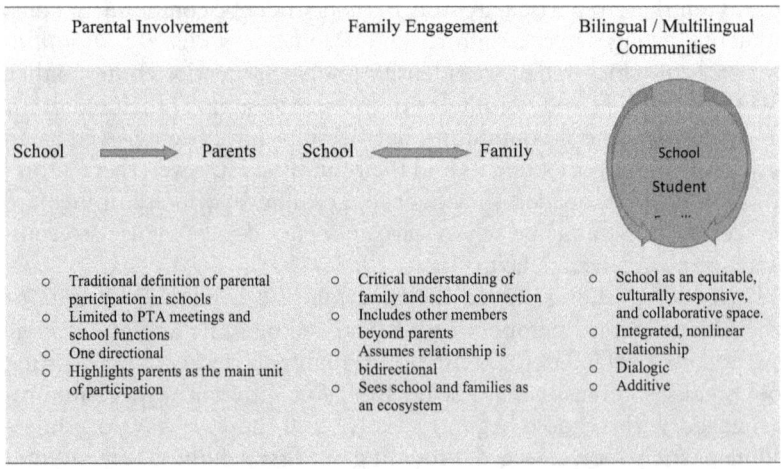

In their work on community and language socialization, Mangual Figueroa, Baquedano-Lopez and Leyva-Cutler (2014) outline sustainable models of bilingual community engagement, and they posit that students best learn to navigate principles of social order in language-mediated interaction. Authentic community development in the context of language socialization requires that members participate in the process of teaching and learning together.

Of particular importance, in the midst of these efforts to build community, is the place of the students. While many school-community partnerships may sidestep the student when establishing direct connections to their families, Dos Puentes places the student at the center of the process. Student-led conferences, as an example of situating student voice, make visible the overarching purpose of their vision: it always comes back to the student.

References

Ferlazzo, L. (2011) Involvement or engagement? *Educational Leadership* 68 (8), 10–14.

Flores, B. (2005) The intellectual presence of the deficit view of Spanish speaking children in the educational literature during the 20th century. In P. Pedraza and M. Rivera (eds) *Latino Education: An Agenda for Community Action Research*. Erlbaum.

Presidents and Fellows of Harvard College (2021) Informing family engagement policy. *Harvard Family Research Project*, 23 November. https://archive.globalfrp.org/family-involvement/informing-family-engagement-policy2

Lave, J. and Wenger, E. (1991) *Situated Learning: Legitimate Peripheral Participation*. Cambridge University Press.

Mangual Figueroa, A., Baquedano-López, P. and Leyva-Cutler, B. (2014) La cosecha/the harvest: Sustainable models of school-community engagement at a bilingual program. *Bilingual Research Journal* 37 (1), 43–63.

Stefanski, A., Valli, L. and Jacobson, R. (2016) Beyond involvement and engagement: The role of the family in school-community partnerships. *School Community Journal* 26 (2), 135–160.

8 Family Diversity as a Strength and a Challenge

Annette Fernandez

Dos Puentes Mother

I was born and raised in Washington Heights, or the Little Dominican Republic. I attended Public School 132, the school that is co-located with Dos Puentes, from kindergarten to 2nd grade. After 2nd grade, my parents sent me to Saint Elizabeth's, a nearby Catholic school, and then I went on to De La Salle Academy, a school for kids from low-income neighborhoods who were 'gifted and talented'. When it came time to choose a school for my daughter, Valentina, I did not want her to relive my trauma that came with being educated in white, heteronormative, wealthy institutions as a Latina. I constantly felt othered by the community and at school as well, where my peers were white, wealthy, and lacked the curiosity to get to know anyone outside of their Upper East Side enclaves. I never felt like I fit in, and it has taken me years of work to uproot all of the white supremacist, elitist constructs that I had ingested and adopted as a coping mechanism and, in my mind, rationalized because I believed that they offered a way to be successful. After all, my Dominican dad, with a 3rd-grade education, wanted us to assimilate to this 'American' culture. So, when it came time to select an elementary school for Valentina, I was focused on ensuring she would be part of the Washington Heights community, and attend a school where her bilingualism would be valued and fostered.

Ultimately, I knew Dos Puentes, led by Dr Hunt and her team, were allies in my quest to support my daughter's growth with an education that not only reflected and celebrated her culture, but also never had her question her belonging. My daughter attended Dos Puentes from kindergarten through 5th grade from 2014 through 2020 and was blessed with talented teachers throughout her time at the school. These teachers saw my child for who she was and inspired her, because they could see her gifts and talents.

At Dos Puentes, the intention to 'build bridges' and create an equitable, diverse and inclusive community has always been at the heart of the school. The principal, Dr Hunt, made a wise choice in partnering with assistant principal Dr Alcira Jaar, a native of the neighborhood, by her

Image 8.1 The author's daughter, Valentina, with her classmates Beatrix and Ruthie, during a performance at International Night. Photo by Monte Isom

side. This team possessed the cultural competence to navigate and unify a segregated community.

The school functions in a way that our children are the bridges for the families. They connected parents from different backgrounds on play dates, and they pushed us to speak to each other even when there were language barriers. If the kids could learn in a bilingual environment, why could we not? The journey in building an organization centered in equity and belonging is not easy because critical, difficult and never-ending conversations are needed to create and sustain an antiracist culture. This chapter focuses on how diversity, equity and inclusion are a strength in community building, while also presenting real challenges to families from different racial and socioeconomic backgrounds, even when we are integrating for a common purpose: the education of our children.

Building a Community of Inclusion

Community is created and nurtured; it does not just come from simply placing diverse people in the same space or school. At Dos Puentes, inclusion is an action word where the administration leads by example. They are supported by the ultimate parent coordinator extraordinaire, Consuelo Villegas, a spitfire, Colombian woman, who was like a *tía* for all of us and the first bridge for families. Consuelo convinced me to become a class parent, then head of the Parent Association (PA), and much more that I could never turn down. After all, how could I say no when I saw her hustling for our kids like her life depended on it?

The involvement of families is critical to the success of a school, but the school has to make it inclusive for them as well. In spite of being a Spanish-English bilingual school, Spanish-speaking parents would share how intimidated and sometimes excluded they felt due to the (English) language barrier. The false and dangerous misperception that Latinx immigrant parents are not involved was still prevalent. However, our focus should not be on deficient views, but on the ways structures such as school leadership teams can remove communication, technological and socioeconomic barriers to enable participation of immigrant and minoritized families. For example, Consuelo would often find a babysitter for certain meetings to ensure that parents could come. I would intentionally recruit some mothers who I could see were too shy to ask what they could do to help. Language and socioeconomic barriers are even more intimidating when we are ingesting social constructs that tell us we are less than.

One of the ways I felt compelled to show up for the community was my annual 'talk' at the first PA meeting. I meant to counter the negative, racist and xenophobic messages that can be present in a neighborhood that is being gentrified by people who do not always understand cultural context or the dynamics of race and class in a segregated neighborhood like Washington Heights. In the ways that it was meant to recruit my fellow Latinx families, it was also meant to smash the stereotypes of what someone who grows up in Washington Heights looks like. You can see the surprise on people's faces when you say you went to independent schools like Hewitt and Trinity, but you do not want that for your daughter. I would do this in service of the school, but also for the love of our community. It was important to set the tone with other parents. I emphasized, '*Como padre, tienes que participar. Tienes que involucrarte en la educación de su hijo* (As a parent, you have to participate. You have to become involved in the education of your child)'. What we were doing as parents was modeling how to build those bridges for our children and sometimes our children were taking us to task. A fellow parent recounted that her son had reprimanded her for not trying to get to know his friend's mother because she did not speak English. This is how we lean into our discomfort. We question our own beliefs about others and then push ourselves to go beyond our assumptions of one another, and our children help us to do just that.

A tradition that has formed over the years at Dos Puentes was the silent auction the PA holds to raise funds for the school. There are public schools in tawny zip codes in Manhattan that are notorious for having six-figure endowments. Our first silent auction showed us what we were capable of as a community because of our socioeconomic diversity, if we shared our resources. It allowed for access to intellectual property and labor that is diverse and experienced in all kinds of areas. We had builders, gardeners, artists, photographers, musicians, dancers, writers, teachers, and all kinds of expertise. The pooling of resources, both monetary and non-monetary, made it successful. In general, the more families we could include in the school's activities, the stronger our community grew and the better the experience for our children. Even conflict resolution was a bit easier to navigate because of the community building and the understanding that we were coming from different lived experiences. This became a tradition as a community where inclusion became the sweet spot where the magic happened.

These auctions raised upwards of $20,000 annually, which was used to fund afterschool enrichment and other PA programs. The afterschool enrichment was made available to all students, the Harvest Festival was for the entire community, and the garden was for everyone's benefit. We were co-creating a supportive community for our children, alongside teachers, administration and shoulder to shoulder with families we might not have worked with, had it not been for Dos Puentes.

However, this was an event where it was still difficult to get the participation of all parents. It definitely felt more affluent and maybe even elitist because of the money that was spent on certain prizes. For example, one year, one of the auction items was a weeklong trip to France. In a beautiful display of their love for the school and an unintentional display of their privilege, the wife joyfully spent her family's money as her husband made funny gestures about how expensive it was. This did support our children, however, looking back on this with a more critical lens, we needed to be more aware of the socio economic divides and the bravado that can be displayed around those with unequal means and opportunities. This makes me think of the many families who did not participate in the auction. Moments like this pushed the parent organizers to be more inclusive in the later years. This is just one example of how the work around equity and belonging never ends, it ebbs and flows and builds.

Building Bridges Across Barriers

In our Dos Puentes community there are cultural, economic, and geographic barriers that show up in the Broadway divide. Specifically this refers to the west side of Broadway, which apartment owners and gentrifiers renamed as 'Hudson Heights', and on the east side of Broadway known as the working class community of 'the Little Dominican Republic'. There are occasions when the cultural complexity, exposure and diversity of backgrounds and life experiences cause conflict. An example of this discomfort arose during school photos where a background that depicted graffiti was included as a choice. A white parent alerted the PA that she believed this background glorified vandalism. As a Dominican and Puerto Rican and raised in Washington Heights, I felt that the graffiti design was a backdrop that represented part of the local culture and hip hop. It was something that community members could identify with. However, this parent reacted with contempt and shock that I disagreed with her

Image 8.2 A graffiti image that was used for an afterschool dance club. Photo by Monte Isom

perspective. I still believe that despite the discomfort of that conflict, we both were impacted. I took what she said personally. It was not personal, it was about her life experience and what she had been exposed to. It had nothing to do with me and vice versa. I saw her contempt as an attack. I saw it as condescension and in that moment I noted it as an aggression. In the end, the background remained as a choice. We all learned that this work of inclusion was challenging and sometimes meant working with people who did not see eye to eye with us. Ultimately, we still had a shared purpose that was bigger than us; we wanted Dos Puentes to thrive, we wanted our kids to flourish and be happy. The beauty is that in that conflict is where the growth lies for all involved.

Conclusion: An honest message for white families in Washington Heights (and beyond) from a Latina mother

Ultimately, the students at Dos Puentes (or any other bilingual school/program) are OUR kids. They are children of the Heights. The pact you make when you cross Broadway from the West Side to the East Side (or whichever community your school resides in) is that you will be a part of the community. No, you are not saving a community, you are immersing yourself in a community. You are offering to contribute to the growth of a community, perhaps in a way that you may not have contributed before. You may be thinking it is going to be so cool when your kid can speak and read Spanish by the time they reach 6th grade and it will be so awesome that your child was exposed to diversity via all kinds of Latinx culture, festivals and rituals. There is just one thing: it cannot be a performative allyship. You were not fully prepared for all of the grit of the East Side of Washington Heights. You were not prepared for the heroin needles strewn around the school. You were not necessarily prepared to see all that is lacking on the East Side. Leave your neoliberalism on the West Side and be prepared to be challenged, be prepared for your whiteness to be off-center in this institution. Be prepared to listen for understanding and take on your unconscious bias. Be prepared to roll up your sleeves and contribute to the work that is building a healthy, inclusive school where all of our children feel a real sense of belonging. Do you want your kid to learn how to speak Spanish or do you want them to learn about Latinx culture and all of its nuances? First, you will have to bravely accept the discomfort of not being centered in the narrative and of doing the real work of dismantling systems of oppression. Then, lead with a curious mind and get past that self-identifying white lens and you will see real community. You will learn the history of the neighborhood and all of its value and nuances. You will learn that Dominicans are entrepreneurial and that we are centered in community. You will become more aware and perhaps admit that uptown is segregated and that gentrification is a force that is like a glacier melting and moving and leaving devastation in its wake. I will continue to work on not holding your whiteness against you and continue to hold you accountable to our pool of shared meaning: getting our children the best education possible that is reflective of them and our community.

Researcher Commentary

Kate Menken

Queens College, CUNY

Annette Fernandez's powerful chapter shares her experiences of Dos Puentes as a Latina mother and lifelong community member of Washington Heights, or Little Dominican Republic. Much of the chapter reads as a love letter to the school, for its significant role in allowing Fernandez to send her daughter to a school where her languages, identity and community would be embraced, thereby countering the trauma that Fernandez experienced in the schools that she attended as a child. She describes not only how she and her family were treated *con respeto* (Valdés, 1996) by school leaders and staff, but also the opportunities that were created within Dos Puentes for meaningful parental leadership. At the same time, her chapter highlights how Dos Puentes works actively to mitigate societal prejudices and inequities. In my commentary, I will locate these points within the academic literature, and then consider both the strengths of Dos Puentes from which other schools can learn as well as the remaining important work to be done.

Context

Several years ago, Ivana Espinet and I interviewed immigrant parents who were bilingual education leaders in New York City schools, and asked them why they fought so hard for bilingual education programs to be available for their children. What we found was that while much of the research about bilingual education continues to focus on the *academic* benefits of bilingual programs (see Baker & Wright, 2021), the parents we interviewed were, like Fernandez, very concerned about the *personal* benefits of bilingual education programs – specifically, that their children are able to attend schools where their languages, cultures and the entirety of their identities would be supported and, ideally, celebrated. In other words, what many parents want is schooling where they and their children will be treated *con respeto* (Valdés, 1996). In this way, research in bilingual education has overlooked what truly matters to families.

Dual language bilingual education (DLBE) programs like that at Dos Puentes hold the promise for students to develop bilingualism, biliteracy and cross-cultural understanding (Howard *et al.*, 2018). These are important aims, particularly within the context of New York City, which is the most racially segregated school system in the United States (Kucsera & Orfield, 2014). DLBE programs often bring together students from different racialized backgrounds, as Fernandez explains is the case at Dos Puentes. However, meaningful integration – whereby efforts are made to mitigate inequities – has historically never been a core component of DLBE (Delavan *et al.*, 2021).

Much recent research has been concerned about the 'gentrification' of DLBE, referring to 'the increasing presence of privileged populations in bilingual education spaces in ways that are frequently to the detriment of minoritized language students, their families, and their communities' (Delavan *et al.*, 2021: 300). Research about middle-class, white children in DLBE has shown how the children dominate classroom talk, receive more attention from their teachers, and how their language practices are positioned as superior (Chaparro, 2019; Palmer *et al.*, 2019), and likewise how their parents typically receive more attention from school leaders and teachers (Burns, 2017; Chaparro, 2019). Ideally, DLBE programs would foster students' critical/sociopolitical consciousness of social injustices (Palmer *et al.*, 2019; Freire, 2020) and otherwise seek to overcome DLBE gentrification.

Discussion

Although schools serving immigrant communities have often approached their relationships with families through limiting paradigms of 'parental involvement', for instance through efforts to change family behaviors to suit the school's agenda and/or PAs focused on school fundraising rather than resistance, increasingly communities and schools are beginning to promote 'parental leadership' instead (see Menken, 2017). Fernandez's chapter shows how Dos Puentes actively promotes parental leadership – an important lesson for others to emulate.

Fernandez's chapter also documents her efforts in partnership with Dos Puentes leadership to manage DLBE gentrification, another essential lesson for all. Specifically, she documents how Dos Puentes worked hard to promote relationships across racial/linguistic/economic lines (e.g. through playdates). Fernandez describes several ways that white supremacy was disrupted within the school, such as by insisting the school maintain a graffiti backdrop as one of its options for school photos, an annual speech to challenge xenophobic ideologies, and the naming of privilege as affluent families brought wealth into the school while ensuring that *all* students benefited from those contributions. In these ways, Fernandez actively promoted critical consciousness.

Key next steps for the field inspired by Fernandez's chapter include:

- centering minoritized groups in bilingual education;
- looking critically at school leadership structures to promote leadership by minoritized parents; and
- challenging white supremacy and fostering critical consciousness amongst students and families in DLBE programs.

References

Baker, C. and Wright, W.E. (2021) *Foundations of Bilingual Education and Bilingualism* (7th edn). Multilingual Matters.

Burns, M. (2017) 'Compromises that we make': Whiteness in the dual language context. *Bilingual Research Journal* 40 (4), 339–352. https://doi.org/10.1080/15235882.2017.1388303

Chaparro, S. (2019) But mom! I'm not a Spanish Boy: Raciolinguistic socialization in a two-way immersion bilingual program. *Linguistics and Education* 50, 1–12. https://doi.org/10.1016/j.linged.2019.01.003

Delavan, G., Freire, J. and Menken, K. (2021) Editorial introduction: A historical overview of the expanding critique(s) of the gentrification of dual language bilingual education. *Language Policy* 20 (3), 299–321.

Freire, J.A. (2020) Promoting sociopolitical consciousness and bicultural goals of dual language education: The transformational dual language education framework. *Journal of Language, Identity & Education* 19 (1), 56–71.

Howard, E.R., Lindholm-Leary, K.J., Rogers, D., Olague, N., Medina, J., Kennedy, B., Sugarman, J. and Christian, D. (2018) *Guiding Principles for Dual Language Education* (3rd edn). Center for Applied Linguistics.

Kucsera, J. and Orfield, G. (2014) *New York State's Extreme School Segregation Inequality, Inaction and a Damaged Future*. UCLA Civil Rights Project/Proyecto Derechos Civiles.

Menken, K. (2017) *Leadership in Dual Language Bilingual Education*. [A National Dual Language Forum White paper]. Center for Applied Linguistics. Retrieved from www.cal.org/ndlf/pdfs/publications/NDLF-White-PaperOctober-2017.pdf

Palmer, D.K., Cervantes-Soon, C., Dorner, L. and Heiman, D. (2019) Bilingualism, biliteracy, biculturalism, and critical consciousness for all: Proposing a fourth fundamental goal for two-way dual language education. *Theory Into Practice* 58 (2), 121–133.

Valdés, G. (1996) *Con Respeto: Bridging the Distances Between Culturally Diverse Families and Schools: An Ethnographic Portrait*. Teachers College Press.

9 Building *Comunidad*

Elga Castro Ramos

Dos Puentes Mother

We were eager to tour Dos Puentes when our daughter was still in pre-K, even though it started in kindergarten. I remember meeting the principal, Dr Hunt, and parent coordinator, Consuelo, and thinking they were a dream team. The presentation about the school's vision and pillars is still glued to my mind. It was the perfect way to start what is now a six-year relationship. We did not need to be convinced about the importance of a bilingual education and a multicultural environment. We were a Spanish-speaking couple born and raised in Puerto Rico who had only spoken Spanish to our daughter. We were attracted by the idea of having her surrounded by other kids who spoke Spanish, and very importantly, teachers who were going to teach her to read and write in Spanish. But we also wanted her to value the meaning of bilingualism and multiculturalism in this city and in this world, for people of all backgrounds.

With Dr Hunt's presentation we learned about the four pillars of the school. Other than the bilingualism and biliteracy pillar, we were attracted to the hands-on learning approach and the partnerships with universities and organizations. But what really stood out and has been the center of this relationship was the focus on families as partners, leaders and advocates. We have come to see that Dos Puentes is more than just our daughter's school, it is our community where we have created bonds that will go beyond the 5th grade when she graduates. This chapter shares some of the stories that illustrate how the school created not only a great educational environment, but where diverse families become one *comunidad*.

Viernes Familiar

Viernes familiar, or Family Fridays, have to be experienced to be fully understood. Whereas in other schools families go to their children's classrooms on special occasions or to meet with a teacher, at Dos Puentes classroom visits are part of the regular school structure. *Viernes familiar* is an open invitation for all families to be an active part of the learning of their children and their peers on a bi-weekly or monthly basis. It is not

Image 9.1 A kindergarten class during a Family Friday where students share the different members of their family. Photo by Elizabeth Menendez

exclusive to younger students, but occurs school-wide during the first period of the school day from kindergarten through 5th grade.

Stepping into a *viernes familiar* allows parents, aunts and uncles, grandparents and even older siblings to experience the classroom dynamics from the perspective of their student. One is able to meet and work with their child's classmates by sitting together to interact around learning tasks that teachers plan for students and families to co-construct knowledge. For some of the activities family members are spectators, but for most they are active participants. Adults become part of the classroom environment as they put faces and voices to all those names that their children talk about. Families see the colorful rug where morning meetings occur, they review the job charts where their kids are assigned specific tasks, skim through all the book titles in Spanish and English – not just the ones that come home in the book baggie – and see their child's work displayed in Spanish, English or bilingually.

Entering an early childhood classroom, adults squeeze themselves into tiny chairs and tables and for a moment they work alongside their 1st-grader. They work together to complete a project about where their family is from as they simultaneously learn about other classmates and families. In a 3rd-grade class the adults work through how to add decimals with their child guiding them through the newest strategy they are learning, perhaps different from the way they learned their math in another time and/or country. In 5th grade the first Family Friday of the year focused on

Image 9.2 A Family Friday where two fathers and their 5th-grade daughters worked on identity cards with the support of their families. Photo by Victoria Hunt

identity cards where students work with their families to write about and visually represent their countries of origin, ethnicity, religion, traditions and more to get to know one another and build connections.

Family Fridays are central to building a Dos Puentes class *comunidad*. This regular experience reminds families of all the things that make this school unique, as they take note of the language of the day, and think about how in two weeks the same dynamics will magically happen in another language. And in the meantime, while changing tables or saying goodbye to one's child, parents talk with other family members, often exchange numbers and even plan a playdate. They comment on how special it is to have ended up at this school and collectively watch their children grow together from year to year.

Recently the school added *viernes familiar* for the clusters or special subjects. This means the physical education (PE), music, science and dance teachers also invite families to learn alongside their children. This has provided more insight into the school as families have had fewer opportunities to meet the cluster teachers and experience what happens in their classrooms. Families are invited to visit as a grade level and circulate through the various cluster subjects. During a dance class we had to create our own improvised dance with a couple of students. It was fun to see so many parents doing different movements at 8:30 am in the schoolyard. On the same day, we transitioned to stretching exercises and cardio with Mr Ronny, the PE teacher, before moving into Tai Chi techniques. I had heard from my daughter about the incorporation of Tai Chi into the PE program, but seeing it in action, and actually doing it was a completely different experience. In science we studied the water of New York, part of the larger project the students were working on that took them to study the East River in Inwood, and prepared students for a three-day camping trip at the Taconic Outdoor Center and Croton Dam (see Chapters 14 and 15). In music we all were given recorders as Ms Lorene explained how to play them with both hands. We learned where we needed to put our fingers and then we attempted to play a song she taught us. It did not sound harmonious, nor as melodic as the children when they played the song back to the families. But in spite of our musical talents, if anyone walked by the school they must have been impressed by the fact that on a random morning, the school opened its door to families to experience what their children's learning looks like each day.

Being a participant and observer during *viernes familiar* is an experience that consistently leaves families feeling we know more about our children, other students, the teachers and all the other adults in the school. Due to different schedules, parents and family members do not always have time for interaction and collaboration, but having the opportunity to attend *viernes familiar* provides a consistent space to ensure access and connection.

Family-Driven Involvement

To achieve deep family involvement, a balanced and cooperative relationship between the school administration and families is necessary. It is not enough for school to provide the space for family engagement if families are unwilling to be active participants. This can only be done through devoted time, coordination and trust. To complicate this further, families often do not know each other, come from different backgrounds and traditions, have different schedules, and diverse visions of what involvement in their childrens' school means. It is important to recall that in many other countries, and especially across Latin America, parent associations and family-driven events in schools are not common. Asking parents to take on leadership roles within the school may be something completely new and foreign to many.

At Dos Puentes family engagement is viewed as a two-way relationship that goes beyond volunteering at school events or with fundraising efforts. Instead, events center community building and most are free of charge. For example, family potlucks in September, a Harvest Festival/ Día de los Muertos celebration, Family Fitness Night and Earth Day celebrations were created by families to get to know each other and work as a school community. Language exchanges, where Spanish- and English-speaking families get together to tutor one another in learning a new language and a school uniform exchange are events created by families based on their needs. In 'regular' times all these criteria lead to a healthy and stable PA, but in difficult times these bonds prove even more critical for sustaining the *comunidad* engagement model. The Dos Puentes commitment to the strength and power of their families was essential to keeping our *comunidad* together during the COVID-19 pandemic as we were able to build on what was already seeded.

Family Lessons Learned through the Pandemic

March 2020 was a shock for everyone, but especially for children whose realities were suddenly changed through the shutdowns. Schools are the center of students' lives and taking that away meant an abrupt interruption in learning routines and the social and emotional aspects of a school community. Parents also suffered these disruptions as we were forced to be home with our kids and do schooling with them. I was the President of the Parent Association (PA) during this challenging time. Reflecting back, I have come to appreciate the autonomy that the Dos Puentes administration supported and encouraged – to the extent possible – to continue many of our traditions online and create new activities and structures to maintain the bonds we worked so hard to establish. The PA had a number of initiatives to support families in need and create bridges between students who were home learning online with those who attend classes through the 'blended' home-school method. One example was when we brought an ice cream truck to the school the last day to celebrate making it through a very challenging year. Although it may sound banal, this was a powerful event as anything that resembled normalcy had added value. Having the whole community together across home and school learning modalities doing something as simple as enjoying an ice cream cone was part of bringing us all back together and feeling that sense of *comunidad* after a very hard year. This event was repeated last year with the school staff and hopefully will remain a school tradition to collectively celebrate the completion of a school year. The PA hosts a book fair of Spanish and English titles that supports the language and cultures of the diverse families. The event not only raises money for the school, but also provides each child a free book of their choosing. Other collective events included a lemonade gathering where parents could network and support with virtual events such as International Night and the Lunar New Year celebration that had to be adapted for the reality of the pandemic.

These events contributed to bringing back a sense of community and for new families, a sense of what being in an actual school means. Transitioning to PA meetings in person, to meeting and welcoming new parents, to understanding that more than half of the school – both kids and their families – have only known hybrid or remote schooling, we wanted to share with them what Dos Puentes was before March 2020.

Conclusion

Comunidad is created and fostered in many ways at Dos Puentes. It is built into the school structure through each *viernes familiar* where classroom learning becomes an opportunity for children and families to learn together across content areas, languages and cultures. It is not a single special event, but a collection of many regular and consistent events that are always special. The PA continues the formation and development of a *comunidad* where activities bring together families during and after the school day to build connections that can only be formed in partnership. With the school population continually in flux due to changing global politics, Dos Puentes is consistently adding newly arrived families who come with different backgrounds and experiences. Our strong sense of community allows us to welcome them in our family and support them as they adapt to a new school and a new country. These are not endeavors that are easy, just like families do not always work in unison and go through struggles, but they are critical to coming together *en comunidad* for our children and the society they will lead.

Returning to the orientation I attended in the library in 2015, I am reminded of the first impression I took away. It was that Dos Puentes was not only going to shape my daughter academically, but also shape her as a human being. This school was going to be our family and *comunidad en Nueva York*, especially since we do not have family here. And now, on the verge of her graduation from 5th grade, we know that Dos Puentes will stay with all of us for its long-lasting impact on our daughter, family and larger community.

Researcher Commentary

Bertha Pérez

The University of Texas at San Antonio

Dos Puentes provides a rich counterpoint to the discussion of parental engagement, illustrating in a parent's voice what is possible. *Building Comunidad* places the agency, or power, of parent school engagement on the families. Immediately conveying to the reader that at Dos Puentes parents are valued integral partners in co-creating learning, teaching, and community. Through a family-driven model, the participation of parents and families builds over the years as the dual language bilingual program evolves into a school model. Elga Castro Ramos describes her six-year trajectory as a parent participant and school leader and how the school views parent engagement as building a *comunidad*. This sense of *comunidad* undergirded the school community response and recovery during the difficult times of COVID and the current sociopolitical 'parental rights' climate.

Context

Historically, beginning in the sixties with Antonia Pantoja, Evelina Antonetty and Genoveva Morales (Ayala, 2022), parents have been some of the fiercest leaders in attaining and sustaining bilingual education. García and Sung (2018: 323) describe how Antonetty's organization, La Coalición Pro Educación Bilingüe 'taught parents to defend bilingual education as a right for their children'. The impact of parent involvement on bilingual students' outcomes has been examined over these sixty years with accumulated evidence showing that educational outcomes are indeed improved. Parent involvement varies on a continuum, e.g. from support for homework and school attendance, in-class/in-school instructional participation, to school leadership. Current models of parent engagement are not that different from the traditional parental involvement models of the past, yet at Dos Puentes they evolved to a more generative and expansive model and called it '*Comunidad*'.

Much of the research on parental involvement in dual language focuses on how parents can assist schools in improving outcomes. Few studies examine how the agency of families and communities, and the development thereof, might become powerful actors in integrating and sustaining parental, family and community engagement. Ee (2017: 145) describes how 'unlike parental interaction, parental participation requires more general contacts with other parents and school personnel…both activities are central to establishing and enhancing parents' social networks…the complementary effects of the two activities show that parents' social networks at the personal and school levels can affect each other in a positive manner and ultimately increase parental involvement in general'. At Dos Puentes, the commitment to equitable participation begins with the inception of the program. The school principal and teachers view parents as knowledgeable partners and guides in the social, cultural and linguistic practices of the families and *comunidad*. This shifts power and builds collective agency on the ongoing familial, *comunidad* school relations.

With deliberate design and organization, the school implemented *viernes familiar*. The *viernes familiar* became a social space where students, families and school staff could come together to create, support, and develop in *comunidad*. Within the Family Friday space, shared norms evolved where individualistic expression of language practices and cultural understanding were valued, while at the same time a sense of collectivity went *mano a mano*. These *viernes familiares* provided spaces and opportunities where families, students and educators could exchange ideas, aspirations, sorrows and a sense of the possible.

Castro Ramos describes how COVID challenged the school-based parent activities and how the isolation and the need for reintegration post-COVID created what Ishimaru and Takahashi (2019) describe as 'turning points' in parent involvement that can lead to 'transformative agency'.

Family engagement at the Dos Puentes *comunidad* took more importance and parents assumed a greater leadership role.

Discussion

When conservative policymakers talk about 'parental rights', they are not speaking of/to diverse multicultural and multilingual parents. Parents who use their languages, culture, and identify in unique ways to create transformative ways of thinking, learning, and being for themselves and their children (Pérez, 2003) are not included in this 'parental rights' discourse. Once again, the challenge for parents, teachers, and school leaders is to fiercely defend educational, cultural, and language rights and to continue the evolution of engagement, empowerment, and leadership of all, but especially diverse parents.

The other sociopolitical wave impacting parent participation is charter schools and school choice. Now dual language programs are becoming more gentrified and marketed to affluent English monolingual parents. Delavan *et al.*, (2022: 14) studied dual language programs in choice schools and found parent contracts commonly used in the student admissions process to secure long term commitment, stating that 'these contracts may have been intended to fulfill a broader purpose that may include the issue of attrition, but it again had the discursive addition effect of sneaking in selectivity'. At Dos Puentes parent commitment is developed through engagement in *comunidad*, not through coercive contracts.

Over the time that Castro Ramos was involved with her child's school, we have gone from global education to COVID isolation and online learning, from building and defending dual language education to seeing its gentrification, from diversity and inclusion to book banning, and from supporting migrant families to seeing immigrants demonized. Through all these trends that have impacted our diverse communities, the families and school staff showed remarkable resilience and leadership in *la comunidad de* Dos Puentes.

References

Ayala, E. (2022) Genoveva Morales. In K. Sosa, E.R. Clark and J. Speed (eds) *Revolutionary Woman of Texas and Mexico: Portraits of Soldaderas, Saints, and Subversives.* Maverick Books.

Delavan, M.G., Freire, J.A. and Morita-Mullaney, T. (2022) Conscripted into thinking of scarce, selective, privatized, and precarious seats in dual language bilingual education: the choice discourse of mercenary exclusivity. *Current Issues in Language Planning* 23 (2), 1–28.

Ee, J. (2017) Two dimensions of parental involvement: What affects parental involvement in dual language immersion? *Bilingual Research Journal* 40 (2), 131–153.

García, O. and Sung, K.K. (2018) Critically assessing the 1968 Bilingual Education Act at 50 years: Taming tongues and Latinx communities. *Bilingual Research Journal* 41 (4), 318–333.

Ishimaru, A.M., Lott J.L. II, Torres, K.E. and O'Reilly-Diaz, K. (2019) Families in the driver's seat: Catalyzing familial transformative agency for equitable collaboration. *Teachers College Record* 121 (11), 1–39.

Pérez, B. (2003) *Becoming Biliterate: A Study of Two-Way Bilingual Immersion Education*. Taylor & Francis Group.

10 Socioemotional Learning and Support

Irving Mota and Kimberly Bautista

Dos Puentes Teachers

Children come to school with myriad experiences within their families and communities. Some students come from homes where they experience stable environments of support whereas others face instability, poverty and/or migration spurred by political forces. In this chapter we highlight the importance of Social Emotional Learning (SEL) (Stanford, 2022) as well as Trauma Responsive Teaching (Minahan, 2019) to ensure students are supported in their challenges at home, school and community. Education goes beyond academics to include development of emotions and social competencies because schooling must focus on children holistically. That includes building self-awareness, self-management, social awareness, relationship skills and responsible decision-making (CASEL, 2020). Such skills are key when working with language learners and immigrant-origin students. These skills help them transition into new environments, build their language practices, and develop cultural competencies as they adjust to life in the United States.

The teachers and school personnel at Dos Puentes support the social emotional development of bilingual students through activities such as holding regular morning meetings, integrating weekly SEL lessons and locating peace corners in classrooms for students to address their emotions. The following narrative showcases one way SEL is put into action at Dos Puentes to support bilingual students, and the strategies and pedagogical practices we put into action to meet the needs of multicultural and multilingual families in our school's neighborhood of Washington Heights. Specifically, we focus on the use of home language to support students through various social emotional phases within a school culture that goes beyond academics to address the holistic development of students and families.

Understanding and Supporting Students' Cultural and Migratory Experiences

Each morning I (Irving) greet each of my 4th-grade students as they enter the classroom. I am happy to see them and welcome them with a warm smile as they slowly make their way up to the fifth floor of Dos Puentes. At the end of the line, José enters the classroom with a serious face, but manages to smile at me when I greet him with a typical Dominican saying '*que lo que*'.

José is a nine-year-old from the Dominican Republic (DR). He moved to New York when he was in 2nd grade and now lives with his father, stepmother and baby brother. In the DR José lived with his grandparents in *el campo* (the countryside). He often draws and writes about his family there and how much he misses them. He shared stories about the friends he left and the many adventures they had together. José often shares how happy he is when he is back home in the DR and cannot wait to visit once again. He visits at least once a year during the summer breaks.

Like most teachers at Dos Puentes, I have taken an active role in getting to know the students in my class. I value the importance of connecting with students, their families and understanding their cultural backgrounds and personal histories. I also understand that in order to have a successful learning environment students need to feel seen and understood. José has struggled with successfully integrating himself into the classroom community and building relationships with his peers. He is often reactive to situations and encounters that result in conflict and altercations.

To support José, I work closely with his family. I often check in with his father on the progress that José is making and am in contact with his stepmother. I have met with them to discuss the areas of growth and development to support José. I acknowledge the cultural differences that José faces being in a school in the US versus a school in rural Dominican Republic. To support José, I have worked with him on connecting to his interests, which include typical music from the DR such as reggaeton and dembow. As a musician myself, I have taken the time to work on songwriting with José as a form of expression.

To further support José, the school counselor and social worker check in with him and his family. The school social worker, Ms Maria has worked with José's family on parenting skills such as establishing routines at home, setting expectations and executing logical consequences that will support his needs. José is also being supported by Ms Kassandra, the school counselor. She sees him weekly to work on self-regulating strategies, conflict-resolution strategies and goal setting. José receives support to propel him to make decisions with positive outcomes that will help him build positive relationships with his peers.

A Classroom Framework for Socioemotional Learning

At Dos Puentes we support students like José through use of the *Holding Space* protocol during morning meeting time. The protocol was

Image 10.1 Fifth grade students listening to one another during a Holding Space session. Photo by Irving Mota

created by teacher educator Arlène Elizabeth Casimir to support teachers as they respond to their students' social and emotional needs in a humanizing, inclusive and trauma-informed way (Casimir & Baker, 2023). During *Holding Space*, students are asked what they need from their peers to support them through their process. Some ask for advice, words of affirmation or silence. This protocol is key to building classroom community and developing intrapersonal, interpersonal and cognitive skills.

During this time students work on not only naming emotions, but also interpreting and appropriately communicating them. This space also provides opportunities to make constructive and safe decisions. In hearing the needs and struggles of peers, students build empathy. This is a key moment in which they can recognize and value the perspectives and emotions of others. They then move a step further by taking action to support them in ways that meet the needs of their peers. This time also nurtures a positive classroom environment that is supportive of the various needs of diverse individuals, teaching students to nurture a positive and supportive community.

During this time students are allowed to share and contribute in either language or bilingually. This is intentional to assure that all voices feel heard. We aim to validate and support the lived experiences of our diverse student population through equitable practices. And although the protocol is modified by grade level, it carries the same importance and provides students with an opportunity to discuss topics and themes of importance to them. Depending on the circumstances facing each classroom, loyalty and structure to the protocol are honored or flexibility is encouraged.

To give further insight into how the social emotional development of students is supported we will walk you through how the Holding Space protocol (see Image 10.2) is adapted and modified to support our bilingual students at Dos Puentes.

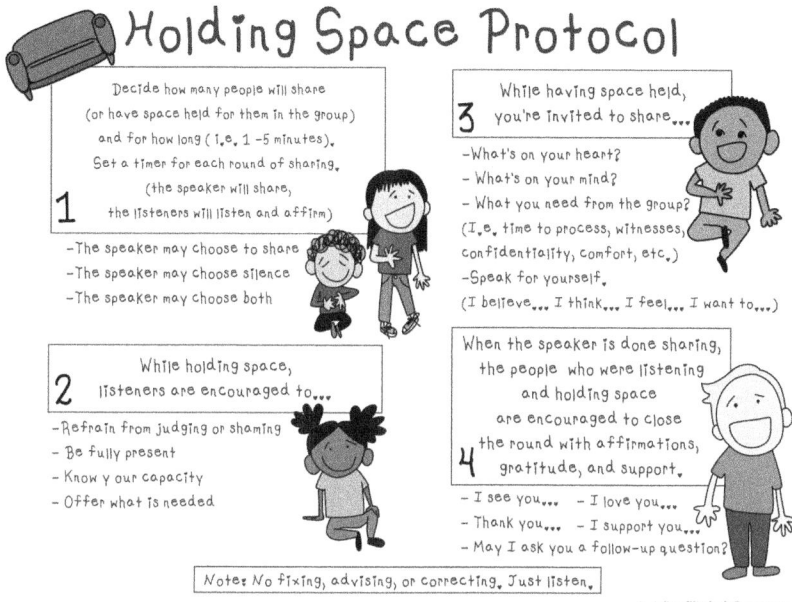

Image 10.2 The Holding Space Protocol from teacher educator Arlène Elizabeth Casimir (Casimir & Baker, 2023: 81). Photo by Arlène Elizabeth Casimir

Holding Space: A Scenario

In the 4th-grade side-by-side classrooms, Holding Space typically takes place during morning meeting time. This became a part of the weekly routine and schedule once the teachers observed the high need to support students' socioemotional wellbeing post-pandemic. The school counselor became an active participant during this time, joining the weekly meetings and alternating between the English and Spanish component classrooms.

The classroom teachers and counselor actively collaborated and planned the weekly sessions. They selected themes and topics based on observations shared by the teachers as well as topics that arose during counseling sessions with the students. During the planning sessions, facilitators discussed alternative themes and topics for discussion in case the original plan fell flat and students were not interested or actively engaged in the discussion. Additionally, a sign-up sheet was provided for students who wanted to take the lead and share their thoughts and sentiments. Regular active participants were encouraged to also be active listeners and motivate their peers to share their thoughts. Let us join a session in progress:

Mr Horowitz rings the chime to regroup and gather the students. He states, 'Let's transition to the rug, so we can begin our Holding Space protocol'. At this point students are well familiarized with the protocol as they enact it in both the English and Spanish classrooms. Once at the rug Arianny, Yeilin, Anderson and Dalexi have their hands up. Arianny asks if she can be the time monitor and track those who will be sharing. Mr Horowitz responds, '*Claro que sí, tu ayuda es muy apreciada* (Of course, your help is very appreciated)'. He calls on Yeilin: '*¿Puedes leer las normas del protocolo en voz alta por favor?* (Can you read the protocol rules please?)' Yeilin reads the protocol on the whiteboard aloud in Spanish very proudly. She is a new arrival and enjoys her time in the Spanish classroom. As soon as Yeilin finishes, Mr Horowitz shares that this is open to share in any language that students prefer and about anything that is weighing on them. He also says, 'For those of you that would like, I think it would be meaningful to share our thoughts around illness, as it was a topic that was mentioned during our last session of holding space'. Immediately, Antonio raises his hand and shares '*¡Yo quiero compartir!* (I want to share!).

'*Gracias Antonio, puedes ser el primero en compartir* (Thank you Antonio, you can be the first to share),' responds Mr Horowitz.

'*En mi familia hemos lidiado mucho con enfermedades* (in my family we have dealt a lot with illnesses),' states Antonio. 'During the pandemic we had to be at the hospital most of the time. For those of you that may not know, I had cancer and was receiving treatment. We had to go to the hospital almost every day and sometimes we would have to sleep there. My mom and dad would take turns staying with me. This was hard for me because I was not allowed to see my little brother and sister because they could get me sick. Sometimes, I would only talk to them on FaceTime and when I did see them we couldn't be in contact,' shares Antonio. As he shares his experience, the class falls silent and attentively listens to all he shares. Antonio continues, 'During the pandemic my aunt also got sick with COVID and it was really hard for our family because we had to take care of her and we were really worried that in DR she wouldn't get the same help and care. This made all of us worry a lot. Thankfully she was okay although it was a difficult time. I hope to go visit her again soon. Like my aunt, I'm still not back to my 100%. I am still in treatment, which is why I have to leave early sometimes and also why I get so tired coming up the stairs,' adds Antonio. He ends by asking the class for words of support.

Many hands go up to provide words of support for Antonio. Olivia begins by saying 'I'm sorry you had to go through all that. We had a family friend go through something similar and it was very challenging'. After Olivia shared, Arryany stated, 'My grandma passed away from cancer and I never got to meet her, talking about her still makes my mom sad so I understand that it's something very hard and scary'. Emmanuel adds, 'My dad is sick now, and he can't work. He has to stay home all the time. So my mom works so much now and is not home a lot of the time. My dad got really hurt at work and now his leg is always hurting. We don't know what exactly is wrong with his leg but we hope he gets better soon. I understand how scary being sick is, I'm sorry you had to go through that'. After Emmanuel, Luis adds, 'Sorry Antonio that you're still dealing with all this. I have a medical condition and I have to see doctors also, it's tiring because sometimes I don't want to go'.

Mr Horowitz thanks everybody who provided support for Antonio. He asks if anybody else would like to share their experience and a couple of students raise their hands as the class continues to hold space.

Conclusion

In addressing the social emotional needs of our students we are centering an aspect of their lives that can act as a barrier to their academic learning and progress. Although students may not openly voice what is going on, some may be experiencing difficulties that take a toll on them in various ways. These experiences may result from their traumatic journeys and arrivals to the US, the challenges they face as immigrants, the lasting effects of the COVID-19 pandemic, and varying degrees of (in)stability at home. Through Holding Space we have an opportunity to learn more about what is happening outside of our classrooms and school and the impact it has on our students and their families. We can then consider providing additional supports that vary depending on need, including referring students for in- and out-of-school services as well as legal or medical referrals. Supporting families through school and community-based resources and promoting the active participation and involvement of families is critical to strengthening their children's academic and social emotional development.

References

CASEL (2020) CASEL's SEL framework: What are the core competency areas and where are they promoted? https://casel.org/casel-sel-framework-11-2020/?view=true

Casimir A.E. and Baker, C.N. (2023) *Trauma Responsive Pedagogy: Teaching for Healing and Transformation*. Heinemman.

Minahan, J. (2019) Trauma-informed teaching strategies. *ASCD*, 1 October. https://www.ascd.org/el/articles/trauma-informed-teaching-strategies

Stanford, L. (2022) Make SEL work by applying these 6 best practices. *Education Week*, 7 November. https://www.edweek.org/leadership/make-sel-work-by-applying-these-6-best-practices/2022/11

Researcher Commentary

Mary Mendenhall

Teachers College, Columbia University

This chapter poignantly captures the efforts that teachers and counselors at Dos Puentes make to nurture their students' social emotional learning (SEL). Irving Mota and Kimberly Bautista capture the intentionality that the teachers and counselors at Dos Puentes embrace to create meaningful spaces for students to share, empathize and support one another. Whether students are engaging with SEL-related topics and activities during morning meetings or regular lessons, or finding solace in established peace corners, the authors demonstrate how these approaches contribute to the holistic development of their students. In doing so, they illustrate the reciprocal relationship between SEL and academic learning and how to constructively bring students' attention to how the realities of their peers' lives, as well as their own, may influence what is happening at school and how to deal with it constructively.

Context

The importance of SEL has garnered much attention in recent years and has only accelerated in the aftermath of the COVID-19 pandemic. As students remained at home and learned online for extended periods of time, the separation and isolation chipped away at children's sense of self, interpersonal skills, and ability to navigate social interactions (Office for Civil Rights, 2021), not to mention the emotional toll of losing family members to the virus. Upon returning to school, teachers and school personnel across the country not only had to worry about learning loss but also the psychosocial setbacks that children were experiencing from not being together for extended periods of time.

Dos Puentes's engagement with SEL activities predates the pandemic and aligns with a mission that focuses on the whole child. A whole-child approach 'understands that students' education and life outcomes are dependent upon their access to safe and welcoming learning environments and rich learning experiences in and out of school' (Learning Policy Institute, 2023). Without attention to their psychosocial needs, students are unable to learn to their fullest potential.

When teachers and other school personnel engage in SEL effectively, it further enriches the types of relationships that students have with the adults at school by establishing safe and secure environments in which to interact. Research conducted by the Center on the Developing Child at Harvard University continues to point to the important role that caring adults play in children's lives, especially in terms of their brain development. The research shows that 'nurturing and stable relationships with caring adults…contribute to the growth of a broad range of competencies, including a love of learning' (National Scientific Council on the Developing Child, 2004: 1). Given the amount of time that children are in school, teachers play a fundamental role as their students form their identities, learn to manage stressful situations, and establish a sense of self.

Within the conversation about SEL, Mota and Bautista point out that 'children come to school with myriad experiences'. In the context of migration, Dryden-Peterson's (2015) work on refugees' educational experiences prior to resettlement in the US identifies several commonalities with the immigrant experience: interrupted schooling, potential language barriers pending the students' home languages, and adjustments to different teaching and learning environments that may prove unsettling. Knowing these details can be helpful to the school and the teachers in smoothing the transition of recently arrived and resettled students into their US classrooms. As teachers work to establish positive relationships with their students, their efforts to get to know their students, their families, and their life circumstances can go a long way to finding opportunities to connect and demonstrate empathy while simultaneously supporting their academic engagement, examples that Mota and Bautista illustrate in this chapter through Holding Space during morning meetings. This approach also helps set the tone for the day, among students and teachers, and creates opportunities for students to express concerns and support in safe and supportive environments.

Discussion

As the potential and popularity of SEL continue to grow, it will be important for school leaders and teachers to ensure that these approaches are meeting the needs of students and do not simply become a superficial checklist of activities amidst competing educational trends and reforms. Teachers will also need ongoing support for both learning about and implementing effective SEL activities in their classrooms. It should not be assumed that all teachers are comfortable with these approaches or know how to implement them. More illustrative examples, like the ones demonstrated in this chapter, are needed to help bring to life what SEL looks like in action, and teachers need to have a range of approaches that span simple to more complex engagements with SEL.

It is also critical that teachers know when students need support beyond the scope of what they can provide in their classrooms and to refer students to school personnel who are professionally trained as counselors and social workers. There is some pushback that teachers should not be implementing SEL (Sheasley, 2022), but clear boundaries and referral pathways should mitigate this trepidation. I can remember more than one occasion when my own daughter came home from school at Dos Puentes and shared how she found solace in the peace corner when she needed to collect her thoughts or regain her composure during the school day. We should applaud the efforts of the Dos Puentes teachers to plan and implement meaningful SEL engagements for their students. Our children's psychosocial and academic wellbeing depend on it.

References

Dryden-Peterson, S. (2015) Refugee education in countries of first asylum: Breaking open the black box of pre-resettlement experiences. *Theory and Research in Education* 14 (2), 131–148.

Learning Policy Institute (2023) Whole child education. *Learning Policy Institute*. https://learningpolicyinstitute.org/topic/whole-child-education

National Scientific Council on the Developing Child (2004) Young children develop in an environment of relationships. *Working Paper No. 1*. http://www.developingchild.net

Office for Civil Rights (2021) *Education in a Pandemic: The Disparate Impacts of COVID-19 on America's Students*. USA Department of Education. https://www2.ed.gov/about/offices/list/ocr/docs/20210608-impacts-of-covid19.pdf

Sheasley, C. (2022) Mental health: Is that a job for schools? *The Hechinger Report*. https://hechingerreport.org/mental-health-is-that-a-job-for-schools/

11 Remote Learning through a Pandemic

Aaron Sidlo

Dos Puentes Father

Have you ever tried to teach and learn during a pandemic? Well, my kids and I have, and…it is HARD! I have been a teacher in New York City for nearly two decades. I am a parent to two children, Auggie and Maya, who were 9 and 11 years old in 2020. In March of that year, just like many other families, we were thrust into the rollercoaster of emergency remote teaching and learning like the rest of the world. In this chapter, I examine my own experiences as a parent-educator, as well as that of my kids, who were both students at Dos Puentes, as well as those of other Dos Puentes families.

A typical online learning day at Dos Puentes began with a morning meeting followed by regularly scheduled small group instruction to teach writing and math in order to meet students' needs in a more individualized way. Two hours of synchronous teaching were followed by independent asynchronous work time in which students completed daily assignments. Teachers also created read-aloud videos for students to watch independently. Finally, at the end of the day, teachers held optional office hours in which students, as well as families, could meet to discuss any academic or social issues they may have been encountering. Teachers continued to follow the model of teaching in both Spanish and English equally, to the extent possible. The model of language distribution varied by grade. In 3rd and 4th grade for example, Mondays and Wednesdays were in Spanish, Tuesdays and Thursdays in English, and Friday was split with half the day in English and the other half in Spanish. However, students were allowed to turn in work in the language(s) of choice so they could receive support from their families at home. The challenges of remote learning, as well as the approaches that Dos Puentes implemented to try to keep students as engaged as possible are explored here.

Challenges to Remote Learning

After settling into the year, Dos Puentes had an organized schedule for the students in their remote learning with a combination of online morning meetings, synchronous instruction, and independent work. In my own house, I was teaching while my own kids were following their class schedules. I considered myself lucky as my daughter Maya was finishing 5th grade and my son Auggie in 3rd, and neither one of them had any major learning issues. When they adapted to learning platforms, they were for the most part independent workers. However, this was definitely not the case for parents who had children in kindergarten and 1st grade. Those parents I spoke to had the overwhelming feeling that remote learning was extremely difficult for their kids. The synchronous lessons were short on the screen because of the children's age-appropriate attention span. This meant the remaining time was devoted to students completing independent work while they were not 'in class'. This configuration also meant that family members had to be present through every part of the learning process, in a way that was never required of them before. Families had to make sure they could connect and use the technology, and then when they did their independent work, constant guidance and supervision were necessary. One parent described her situation: she had a daughter in kindergarten and a son in 4th grade and a job that required her to be physically present, as completely chaotic as it was for her youngest. She put in as much time as she could to assist her kindergartener, however it was impossible for her to dedicate the time necessary for her to stay consistently engaged. Another parent essentially stopped working to be present for her child's learning. However, many immigrant parents and those from lower socioeconomic statuses did not have the financial means to be there all the time for their children, as their challenges were even greater. Since Dos Puentes families come from various economic, racial and immigrant/US-born backgrounds, some had to learn how to use the technology themselves for the first time. On top of that, parents faced job losses related to the pandemic that made it difficult to meet their basic needs, as well as afford the internet for their children's schooling. Many had to confront these issues and seek out assistance when they were still learning to speak English. The next section highlights the experience of just one of many families for whom even entering the online learning world was a major barrier.

Struggling to Connect

It was early November 2020 and Ana was hopeful her son Iker would finally be able to attend school remotely on this day after months of being unable to connect. Although nobody had been attending in-person school for several months, Ana knew that some of her friends had begun to get their kids to use a computer to take classes with their teacher by using the internet. Ana did not know how to use a computer herself and was hopeful she could learn something when the school provided her with a free device. She had spoken to Consuelo, the parent coordinator at the school, about how important it was for Iker to be able to attend the online classes. Ana's mother passed away in September due to complications from COVID and neither she nor her husband Nestor had been able to continue working at the laundromat. Ana was also taking care of three children: Iker, who was a 2nd grader, and his two baby sisters. There were many distractions at home with the little ones, and she never felt she had enough time to focus on getting Iker up and running with school. Additionally, they had not been able to afford the internet because of their financial situation. She was encouraged by the fact that Consuelo told her that the New York City Public Schools had recently begun to give out iPads that came with free internet service. They completed an application with Consuelo's help and Nestor passed by the school to pick it up.

Ana relied on her 12-year-old niece, Belinda, who lived next door, to help set up the device as the family's technology expert. She rang the bell, came in and sat down next to Iker, who was watching TV at the kitchen table. Ana handed her the box with the new iPad inside and Belinda pulled it out and exclaimed, '*No va a funcionar. Yo traté con mi propio iPad y la señal no entra aquí* (It's not going to work. I tried with my own iPad and the signal doesn't reach)'. Ana told her, '*¡Hay que tener fé, mi niña* (You have to have faith, my girl)!' Belinda rolled her eyes and pushed the power button. The computer sprang to life. She put in Iker's student username and password, but the iPad was not responding. She pointed out to Ana that there was no internet signal, but Ana said that the school had told her the iPad had its own internet. Belinda picked up the iPad and began wandering around the basement apartment, and finally stated, '*No hay señal* (There's no signal)'. Then she said to Ana, '*Ven conmigo* (Come with me)' and walked out the apartment door. When she walked through the lobby and out the front door of the apartment building, Belinda held the iPad in the air and showed her the internet signal producing one bar of service. Then she explained to Ana that if she wanted Iker to learn, she'd better get a table and set it up outside since that's the only place they would be able to get a signal. Ana shivered in the cold, and with the realization that today was not going to be the day Iker would get to go to school after all. Unfortunately for Iker this was the beginning of many months of missed instruction because attending school outdoors in New York City was not feasible during the winter.

Special Projects and Successes

Although there were myriad challenges to learning in the elementary setting, Dos Puentes teachers were continually learning how to improve instruction by coming up with new and creative ideas that encouraged students to take ownership over their own learning. In a personal example, very early on in the pandemic, Ms Lorene, the music teacher along with other collaborators, came up with the idea of writing a theme song for Dos Puentes which would be performed at the online 5th-grade graduation (see Image 11.1). She asked my daughter Maya and me to help write a few verses after she saw us perform a song we had written together at a talent show at the school. This was the one time I really saw my daughter become excited to be involved in something during the pandemic and, as an added bonus, I was also able to participate. It tapped into something she was interested in (music), and helped her to practice both languages as it was a bilingual song. The activity also gave us something to connect over and taught us to use new recording platforms. For Maya, working on the song offered engagement at a time when it was hard to come by and it went like this:

> **Somos Dos Puentes**
> *'Riendo juntos*
> We laugh together
> *Con familiares*
> On Family Fridays
> *Podemos crear*
> We could create
> A new awareness
> *Todos unidos*
> We're all united
> *Sembrando cariño*
> You're all invited
> It's all for one
> *Y uno para todos*
> Somos Dos Puentes'

Parents noted other special projects or strategies that helped engage their younger children and break through their disconnection. Teachers made efforts to collaborate and make learning fun. In math class students were encouraged to make learning relevant through modeling problems with imaginative drawings and household objects they found to use their natural creativity. Ms Poms included music in her teaching and made sure to sing songs with the students in Spanish to try and reach learners in a creative way. Read-alouds were a consistent part of the programming and done in 'beautiful ways' as the teachers acted out the stories, according to one parent. This kind of dedication showed children the power of literature to take us to places and times beyond the pandemic while also pushing students to see the value of reading. Mr Armando made sure to include a puppet named 'Lobo' (wolf in Spanish) as a regular part of his teaching. In fact, Lobo sometimes took over the 1st grade class as the substitute 'teacher'. For students in the youngest grades this creativity and pretend world was absolutely riveting and hilarious and, most importantly, effective, as students seemed to hang on Lobo's every word.

Image 11.1 My daughter Maya, myself, and our dog recorded part of the theme song '*Somos* Dos Puentes' in June 2020. Photo by Aaron Sidlo

For students in the upper grades, regularly scheduled small group sessions were also in place. My son Auggie mentioned that one of the things he liked about the small groups was that he and the other students did not always have a teacher present. This design was intentional as teachers wanted students to have the time to discuss amongst each other in a way that lent itself to debate, open-ended answers and collective strategies for how to carry out classwork. Another mother mentioned how she got a view into her son's limited effort during independent work. However, she felt the small group sessions with Mr Horowitz were helpful in pushing her son to show more effort and understand how to complete the work and what was expected of him. Students were also given the freedom to use some of their developing knowledge of technology for special projects in a way that most suited them. For instance, they were given a choice in how they wanted to present their work, through videos, PowerPoints, or written documents. For one school project, my son got our whole family involved in creating a video about the Haudenosaunee tribe. We were able to make it informative and use our creativity, making it fun and interesting. Another friend of his was able to design a Haudenosaunee Iroquois living structure called a Long House by using the building video game Minecraft. These unique opportunities from the home learning environment and strategies chosen by Dos Puentes's teachers made some parts of the virtual learning come alive.

Conclusion

Pandemic online learning for elementary students was a tremendous challenge for the students, families and educators, although those who were the most vulnerable due to their economic and/or migration status suffered disproportionately. Hopefully, it is something we will never have to face again! The lack of social connection was something that could not truly be recreated through a computer screen and impacted children (as well as adults) greatly. On top of that, the level of family guidance necessary for the youngest students was essentially impossible for most family members to provide, as they also had to work either outside the home or without outside childcare. For upper elementary students, the disengagement lent itself to students sometimes doing less than their best and for many engaging with a screen more than most parents would prefer. However, students and their families did learn to use technology in new ways that most had never accomplished previously. Dos Puentes teachers worked hard to adapt to their new teaching environment by showing a dedication to their craft and an interest in tackling the disengagement that so many students felt. Although remote learning is most likely not the way of the future for elementary children, some of the lessons we took away from it are certainly valuable for teaching and learning in general.

Researcher Commentary

Devon Hedrick-Shaw

University of Colorado Boulder

The stories in this chapter illustrate the complexities that families faced when instruction moved online during the early days of the COVID-19 pandemic. As teachers were catapulted into creativity, trying to design learning experiences that for so long required in-person participation, families were forced to quickly adapt to this new reality. While the abrupt transition to online instruction is a time few want to relive, the experience nevertheless prompts the question: What did remote learning make possible, and what stays? By centering family perspectives during this unique and challenging time, this chapter provides educators with guideposts for reimagining meaningful family partnerships within and beyond remote learning.

Context

As the cases in this chapter depict, families faced complex challenges at this time, the impacts of which were disproportional along social isolation and identity markers such as race, language, gender and socioeconomic status. Immigrant families, parents without college degrees, and mothers were among the most impacted, especially while navigating childcare decisions (Cioè-Peña, 2022). Soltero-González and Gillanders (2021), for instance, highlight how mothers were forced to choose between maintaining employment and supporting children at home. Additionally, research describes how even when school districts provide families with technology like tablets, challenges still remain such as accessing internet connection and configuring devices programmed exclusively in English (Cioè-Peña, 2022).

Such inequities are not a result of the pandemic but rather constitute a longstanding 'digital divide' (Jacobsen, 2020). Ana's story in particular illustrates how these inequities became barriers when attempting to connect her son to remote classes. Unfamiliar with how to use a computer, Ana reached out to the school to receive a tablet for her son. Even though the district assured her that she could use the device to connect to the internet, the signal in her home was weak, making it difficult to connect to remote instruction. Yet, despite her discomfort with technology, Ana used a variety of strategies to navigate the situation, including enlisting the help of her niece. These actions represent families' resourcefulness during the pandemic to creatively support their children (Carrell Moore, 2022; Cioè-Peña, 2022).

Additionally, a widespread challenge was the disengagement that families observed in younger children. As the home became the classroom, Carrell Moore (2022) describes how parents of early-childhood students quickly took primary responsibility for keeping children engaged. In this chapter, Aaron Sidlo outlines how his children in 3rd and 5th grades were able to manage remote learning independently, while parents of younger students had to be constantly present. Teachers consequently managed this dilemma by designing activities that were shorter in length, multimodal and allowed for social interaction.

Some of the successes of these strategies and special projects were due to how teachers, families, and students engaged with each other through music and imagination. The Dos Puentes theme song, for example, was an opportunity for students to participate bilingually in a creative project with an authentic audience. Similarly, using puppets, acting out read-alouds, and designing models through video games all offered examples of how to increase connection through play, discovery, and choice. Soltero-González and Gillanders (2021) note how these motivating factors not only facilitate student engagement but also encourage families to participate in experiential learning activities that draw on community math and literacy practices. Taken together, these activities rest on an understanding of learning *through* language (Halliday, 1993), meaning that the learning process is fundamentally a linguistic endeavor that considers approaches like imaginative play as tools for making meaning of the world. Authentic tasks and audiences with explicit opportunities for social and linguistic interaction are thus essential, especially when technology is one of the primary learning tools.

Discussion

Out of necessity, the pandemic prompted a much-needed dialogue between schools and families as the home became a more direct site for facilitating school-based learning. Families, especially those of younger children, became active participants in classroom activities, which allowed space for school tasks to become more grounded in children's home lives. Remote learning also necessitated the design of imaginative, multimodal instruction which utilized a variety of meaning-making tools to enhance student engagement. Going forward, educators can reflect on the limits and possibilities remote learning offered with attention to how in-person instruction might continue to leverage technology as a significant meaning-making resource. For example, educators might consider how technological tools embedded in remote learning tasks might continue to expand bilingual students' agency in selecting how and for whom to communicate their learning, including families.

Remote learning also put a spotlight on the challenges that, while seemingly unique to the pandemic, were in fact longstanding. The disparities that remote learning illuminated require schools to develop family partnerships that are dialogic and dynamic, having the ability to responsively change based on the contextual demands of the time. Approaching family partnerships in this way is thus a project of listening to what families communicate *they* need (Cioè-Peña, 2022), especially alongside district initiatives like distributing devices to students' homes. Lastly, building family partnerships must continue to consider the multiple, intersecting identities and lived experiences that families bring to school in order to better understand how to address institutionalized inequities that cause such disparities to exist in the first place.

References

Carrell Moore, H. (2022) 'The whole experience is still very high touch for parents': Parent moves to support young children's remote learning during the COVID-19 pandemic. *Journal of Early Childhood Research* 20 (4), 624–636.

Cioè-Peña, M. (2022) Computers secured, connection still needed: Understanding how COVID-19-related remote schooling impacted Spanish-speaking mothers of emergent bilinguals with dis/abilities. *Journal of Latinos and Education* 21 (3), 224–238.

Halliday, M.A.K. (1993) Toward a language-based theory of learning. *Linguistics and Education* 5 (2), 93–116. https://doi.org/10.1037/030051

Jacobsen, L. (2020) Digital and economic divides put U.S. Children at greater educational risk during the COVID-19 pandemic. *Population Reference Bureau.* https://www.prb.org/economic-and-digital-divide/

Soltero-González, L. and Gillanders, C. (2021) Rethinking home-school partnerships: Lessons learned from Latinx parents of young children during the COVID-19 era. *Early Childhood Education Journal* 49, 965–976.

Pillar 3 Introduction
Investigaciones and Hands-on Learning

Alcira Jaar

Dos Puentes Co-Founder and Assistant Principal

During the planning stages of Dos Puentes as a dual language bilingual elementary school, Dr Victoria Hunt, founding principal, felt it was essential for language learning that students ask questions and have tactile, real-life experiences that support content learning. As the co-founders were in dialogue to determine the school's pillars, we took the opportunity to reflect on our collective language learning experiences and being educators of multilingual learners. Our team agreed that consistently integrating inquiry-based learning, and making sure students have ongoing hands-on or interactive experiences with materials at school and through field trips across all grade levels had to be one of the four pillars of the school.

Inquiry-Based Learning

Inquiry-based learning is an educational strategy in which students follow methods and practices similar to those of professional scientists in order to construct knowledge (Keselman, 2003). When it pertains to language learning, inquiry-based teaching stimulates students to actively engage in cognitive and exploratory activities (Lee, 2014). At Dos Puentes, inquiry-based learning encourages curiosity by asking students what they want to know about a particular topic. Once students have developed their inquiry questions, they research the topic in various ways. In the lower grades, it may be through the teacher's read-aloud and by watching videos. As students are able, they begin to research topics by reading teacher-gathered texts. Eventually, students can research by reading physical and digital texts on their reading levels and watching videos pre-selected by the teacher. Individually or as a group, students are then asked to present what they have learned by way of a culminating project, where they create artifacts such as posters, articles, models, or a slide presentation. Inquiry-based learning is unique at Dos Puentes because students can read, discuss, research and present in Spanish and English and are encouraged to connect with and add their multicultural perspectives. Through inquiry-based learning, language learners strengthen their linguistic skills, while at the same time gaining different cultural and social perspectives as they discuss and research content (Escalante Arauz, 2014).

Hands-on Learning

Hands-on learning can be defined as learning by doing. At Dos Puentes, we believe that students can learn new concepts and become bilingual and biliterate through action and experiences, rather than just being told about content by teachers or texts. Hands-on learning leads to higher engagement as it is a more interactive and engaging way to learn. For example, when learning about structures students can build them using different materials instead of simply looking at pictures and reading about the buildings or landscapes. It allows for experiential learning, as theorized by David A. Kolb (1984); it is the process by which students interact physically with an experience, reflect, conceptualize and then act on what they have learned in multiple ways. Recent practices in language learning emphasizes the significance of the student's own contribution to the development of their language practices through active involvement (Mollaei & Rahnama, 2012). By interacting physically with materials and other students and adults while they are learning, Dos Puentes students are simultaneously expanding their linguistic repertoire as they learn in and through two languages; as well as develop multicultural understandings. For example, when students make and maintain a compost bin by using organic waste from the lunchroom, they figure out what works and does not work to keep a healthy environment for the worms, then use the soil for the school's garden. At the same time they may discuss how/if composting is done in their homes or countries of origin in order to expand multicultural perceptions. Throughout this hands-on learning project, students are authentically using scientific vocabulary in two languages and developing a deeper understanding of recycling, compared to students who only read about it in a textbook.

Inquiry and Hands-on Learning at Dos Puentes

Science Program

In my first year as a founding teacher at Dos Puentes, I was the science and movement teacher for three kindergarten classes (I became the assistant principal in 2019). The school's founders felt that bringing real-world experiences to students' learning would lead to high engagement, increased opportunities for students' bilingualism and eventually an inquiry stance.

When I started planning the animals and habitats unit, having real-life animals in the classroom was essential. I knew that having classroom animals would awaken students' curiosity and lead to many questions. For my first animal habitat unit, our science classroom had a tarantula, a fish, an ant farm, red belly frogs and beetles. Student faces lit up when I told them they would be scientists researching how these animals lived in our classroom habitat. It was hard to contain the excitement when students held magnifying lenses for the first time to observe our classroom animals' body parts and behaviors. They asked many questions, such as 'Why does the fish always open and close its mouth?', '¿*Cómo pueden ver las lombrices de tierra si no tienen ojos* [How can earthworms see if they don't have eyes]?', 'Why does a tarantula have hair (see Image P3.1)?'. Some

Image P3.1 A kindergarten student's observations about the class tarantula. Photo by Alcira Jaar

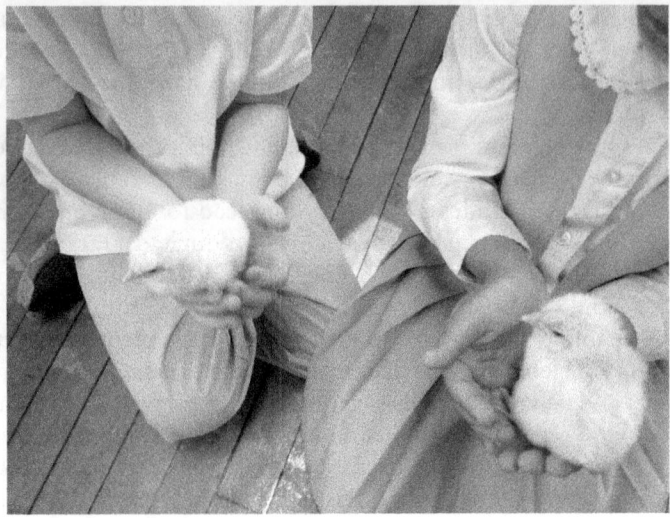

Image P3.2 Kindergarten students holding chicks after they hatched in the classroom. Photo by Alcira Jaar

questions were answered through observations and others by reading books or watching videos.

To deepen our science instruction, we partnered with the Leave It Better foundation (LIB) in our first year. I had previously worked with them at another school and found their approach powerful. LIB weaves in hands-on learning in Science, Technology, Engineering, Art and Math (STEAM) projects, gardening and mindfulness exercises so that students develop environmental consciousness as early as possible. This partnership helped us build garden beds in front of our school and taught our students how to plant lettuce seeds. With Leave It Better, students learned all about worms, how to make a compost bin and how to maintain it so the soil could nourish our garden. We kept the composting bins in the science room and students checked them daily to ensure the worms were happy eating organic matter to produce rich soil. At the same time, students learned how to film themselves using the six basic film shots and made a short documentary educating our community about how to leave our Earth a better place by composting, planting and eating healthier.

Families were so excited with all this work that they began sharing ideas on further enriching the curriculum with other hands-on opportunities. One parent contacted a farm that had a chick hatching program. Our students learned the life cycle of a chicken and saw up close how a chick is born from a fertilized egg. Before we knew it, we had 12 little chicks in the classroom that everyone got to hold and observe (see Image P3.2). For most of our students, it was the first time watching a baby chick hatch

Image P3.3 The kindergarten representatives of the fish study at the New York City Science Exposition. Photo by Alcira Jaar

from an egg and seeing them feed for the first time. We learned '*los pollitos dicen*' a song many children learn in Spanish-speaking countries, to sing when learning about what baby chicks eat and how they huddle when they are cold. There were many sad faces when the chicks had to return to the farm but, at the same time, they understood that it would be hard for them to live at our school as it was not the ideal habitat for these chicks to survive to adulthood.

To reinforce the learning of life cycles, the parent association purchased butterfly larvae. Students could see the differences between a chicken's life cycle and an insect undergoing metamorphosis. Most students had never seen the stages of a butterfly up close (especially those from NYC) and it generated many questions. Students started noticing differences between insects. '*¿Por qué algunos insectos vuelan y otros no* [Why do some insects fly and others don't]?' 'Why do larvae eat certain kinds of plants?' '*¿Por qué son todos de diferentes colores y tamaños* [Why are they all different colors and sizes]?' Students had lots to say about animals and used rich vocabulary in both languages.

Towards the end of that first year, the New York City Public Schools was hosting its first annual science fair. We had done such exciting work that I entered a research project for each kindergarten class. Students voted on one animal to focus on for the science fair. They were excited to have their class display board with their bilingual work exhibited alongside the work of many older students throughout NYC. We were all very proud to have the only kindergarten poster boards on display that year. Student representatives answered questions from fair participants as they came to their science poster boards. Many visitors were impressed with the amount of knowledge and ability of our students to answer questions. All kindergarten students received medals that they displayed very proudly (see Image P3.3).

Exploration, Investigation and Inquiry

The inquiry and hands-on learning pillar places students at the center, leads to high levels of engagement and multiple entryways into learning, and moves students towards independence. Although science instruction at our school upholds this pillar, it lives at the school in various ways. In early childhood (K-1) classrooms, inquiry and hands-on learning is also built in during a daily exploration period. During explorations, teachers introduce new words and model how to explore with friends. Students can participate in various centers that change throughout the year. Students choose between the kitchen, building blocks, art, dressing-up or the writing station. This choice naturally leads to engagement as students decide where to spend their time. At exploration centers, students learn how to play with peers as they navigate the space and materials, which leads to learning new words in multiple languages. Explorations at Dos Puentes allow students to be creative in different modalities. Some students may use blocks to build a skyscraper, while others make a collage of the buildings in their community. While some students role-play in the kitchen area, others create a menu for their restaurants. Explorations push students to interact with one another and teach each other words across languages and without restrictions. It is a period where translanguaging is encouraged and naturally occurs. Students think they are just playing and having fun, but we know they are simultaneously learning content, language, and multicultural understandings through inquiry and hands-on learning.

In 2nd grade, we transition from explorations into investigations. Investigations are units that integrate social studies content with inquiry and hands-on projects. Teachers begin each unit by having students share what they know about a topic, then have students generate questions about what they want to learn more about. In a New York City landmark unit, students first review photographs of landmarks around the city and write down what they notice. Then they write down their wonderings and use different resources (i.e. texts, videos, visits to museums and cultural institutions) to answer their questions. As one of the culminating activities, students work in groups to build a chosen landmark out of cardboard, paint and other materials. Families are invited into the classroom to help students build their landmarks and reinforce their learning by sharing facts they have learned based on their inquiry questions. At the end of the unit, students proudly present their projects to classmates, staff and families bilingually.

Similarly, in 3rd grade, Dos Puentes students begin their investigation units by exploring a geography unit of our community and end with a social issues unit that explores racial, gender, immigration and environmental justice. Topics are chosen based on student interest, current events and the availability of age-appropriate resources. Throughout each unit, students ask questions that shape the direction of their learning and create a culminating project. In the geography unit, students ask questions about borders and map representations. They make community maps that allow them to get to know their neighborhoods and begin to wonder about specific issues affecting them and those around them such as lack of green space or overflow of trash in more condensed areas. By the end of the year, students are ready to take action in the social issues unit. They choose from a menu of options as they decide whether to write a petition for change, write an op-ed, make signs to post in the school or community or create a public service announcement addressing their topic.

In our upper grades, we see a shift from investigations to inquiry. While the foundation of asking questions about a topic and researching it solidifies in 2nd and 3rd grades, the work shifts to include more student choice and voice in the 4th and 5th grades. Teachers plan units that center student inquiry around topics that the NYC Social Studies Scope and Sequence determine. For example, the 4th graders learn about the Native Americans of New York State. In one of the inquiry units, students investigate the Haudenosaunee and work on projects based on their interests and inquiry questions. Students choose an aspect of the Haudenosaunee's way of life to research, such as housing, food, clothing, and the role of women, among others, and also choose how they will present the information they learn. Since mathematics and literacy are carefully planned in terms of language allocation, inquiry units are usually linguistically fluid, teachers work with students to decide the language(s) of culmination and presentations; this gives students additional choice and opportunity to bring in their voice and identity.

Inquiry units evolve even further in the 5th grade as students are made aware that they are bilingual ethnographers/historians with unique bilingual perspectives. During a European exploration unit, students explore the essential question: 'How do issues of power and language influence exploration and colonization?' Teachers push students to look at European explorations through a critical linguistic lens to determine the extent to which language was a factor in colonization. Students are also made to analyze their language use to develop metalinguistic awareness and ultimately look at primary sources for whose voices are missing and why. Students create artifacts, including dioramas, galleries of photos, speeches and bilingual videos to highlight the results of their inquiry.

Field Trips

The inquiry/hands-on pillar also means that Dos Puentes embraces field trips as experiences that enrich classroom learning and build bridges to our surroundings. Our school works with outside partners and organizations such as the Bronx Zoo, New Victory Theater and the Leave It Better Foundation to enrich our curriculum and give our students another entryway to learn content and make real-life connections.

For some of our students, going on a school trip is the first time they leave the neighborhood and visit the renowned cultural institutions our great city offers. For some of our families who are new to speaking English, staying within their Spanish-speaking neighborhood is a haven. There are also a range of structural barriers that keep minoritized families out of arts-based institutions. They range from outreach and advertising that targets English speaking clients, exhibits that center and value European forms of art over other groups and the cost of public transportation and admission. Families may also fear the unknown when it comes to the etiquette/procedures for these unfamiliar spaces and may choose to avoid them altogether. For all these reasons, Dos Puentes is committed to taking students on field trips, whether we ride a yellow school bus, go underground on the subway, or do walking tours of our neighborhood.

Walking trips near our school allow students to see their community differently. First grade students look for numbers or mathematical symbols in the community on a math walk and discuss their daily use. We also venture outside the surrounding community. Students visited the Metropolitan Museum of Art and other art institutions throughout the years. Studio in a School, a visual arts organization, provides schools with teaching artists that have students create art through a variety of media. Because we partner with Studio in a School, it is essential to have students observe different art media up close and learn the process from working in a studio to the art displayed at a museum or gallery. Some of our students have had the extraordinary opportunity to exhibit their work at galleries like Christie's New York. Visiting art museums also gives students another way to learn about culture and history. When studying India, our 3rd-grade students visited the Rubin Museum of Art to see sculptures and paintings they were learning about at school in person. Going on this field trip gave students another perspective and deeper understanding of the culture and history of India than they had before visiting the museum.

Architecture is an integral part of New York City; therefore, we believe that having students visit iconic landmarks leads to a greater understanding of our city's history. As part of a 2nd grade investigations unit on city landmarks, students have taken the subway to walk across the Brooklyn Bridge, rode on the Staten Island ferry to see the Statue of Liberty, and walked to see the Little Red Lighthouse that sits under the

George Washington Bridge in our very own neighborhood. Our 4th grade students have walked Highbridge, which connects our Washington Heights neighborhood to the Highbridge neighborhood in the Bronx. They learned its primary purpose was to carry an aqueduct that brought fresh water from upstate New York. Later in the year, these 4th graders visited one of the manufactured reservoirs upstate that house some of the city's fresh water before it travels down via one of the new aqueduct tunnels. These experiences gave our students a new perspective on our water supply and all the work that went into and continues to this day to maintain NYC's water supply.

At Dos Puentes, allowing our students to experience the outdoors for an extended period is vital. Since many of our students have never gone camping or been to the upstate New York region, every year we organize a two-night, three-day camping trip to a campsite about two hours north of our school. In science, our 4th grade students learn where their drinking water comes from and how the water cycle helps produce the water needed to sustain our city's needs. This camping trip includes a stop at a reservoir upstate. Students get to see firsthand one of the reservoirs that hold their drinking water before it makes its way down to the city. This visit helps them appreciate our water supply and learn about the need to protect it. This camping trip gives most of our students an experience they will never forget.

What is learned during the field trip experiences is extended once students return to the classroom. Students can then compare their experiences with what they have learned at school. Did it confirm or extend a concept? Did we change our opinion or do we now have more questions? In addition, these field trips strengthen student bilingualism as content vocabulary in both languages fortifies real-world usage, connection to concrete experiences builds cross-cultural connections and later application to products of learning is increased.

Inquiry and hands-on learning for bilingual learning

Inquiry-based and hands-on learning are essential for teaching and learning in general, but especially for students learning to become bilingual and biliterate. When students are at the center of the curriculum planning, they will be highly engaged in learning new content and skills as they grow their linguistic repertoire with features of Spanish and English, and perhaps other languages too. Field trips add another level of conceptual understanding, as students can experience content while interacting through models, exhibits, experts, and authentic artifacts. Content and vocabulary come to life differently when you can interact with them alongside books, images, videos, or school spaces. Students come to new understandings, come up with new questions, and are motivated to further their learning. Due to a high level of engagement that allows for autonomy and curiosity through choice, students are also more eager to take on new tasks, become risk-takers and develop more independent in their learning. The pillar of inquiry-based and hands-on learning has dramatically impacted learning and languaging at Dos Puentes.

Section Overview

The four chapters in this section delve deeper into the inquiry-based and hands-on learning pillar and how it comes to life at Dos Puentes. In Chapter 12, '*Exploraciones en* Early Childhood', Elizabeth Menendez and Catherine Velásquez-Lealock bring you into our early childhood classrooms and explain the importance of the exploration period for language acquisition as they show why it is almost every student's favorite subject. In Chapter 13, 'Transition to Investigations and Inquiry in the Upper Grades', Hazel Garcia-Banguela and Carmen Morel show how 2nd and 3rd grade classrooms transition from explorations into more structured investigation units, while Michelle Madera Taveras demonstrates how 4th and 5th grade classes fully evolve into inquiry-based units where learning is student-driven and centered in their voice. In Chapter 14, 'Learning Science through Hands-on-Experiences and Animals', Karín Dejesus and Yesenia Moreno continue to deepen science content learning in Spanish and English through an inquiry-driven curriculum that includes many hands-on activities, field trips and animals in the classroom. In Chapter 15, 'Field Trips as *Paseos* to Real World Connections', Peggy McQuaid and Kristen Minno-Bingham take you on field trips, conceptualized as *paseos*, to illustrate how teachers make real-life connections to content and immerse students in learning two languages to deepen and enrich classroom learning.

References

Escalante Arauz, P. (2014) Inquiry-based learning in an English as a foreign language class: A proposal. *Revista De Lenguas Modernas* (19). https://revistas.ucr.ac.cr/index.php/rlm/article/view/14031
Keselman A. (2003) Supporting inquiry learning by promoting normative understanding of multivariable causality. *Journal of Research in Science Teaching* 40, 898–921.
Kolb, D.A. (1984) *Experiential Learning: Experience as the Source of Learning and Development*. Prentice Hall.
Lee, H.-Y. (2014) Inquiry-based teaching in second and foreign language pedagogy. *Journal of Language Teaching and Research* 5 (6), 1236–1244. https://doi.org/10.4304/jltr.5.6.1236-1244.
Mollaei, F. and Rahnama, H. (2012) Experiential education contributing to language learning. *International Journal of Humanities and Social Science* 2 (21), 268–279.

12 *Exploraciones* en Early Childhood

Elizabeth Menendez and
Catherine Velásquez-Leacock

Dos Puentes Teachers

It's 1:30 pm and every kindergarten class is bursting with excitement to start a lively part of the day, *Exploraciones*. Every hand is raised, they all want to pick a center. Each center or theme-based area for students to play and explore is listed on a chart making it easy for the children to choose. As the children choose a center, the teachers will fill in a chart with that child's name. Some centers fill up fast. Leandro starts by saying, '*¡Yo quiero jugar en la casa de muñecas* (I want to play in the dollhouse)!'. It's Citlali's turn and she says, '*¡Yo quiero jugar en los bloques* (I want to play with the blocks)!'. Angel is next, but he wants to wait, '*Yo quiero esperar for Gabriel* (I want to wait for Gabriel). He will pick and then I will pick'. Explorations are a fundamental part of our Dos Puentes daily schedule. It is the time of the day when every student gets to choose a play space to work. Every early-childhood classroom is filled with Lego bricks, blocks, a dramatic play space, art supplies, trains, playdough and many other bins filled with endless possibilities for five- and six-year-olds. We could not think of a better name for when the students get a chance to explore, ask questions, and experiment with materials and language - all the while forming friendships. Explorations are an essential part of the school day because they allow for language learning, parallel play and social emotional learning through student choice and student agency. The creative freedom provides a comfortable environment in which to learn language.

Explorations comes alive across the early-childhood classrooms because of how we organize our materials and spaces around play and language. In the areas for dramatic play, we include dolls of different skin colors so that all students are represented. We have an art center where students can create using crayons, markers, paints, scissors, glue, paper and fabric. Dramatic play is a an essential center available for students to choose from, with bins that include different types of clothing, shoes and accessories. We equip the kitchen not only with appliances, dishes and

Image 12.1 Students playing at the magnetic tiles center. Photo by Elizabeth Menendez

silverware, but also with notebooks or pads of paper which students often use to take orders or to create their own menus. Many classrooms across the grades have stuffed animals in the block center and in the dramatic play center for children to interact with. In the 1st grade classrooms, we have a center with medical equipment where students take on the role of a doctor, nurse or patient (see Image 12.2). These materials allow students to use their imagination and skills to create freely and develop language, all while forming friendships, learning social skills and making sense of the world they live in.

Once everyone has chosen their desired spot in the room, the play and work begins. There is an energy and a buzz in the room. The students are engaged, their hands busy, and everyone is talking. They are communicating in Spanish, in English, bilingually and even bringing in additional home languages, as they are compromising and sharing (see Image 12.3). In the dramatic play center, Ava and Jade are working on dressing up in tutus and firefighter costumes. In the Lego center, Daniel and Ikal are working on creating flying cars. In the art center, Yana and Avery are making pop-up monsters. Dayana and Camila are walking around the room with a plate full of playdough pancakes. They want everyone to take a bite. As centers are in progress, teachers walk around the room pretending to be the sick patient who needs to get checked by the doctor, or sampling playdough creations. We find ourselves bouncing from center to center taking pictures of their creations to share with families, or to

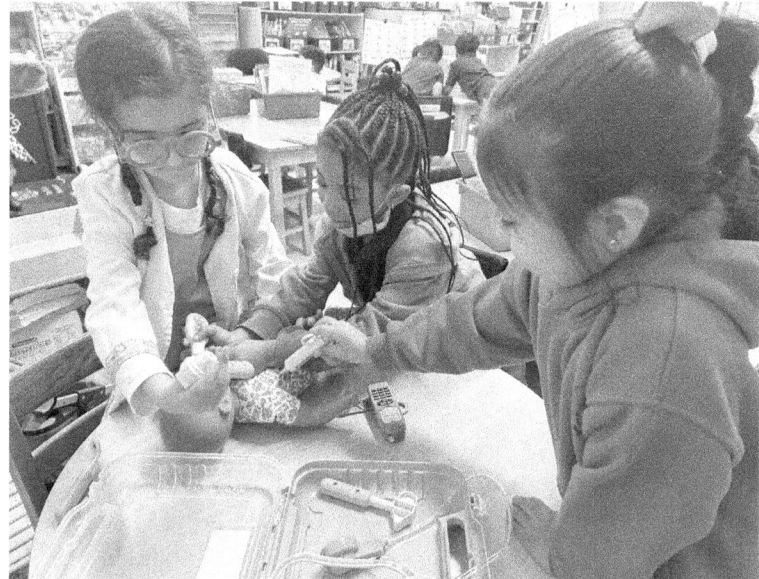

Image 12.2 Students at the dramatic center attending to the medical needs of a baby. Photo by Elizabeth Menendez

showcase in our classrooms and bulletin boards. Often, we are not needed at all when students reach an independent level. The students are so engaged with their work or pretend worlds, it allows teachers to observe and learn from them (see Image 12.1).

Language Learning

Language learning is a critical part of explorations. The children are acquiring language from the moment they choose their spot with a well-rehearsed, '*Yo quiero jugar en*' or 'I want to play in', to the translanguaging that naturally occurs for bilingual children while playing. Since each child chooses where to explore, each center has a different mix of Spanish-dominant speakers, English-dominant speakers or bilingual speakers who can move easily between languages. The children learn to communicate with one another through play. They observe the materials, they observe each other, and they look for the right moment to jump in. Even when our days are labeled with '*Hoy estamos hablando en español*' or 'Today we speak in English', explorations are an open time where both languages co-exist and additional languages are welcomed. It is a perfect time to experiment with a new language in a comfortable, low-stakes environment. Listening to their conversations, you can hear English being spoken in the art center, Spanish in the blocks center, and a mix of both in the kitchen and the dollhouse. Every day the language practices across centers

Image 12.3 Students having a conversation at the Lego center. Photo by Elizabeth Menendez

change because the children choose different spots. Every day is a new opportunity to strengthen one's home language or develop in the new language. The opportunity to use language through play mimics how one's home language is learned as the desire to create with a friend is strong enough that communication will break through.

Play Motivates Language

Angel primarily speaks Spanish and he loves playing with Gabriel, who only speaks English at home. Angel uses all the English he knows to compromise and share the Lego bricks with Gabriel. He wants to work on a project together to build a zoo with slides and pools for animals. Angel, who mostly speaks Spanish, says, 'This the *piscina* (pool)' as he shows Gabriel the blue bricks. Gabriel, who only speaks English, sees the blue pool and understands, 'Okay, the *piscina* (pool) for the tigers'. They each have enough Spanish and English exposure to communicate with one another. They are both building their language skills, but because they are immersed in play, language learning is purposeful, natural and comfortable.

Parallel Play

In the beginning of the year, some children parallel play as they are in the same exploration spot, without talking or playing with one another directly. This can happen when children are still getting to know one another and have a language in common, but it almost always happens when children do not speak the same language. In the kitchen dramatic play center, Leah, who speaks only Spanish, takes out all the play food from the kitchen. Elodie, who speaks only English, takes out the notepad and pencil. Leah wants to play by cooking the food and serving it to the class. Leah proudly says she is making *'arroz con pollo, habichuelas y tostones'*. She also enjoys charging for the food she is making. Leah has pretend money and says, *'Tengo mucha plata y voy a ganar más* (I have a lot of money and I'm going to make more)'. Elodie wants to walk around the room and ask people what kind of ice cream they like. She is taking notes (writing random letters) in her notepad and running back to the kitchen to collect everyone's favorite flavor. Elodie says to Leah, 'Get the ice cream ready!' but Leah continues stirring her pot because she is still cooking. Elodie realizes Leah does not understand. The girls look quietly at one another and smile. Elodie offers Leah a compromise and starts using her hands for communication. She puts her hand out over the pot to indicate stop with the *'habichuelas'* and shows Leah the play ice cream cones. Elodie says, 'Yummy' to entice Leah over to her idea. Leah agrees, 'Okay, ¡*pero vamos a usar la plata* (but let's use the money)!'. Elodie knows how to say 'chocolate' in Spanish but asks the teachers to help her with strawberry and vanilla. Once she knows, she runs to Leah and says, *'fresa'*. Leah knows Elodie is serving strawberry ice cream. She scoops the strawberry flavor on the cone and hands it to Elodie knocking down all the other scoops. They start giggling when all the ice cream falls on the floor. Both seized key moments to try their new emergent language in a safe space with peers. Even when there is minimal communication, it evolves over time because of the authentic purpose to learn a new language and connect with their classmates. They think, I want to have fun with this person and I am going to make this work. Today they play with the ice cream and tomorrow they will sell *tostones*.

Social Emotional Learning

Play is an important part of children's social emotional development. Through play students learn to embrace diversity, learn real-world skills and interact and work with others. During explorations, students are able to embrace and capitalize on their differences for the benefit of their play while at the same time bonding over their similarities. One of the centers where you can see this is in dramatic play, where students can explore a play kitchen with costumes and dolls. In this center, small groups of children come together to negotiate and role play. They have to decide the story line that they will follow, who they will be while playing as they lay out the rules. Through this play, children are able to speak up their ideas, likes and dislikes. They do this in their language of choice or through translanguaging. Children learn how to share the space and materials if they want to play with each other. They learn when to lead and when to follow. They have to learn to communicate with each other if differences in language are a factor while at the same time learning about cultural and familial diversity.

Isaac and José are playing with trains and tracks. Isaac is English-dominant while José is Spanish-dominant. José mentions that he is taking the train *'para ir a pescar con mi tío* [to go fishing with my uncle]'. Isaac looks puzzled and José quickly says 'fish' while using hand gestures to explain one of his favorite activities. Isaac mentions that he has also gone fishing with his uncle when visiting family with both of his mommies. Both boys share a smile and have now made a connection through uncles and fishing while acknowledging their familial differences. Explorations are the perfect time for our young learners to develop their language practices, not just in a new language but their home language as well. Students use vocabulary that pertains to the activity that they are participating in. They also learn vocabulary through acknowledging each other's language varieties. Audrey, Lila and Keyla are creating at the playdough center. As I walk past, Audrey tells Lila '*Necesito el playdoh rojo to work on a heart* (I need the red playdough para trabajar en un corazón)'. Lila responds '*aquí tienes la plastilina pero yo voy hacer una flor* (here you have the playdough but I'm going to make a flower)', meanwhile Keyla reminds the girls to close the tubs when they are not using them to avoid '*la masilla* (the putty)' drying out. At this moment the girls are not only learning and acknowledging the various names for playdough; they are also learning to compromise and set expectations. These are the building blocks for the skills that they will need to navigate the real world.

Explorations allow teachers insight into what is going on in children's personal lives. At the art center there is a little girl working quietly on a family portrait. Jennifer is a very bright and happy little girl. When speaking with Jennifer about her picture you hear her mention her big sister, and how she is her best friend. Once you get to know Jennifer better she will tell you that her big sister passed away. In this case, explorations are giving Jennifer time and space to grieve, honor her sister and also open up to those she feels comfortable sharing her story with. And it also allows her teachers to better understand her family dynamics and look out for times Jennifer may need additional support or space to come to terms with this loss.

Laying the Foundation

Explorations is the foundation that gives our youngest learners space to experiment with materials, language, independence and friendship. They learn to take risks and make connections to real world situations.

The children will continue the work of asking questions, researching and making conclusions as they move on to 2nd grade where 'Explorations' are replaced with 'Investigations' and 'Inquiry', as the work becomes more sophisticated and they pursue their wonderings on a grander scale that goes beyond their role playing to actual research. The students grow taller and move on, but they never forget how explorations was their favorite time of the day. When the kindergarten classes visit the Lego Robotics exhibition, Emmanuel, a 5th-grader, shows off his remote-control vehicle with a crane as the kindergarteners look in awe at his structure. Emmanuel, who was a new arrival labeled as an English Language Learner when he came to Dos Puentes for kindergarten, exclaims, 'I remember when I used to make bridges and other structures with blocks and Legos during explorations when I was in kindergarten! You, too, will be able to join the Lego Robotics team when you are in 5th grade'. Through this exchange, it is evident that explorations are an experience that he has held on to which he is excited to share with the younger children, and that has encouraged his language acquisition and creativity.

Researcher Commentary

Dina López

The City College of New York, CUNY

In this chapter, kindergarten teachers Elizabeth Menendez and Catherine Velásquez-Leacock give us a wonderful peek into the vibrant, creative, productive, and joyful learning that takes place during the part of the Dos Puentes school day called *Exploraciones*. They call attention to some key themes that emerge from the daily interactions students have during this period, when they are allowed the freedom to play, explore, experiment and create using their entire linguistic repertoire.

Context

Play and early-childhood learning

It is a well-established research principle that young children learn and develop through play, and that it is a crucial component of developmentally appropriate practice (NAEYC, 2009). This understanding has been demonstrated in the research on child learning and development and, more recently, in the neuroimaging science of brain development (Hassinger-Das *et al.*, 2017). As such, the time that children spend playing freely and creatively during *Exploraciones* is critical to their ability to develop their language and literacy skills, process information, and engage in social emotional development (Hoffman & Russ, 2012).

Language as a social practice

What is clear from the examples of emergent bilingual children's interactions featured in this chapter is that language learning is a socially and culturally mediated process (Lave & Wenger, 1998; Vygotsky, 1986). From a bilingual education perspective, it highlights the social complexities in school-based language practices that go beyond 'dual language' or two named languages. Bilingual classrooms can be thought of as unique communities of practice, in which students participate in language socialization processes that include both explicit and implicit guidance by teachers as well as more proficient peers (Duffy, 2010). Thus, *Exploraciones* provide a unique opportunity for emergent bilingual children to use language and develop their language skills through play-based social interactions with peers in a safe learning environment.

Dynamic bilingualism of early-childhood bilingual learners

Regardless of whether it is an English or an *español* day, kindergarteners at Dos Puentes are allowed and encouraged to use their entire linguistic repertoires as they play and create with one another during *Exploraciones* (Axelrod, 2014; López, 2019). This intentional stance acknowledges the dynamic bilingualism of emergent bilingual children as they construct meaning and develop language and literacy skills – a perspective that emphasizes one language repertoire from which children draw to use linguistic features associated with more than one named language (García, 2009; Gort & Pontier 2012).

Discussion

Lessons learned

The cases presented highlight the importance of prioritizing play for young emergent bilinguals in kindergarten and beyond. As the emphasis on academic standards and instruction is felt across grade levels, it is not uncommon for schools to do away with center time, choice time, and time for play in the lower grades. For dual language bilingual educators, the task to teach academic content in two languages might make this even more challenging. However, I would like to highlight some important lessons learned:

- *Translanguaging through play:* Emergent bilingual children use all their linguistic resources to make meaning through play. With varying levels of competence in named languages, this often involves language learning, including developing metalinguistic awareness about the different language varieties of the same named language. A key aspect of *Exploraciones* is a complete freedom for children to use language

however they want, and that teachers should not be limiting their expression regardless of the language of the day.
- *Student agency and teacher as learner:* In *Exploraciones*, children are in charge of setting the scope and pace of their learning. They certainly negotiate and make compromises with their peers/friends but ultimately, they have more control over their own learning as compared to other parts of their school day. Meanwhile, teachers have the unique opportunity during this time to learn from and about their students in order to better support them as whole bilingual learners.
- *Joy, wonder, and curiosity:* Children find so much joy, purpose, and meaning during *Exploraciones*. They are provided with the space, materials, and time to play, to wonder and to pursue their curiosity through social interaction and experimentation. It is no surprise that this is their 'favorite part of the day'!

Implications for the field

Bilingual elementary school leaders and educators might consider how to prioritize and incorporate this kind of joyful and exploratory play into their school day – seeing it as a matter of a right to play rather than a privilege (Souto-Manning, 2017). Just as important as making the time for play is embracing translanguaging as a stance, which allows for students to use their entire linguistic repertoire without contending for the 'language of the day'. Finally, a question for all to consider: How can we incorporate open-ended and student-centered play into ALL of our bilingual classrooms?

References

Axelrod, Y. (2014) 'Todos vamos a jugar, even the teachers' – Everyone playing together. *Young Children* 69 (2), 24–31.
Duffy, P. (2010) Language socialization into academic discourse communities. *Annual Review of Applied Linguistics* 30, 169–192.
García, O. (2009) *Bilingual Education in the 21st Century: A Global Perspective.* Wiley-Blackwell.
Gort, M. and Pontier, R. (2012) Exploring bilingual pedagogies in dual language preschool classrooms. *Language and Education* 27 (3), 223–245.
Hassinger-Das, B., Hirsh-Pasek, K. and Golinkoff, R.M. (2017) The case of brain science and guided play: A developing story. *Young Children* 72 (2), 45–71.
Hoffmann, J. and Russ, S. (2012) Pretend play, creativity, and emotion regulation in children. *Psychology of Aesthetics, Creativity, and the Arts* 6 (2), 175–184.
Lave, J. and Wenger, E. (1998) *Communities of Practice: Learning, Meaning, and Identity.* Cambridge University Press.
López, D. (2019) Jugando y explorando together: Translanguaging and guided play in a bilingual kindergarten classroom in NYC. *Journal of Bilingual Education Research and Instruction* 21 (1), 1–16.

National Association for the Education of Young Children (2009) *Position Statement: Developmentally Appropriate Practice* (3rd edn). NAEYC.

Souto Manning, M. (2017) Is play a privilege or a right? And what's our responsibility? On the role of play for equity in early childhood education. *Early Child Development and Care* 187 (5–6), 785–787.

Vygotsky, L.S. (1986) *Thought and Language*. MIT Press.

13 Transition to Investigations and Inquiry in the Upper Grades

Hazel Garcia-Banguela, Michelle Madera Taveras and Carmen Morel

Dos Puentes Teachers

As explained in the previous chapter, Dos Puentes's *exploraciones* are a very social, joyful, exploratory, and interactive space for students in kindergarten and 1st grade. In the upper grades, we carry forward the same energy as we support students to apply their collaborative skills and curiosity with more academic rigor, through what is referred to as *investigations* in 2nd and 3rd grade, and *inquiry* in 4th and 5th grade. This chapter will describe two examples of units in each grade span: one on community investigations in 2nd grade and a country comparison in 5th grade.

Our investigations/inquiry units use a general inquiry structure, centered around an essential question to guide content learning, while also flexibly centering students' diverse strengths, interests, backgrounds and wonderings. Collaborative structures such as partnerships of varied abilities, multiple opportunities to share learning, revised understandings and asking questions all allow students a space for reflective conversations and provide support for deep learning and engagement. Let us dive deeper into two specific case studies that will showcase how inquiry comes to life in our classrooms.

Investigations

In 2nd grade and 3rd grade, students take part in *investigations* daily during their social studies time. Each unit begins with an essential question planned by the grade level teachers in order to integrate the school community and experiences into the curriculum. It also anchors the lessons as students engage with their prior knowledge and draw on new ideas for the unit.

A community investigations unit

In 2nd grade students work to answer: How and why do communities develop differently? This essential question allows students to take ownership and develop more specific inquiries. For example, a student last year wanted to learn why there were so many *bodegas* in our urban neighborhood and another student wondered why there were so many people in our community.

Next teachers activate students' prior knowledge through activities such as KWL (Know, Want to Know, and Learned) charts and a See, Think, Wonder activity in the language of the day. However, students are free to share in any language(s). For the See, Think, Wonder activity, students are presented with an image related to the inquiry unit to share their observations. These may be recorded on individual post-its or on a class chart. Then students jot down what they think is happening in the photograph and then list their wonderings about the topic or photograph. This activates students' curiosity and critical thinking.

For this unit and throughout investigations students are introduced to 'purple time' (as opposed to blue that represents English and red that represents *el español*). At Dos Puentes, purple time is a space in which translanguaging is most encouraged and students feel free to work in a ways that are inclusive of their linguistic repertoires and cultural backgrounds.

Small group work

Once students have built background knowledge and viewed videos about geographic communities, they begin to apply and extend their knowledge through hands-on activities in small groups. Student choice is essential to forming these groups as they will ultimately collaborate on a summative project of designing and building a model of one community type. Students choose which community they would like to learn more about and work in small groups to go deeper within the unit. Small group inquiry work allows students to learn social skills such as negotiating and problem solving while working towards a common goal. This is when the skills learned in kindergarten and 1st-grade *explorations* contribute to student success in *investigations*.

Students work on sorting pictures and clues of communities. They review a variety of images from different communities as well as clues such as, 'in this community there are very tall buildings called skyscrapers'. Students work together by discussing with their group which community each picture and clue belongs to and why. They also read books and listen to recorded facts about the different communities, draw a map of a community, or label photographs. Working on these kinds of activities allows students to continue to build background knowledge that prepares them for the final project.

The culminating community building project

The final project affords students opportunities to be architects, cartographers, masters of geometry and artists as they collaborate to construct an urban, suburban, or rural community using recyclable materials. While this seems simple, straightforward and fun, this project-based learning is also full of opportunities for social and academic learning. What you are likely to find, however, is a messy classroom where students are elbow-deep in paint and loudly discussing whether the *rascacielos* (skyscrapers) in their urban community are tall enough or whether the houses should be the same or different in their *comunidad suburbana* (suburban community).

Each group begins the process of building their community by coming up with a plan. They have complete creative freedom to design what the community will look like as long as it fits the description of the community type they have chosen. They first create a sketch of the community, although as 2nd graders, their ideas are not always in sync. As teachers circulate around different groups, you can overhear frequent reminders to 'listen respectfully to everyone's ideas' towards the more vocal students and *'¿quieres compartir tus ideas* (do you want to share your ideas)?' towards those who are quieter. All the while, students practice conflict resolution and respectful negotiation as some ideas make it to the final design, while others are met with rejections.

By this point, students have a group and a plan, and are ready to construct with plenty of recyclables, masking tape, paint and determination. It is not uncommon for students to show up to school in the morning with their arms full of boxes of breakfast cereal they have been collecting from home. It is rewarding to watch children smile with pride as they turn their two-dimensional drawings into shaky piles of boxes and eventually into three-dimensional models that showcase what they have learned about their communities. This type of project is also the perfect activity for Family Fridays (see Chapter 9), allowing families to get involved in constructing the communities while also getting to witness and support their child as they continue the challenge of working with others towards a common goal. The final step is to paint their models. This step may require reminders of *'tienen que escoger colores realistas* (you have to choose realistic colors)' so as not to end up with a purple barn with green polka dots in one of the rural communities. An afternoon spent in cooperative learning with fun materials and paint makes answering the essential question of 'how and why do communities develop differently?' just as engaging and appealing as an afternoon spent engaging in cooperative play.

Throughout the unit, students learn social studies content, but they also practice reading, writing, math (geometry) and social studies. They practice sharing and listening to ideas with respect, and handling frustrations appropriately. They are immersed in opportunities to practice new vocabulary in both languages, and possibly in additional languages. Project-based learning in 2nd grade allows students to investigate, create, and reflect as their minds start to consider what life is like outside of the urban community of Washington Heights as they prepare for the inquiry work of 3rd grade where they will investigate what life is like in other countries around the globe.

From Investigations to the Inquiry Structure

Our upper elementary, multidisciplinary inquiry units allow 4th- and 5th-grade students to have more independence and flexibility in how they engage in the research process. Each student begins with curious questions they have about a topic and uses those questions to plan, collect and interpret data, create an artifact and present their findings (see Image 13.1).

As educators we take care to teach perspective taking, source analysis, and analytical skills to prepare students to be more thoughtful and critical about the content they interact with during the inquiry process. The units also begin with essential questions to guide the creation and compilation of specifically curated resources for students to explore. These resources build upon the exploration they did in the younger grades using personalized book baskets curated by the teachers, dramatic play and artwork. Inquiry also involves analysis of complex texts and sophisticated digital tools with links to websites, articles, videos and images in Spanish and English.

Country Comparison Inquiry

Student voice and choice is also at the forefront of the inquiry model. The topics chosen for study, as well as the means for creating and sharing their learning, are a reflection of student interest and identity. Since the units are shaped by the students' specific interests and line of inquiry, they look different each year. To illustrate what a unit may look like, we walk you through last year's 5th-grade country comparison which was aligned with the NYC Social Studies Scope and Sequence curriculum. The unit offered an authentic opportunity for students to tap into their intellectual and cultural curiosity, learning deeply about themselves, their family members and/or the local community. It's a comparative case study of cultures of the Western Hemisphere that allows students to take on roles as historians, ethnographers and researchers to truly hone their investigative skills.

'¿*De dónde eres* (where are you from)?' is the standard national identity question most school-aged students explore. However, in this unit we wanted to push students beyond the surface learning of memorizing fun facts about a country to deeply synthesizing the country's government, economics, culture, geography and history, and their own roles within it.

Image 13.1 The Inquiry process that students in the upper grades (3rd–5th) follow throughout each unit as they learn about their topic. (Translation: The Inquiry Process: 1. Ask curious questions about your topic. 2. Make a plan. How will you explore your questions? 3. Collect data. Take lots of notes. 4. Interpret your data. What conclusions can you make? 5. Create an artifact that demonstrates your conclusions. 6. Share how we understand this topic together). Chart by Devon Hedrick-Shaw

Through their research, partnership work and small group conversations, students created authentic spaces to share their cultural experiences, process hardship and loss and mobilize as advocates.

Students were presented with the essential question for the unit: How do key forces and events shape nations? The case study unit was organized into learning and researching Mexico and the Dominican Republic (DR). Students were then presented with the choice of studying the Dominican Republic or Mexico, and voted online for the country they were most interested in researching as a class. Then they were split into small groups across the four teachers on the grade. These groups were created heterogeneously, by considering aspects such as student content knowledge and linguistic profiles.

While students chose the country they would each be researching, they in turn were also learning about the other country, through teacher

Image 13.2 Curated research pages created on Padlet for student research, covering the subtopics of government, economics, culture, geography and history. Photo by Kristen Minno-Bingham

modeling. For example, students who chose to research and complete their project on Mexico, learned about the DR (and vice-versa) through teacher-presented slides and facilitated conversations. Research and notetaking skills were modeled as teachers taught about each subtopic (i.e. government, economics, culture, geography and history). This way, students learned about both countries, one modeled by the teacher and the other through their own research and shared conversations. The purpose of this was to model and teach to the cultural components we wanted students to think about as they explored the factors and events that shaped each country.

The unit began with an invitation for students to brainstorm everything they knew about their selected country. This web included their ideas about Mexico's and the Dominican Republic's languages (Indigenous and national), food, traditional clothing, music and festive celebrations. From here students developed connections for the deeper work that was to come. *El orgullo de los estudiantes* (students' pride) was felt as they shared stories about their summer travels to, or migrations from, Mexico and DR, as well as anecdotes they overheard during *el tiempo de cafecito* (coffee time) when their grandparents, aunts and parents gathered to reminisce about *los viejos tiempos*. Students spoke about playing with other kids in the *campos* (countryside); tasting their *abuelita's* (grandmother's) exceptional cooking and exploring traditional spices not commonly found in the US supermarkets or on Amazon Prime; packing old clothes and toys to distribute to younger cousins, and immersing themselves in the local music played at family gatherings, holidays and birthday parties. These introductory sharings to the unit were also powerful because they allowed students to compare and contrast both cultures.

Una Guía para tu visita a México

Muchos viajan a México pero no saben nada de México

Aquí te voy a enseñar que tienes que saber antes que viajes a México y cuando regreses dime cuanto esto te ayudo.

Geography

Its territory is very varied approximately 85% of the country is made up of mountain ranges, plateaus and numerous valleys, it has a variety of climates and its ecosystems thanks to its Geography. Mexico is one of the most diverse countries in the world.

La Cultura

Hay mucho que hablar de la cultura en México hay Pintura, Literatura, Culturas Mestizas, Arqueología, Gastronomía, Música Popular, Tradiciones pero hay mucho más de que hablar más adelante podrás ver toda la información.

Image 13.3 Student's final project: brochure based on his study of Mexico, which included the subtopics of geography, government, history, economics and culture (traditional music, food and clothing). Photo by Michelle Madera Taveras

The initial lessons included a launch of the unit and teaching into each of the subtopics of geography, government, history, economics and culture. By lesson four, students began discussing cultural aspects of each country. Student research became real when they connected it to their family and life experience. Student sharings ranged from how sad it was for one student's family to add his *abuelo* (grandfather) and *tío* (uncle) to *el altar* (the altar) due to COVID, during his family's celebration of *día de los muertos* (Day of the Dead), to another student identifying with the social movement of *las hermanas Mirabal* (the Mirabal sisters), and stating she too would have been a *mariposa* (butterfly) if she lived during the age of Trujillo. Through these cultural discussions, students truly began making those deeper and personal connections.

The exploratory work being done in the classroom transcended to the home, when a student created a playlist of Mexican songs with his mother for the class to listen to while we worked on our projects. Songs and cultural dances permeated in the classroom including *'La bamba', 'Cielito lindo'*, a few of Maná's greatest hits and the class favorite: *'Payaso del rodeo'* with its fast-paced movements. Describing the popular music genres and artists in DR and contrasting those with the Mexican mariachi music suggested by the student and his family enabled rich exchanges between the children. Cultural pride could not have been more evident as when a student who was a recent arrival from the DR spoke about the different styles and colors of the homes based on socioeconomic class, as well as the food commonly eaten during *el almuerzo* (lunch), and why that is always the heavier meal of the day. These were clear moments when students proudly tapped into their funds of knowledge by expertly sharing about their cultural identity.

To conclude the unit, each student created a digital brochure, using all they had learned through their research and conversations at home and in the class. While students worked in partnerships or groups to collectively research and share sources, each student was required to produce their own brochure. Their answers to the essential question of the unit, 'how do key forces and events shape nations?' were reflected in their research and what they shared about the geography, government, history, economics and culture of Mexico and the Dominican Republic (see Images 13.2 and 13.3).

Conclusion

We hope these examples have demonstrated some of the ways that upper elementary students experience joyful hands-on learning through investigations and inquiry. While curiosity and collaboration remain the driving force in our school, the introduction of academic questioning and curiosity as well as the thoughtful and intentional development of inquiry skills that allow for linguistic and cultural connections in the upper grades specifically helps prepare students to be analytical, critical and collaborative lifelong researchers and learners.

Researcher Commentary

Gladys Y. Aponte

Arizona State University

This chapter demonstrates how effective and impactful inquiry-based learning in dual language bilingual settings can be. Not only are the *Investigaciones* and Inquiry units highlighted in this chapter strong examples of child-centered pedagogy, they also exemplify linguistically and culturally sustaining teaching practices.

Context

A growing body of literature calls for educators to engage students in authentic educational curricula that provide opportunities for genuine knowledge production (Darling-Hammond *et al.*, 2008; Hammond, 2015). Through inquiry-based learning, students take an active role in building their knowledge and benefit from increased self-efficacy, intrinsic motivation and task commitment (Saunders-Stewart *et al.*, 2012). This student-driven approach inspires a lifelong love of learning as students become enthusiastic to investigate answers to their own questions. We see this at Dos Puentes Elementary where students are positioned as bilingual experts (i.e. geographers, mathematicians, ethnographers, etc.) as they lead inquiries into their communities and other countries. Through asking questions, thinking critically and problem solving, students develop social, emotional and intellectual skills that are needed throughout their whole lives (Darling-Hammond *et al.*, 2008).

The Dos Puentes Investigations and Inquiry units are also excellent examples of culturally sustaining classroom practices. *Culturally sustaining pedagogy* (Paris & Alim, 2017) calls for schools to foster students' linguistic, literate and cultural pluralism as a means of sustaining, rather than diminishing, the cultural ways of being of communities of color. Entering the *Community Investigations* unit by inquiring about their own neighborhood in 2nd grade, and delving deep into Mexico and the Dominican Republic in 5th grade – two countries largely represented in the school population – allowed students to leverage their funds of knowledge (Moll *et al.*, 1992) as they made deep personal connections and constructed new understandings. Moreover, creating spaces for students' bilingual creativity to flourish through *purple translanguaging spaces* (Solorza *et al.*, 2019) allows students to express themselves authentically as they explore new ideas in English and Spanish. 'Purple time' at Dos Puentes invites students to use their full linguistic identities as opposed to maintaining separate language spaces, in which Spanish is represented in red and English in blue. Because students learn best when the curriculum validates and builds on their multimodal linguistic repertoires (García & Kleyn, 2016), it is also fundamental that students in this bilingual public school are given the opportunity to express themselves freely through art, multimedia and dramatic play.

Discussion

The teachers in this chapter remind us that learning in the upper-elementary grades can and should be engaging, child-centered and culturally sustaining. Too often, inquiry-based learning is only accessible to students from privileged socioeconomic backgrounds in private school settings. The *investigaciones* spaces demonstrate the value of inquiry-based instruction for students from marginalized identities, including emergent bilingual (im)migrant students of color and students with diverse learning styles and needs. The examples in this chapter illustrate the types of intricate and instructive conversations that emerge when the rich cultural and linguistic repertoire of each child is valued and leveraged in the classroom.

To support the availability and effectiveness of inquiry-based learning in bilingual public school settings such as Dos Puentes, we must address several factors within the field of education. First, education policy that elevates traditional teacher-centered instruction must be re-examined. Interrogating how standardized assessments and mandated standards avert inquiry-based practices is particularly important. In addition, it is imperative to acknowledge the preparation and ongoing support teachers need. Teaching through inquiry is a skilled practice that requires the use of subtle strategies to spark curiosity and inquiry. Teacher training programs must commit to preparing inquiry-based teachers, and school administrators must be supported in providing teachers with professional development and ample time to collaboratively plan across grade levels. This vertical alignment sets the stage for students to make connections and constructively build on skills they have acquired in previous years of inquiry, just as we see in this chapter.

Finally, inquiry should be used to address social injustices and cultivate the type of critical consciousness that scholars have been calling for in dual language bilingual education (Cervantes-Soon *et al.*, 2017). While the original purpose of this model of bilingual education was to equitably educate marginalized communities of color, it has come under scrutiny for its 'gentrification' (Valdez *et al.*, 2016) and for upholding hegemonic ideologies (Flores & García, 2017). It is instrumental to create opportunities for elementary-age students to examine and inquire about social inequities as they play out within and *beyond* dual language bilingual classrooms.

References

Cervantes-Soon, C.G., Dorner, L., Palmer, D., Heiman, D., Schwerdtfeger, R. and Choi, J. (2017) Combating inequalities in two-way language immersion programs: Toward critical consciousness in bilingual education spaces. *Review of Research in Education* 41 (1), 403–427.

Darling-Hammond, L., with Barron, B., Pearson, P.D., Schoenfeld, A.H., Stage, E.K., Zimmerman, T.D., Cervetti, G.N., Tilson, J.L. and Chen, M. (2008) *Powerful Learning: What We Know About Teaching for Understanding*. Jossey-Bass.

Flores, N. and García, O. (2017) A critical review of bilingual education in the United States: From basements and pride to boutiques and profit. *Annual Review of Applied Linguistics* 37, 14–29.

García, O. and Kleyn, T. (eds) (2016) *Translanguaging with Multilingual Students: Learning from Classroom Moments*. Routledge.

Hammond, Z.L. (2015) *Culturally Responsive Teaching and The Brain*. Corwin Press.

Moll, L.C., Amanti, C., Neff, D. and Gonzalez, N. (1992) Funds of knowledge for teaching: Using a qualitative approach to connect homes and classrooms. *Theory into Practice* 31 (2), 132–141.

Paris, D.H. and Alim, S. (eds) (2017) *Culturally Sustaining Pedagogies: Teaching and Learning for Justice in a Changing World*. Teachers College Press.

Saunders-Stewart, K., Gyles, P.D.T. and Shore, B.M. (2012) Student outcomes in inquiry instruction: A literature-derived inventory. *Journal of Advanced Academics* 23 (1), 5–31.

Solorza, C., Aponte, G.Y., Becker, T., Leverenz, T. and Frias, B. (2019) *Translanguaging in Dual Language Bilingual Education: A Blueprint for Planning Units of Study: A CUNY-NYSIEB Guide*. City University of New York–New York State Initiative on Emergent Bilinguals (CUNY-NYSIEB), The Graduate Center.

Valdez, V.E., Freire, J. and Delavan, G. (2016) The gentrification of dual language education. *The Urban Review* 48 (4), 601–627. https://doi.org/10.1007/s11256-016-0370-0

14 Learning Science through Hands-on Experiences and Animals

Karín DeJesus and Yesenia J. Moreno

Dos Puentes Science Teachers

Increasing student engagement, capitalizing on students' curiosities and building from students' linguistic strengths is at the heart of the bilingual science program at Dos Puentes Elementary. We are the bilingual and biliterate teachers who lead the science program. The lower grade science teacher (Karín) teaches 1st, 2nd and 3rd graders while the upper grade teacher (Yesenia) serves the 4th and 5th graders two to three times a week, respectively. We act as bilingual models and work collaboratively with the administration to make sure that the science curriculum has a strong Spanish component with supporting resources that include books, worksheets and videos. This helps ensure the science program is aligned with our larger bilingual program. In the early years of Dos Puentes we used the FOSS (Full Option Science System) curriculum but then transitioned to Amplify Science due to a city-wide mandate. Fortunately, Amplify Science met both the content and linguistic needs of our students. We also selected a supplemental curriculum called Mystery Science due to its Spanish component resources, real-life problems and hands-on activities.

The science program follows a 50/50 bilingual model. For example, lesson 1 is taught in Spanish, lesson 2 in English, and the pattern continues. Therefore, the goal is to build upon each lesson by making vocabulary and content connections from one lesson (and language) to the next with little to no repetition, unless we are extending the learning or reinforcing a concept. However, within this framework, we are also flexible when certain resources may be more abundant in one language or another, so adjustments are made but the language allocation goal for each unit remains 50/50. Each science classroom is flooded with cognates, content vocabulary that is supported by visuals and bilingual teaching slides that are strategically color-coded in red for Spanish and blue for English. This strategy provides students with the opportunity to see connections and differences between key vocabulary words and so when they take the end-of-unit assessments in their preferred language they are able to connect content and language.

These are some of the ways that linguistic barriers are reduced in the science classroom as a means to cultivate bilingualism, increase student engagement and *orgullo* (pride) in a bilingual classroom setting. Hands-on activities and inclusion of live animals are also important to increase student engagement and ignite students' curiosities.

Language Development through Hands-on Experiences and Field Trips

Common themes you will find in the science classroom are building on students' wonders, curiosities and backgrounds to solve hypothetical real-world problems in collaborative groups. For example, students tackle open-ended questions such as 'By 2030 we will have no more drinkable water, unless we _____.'. To complete these hypothetical questions students have the opportunity to consider their entire scientific repertoire that ranges from what they formally learn at school to their home and cultural experiences. Throughout the years we have noticed that the more personal connections students make with the science content, the more invested they are in solidifying their knowledge base. By combining their scientific and linguistic repertoires they are able to generate endless possible solutions.

The above problem was explored in great depth with 4th-graders during the unit on water. The unit was launched with students reflecting on how they use water in their daily lives in groups and ended with a two-night camping trip to the Croton Watersheds, which provides drinking water to New York City residents (see Image 14.1). After exploring how we use water today and in our current community contexts we jumped into the past to think about the future. Many of our students are Dominican, with strong ties to their country of origin. Some have personally had to get water from *cisternas* or *pozos* (wells). These cultural connections are validated in the science classroom as key prior knowledge to build upon and further enhance learning as students are allowed to express themselves in Spanish, English or bilingually when generating ideas.

As bilingual science teachers, we anticipate some of these cultural connections and make sure to have visuals or videos that highlight these exact ideas across languages. By validating these cultural connections, Spanish vocabulary is simultaneously increased for Spanish learners. For example, after a student mentions *pozos* as one way to get water, I (Yesenia) will show an image of it and ask the students for the English word for it or vice versa. Recognizing students as equivalent valuable sources of knowledge is also prevalent in the science classrooms and critical for giving bilingualism a purpose.

Figure 14.1 Students complete the sensory challenge in partnerships during the 4th grade camping trip. Photo by Yesenia Moreno

The water unit is a powerful example of building from small-scale classroom experiences to larger-scale life experiences. In order to address the hypothetical real-world problem, questions are strategically posed, so students can begin to visualize concepts. For instance, the question, 'where does our drinking water come from?' is explored in the unit. Students tackle this question across a six-week period, simply to realize that it is a lot more complex than just turning on our kitchen faucet. During this unit students learn about water conservation, as they reflect on how sources of water have changed over time and the engineering of aqueducts meets the needs of growing populations.

A hands-on activity that helps students truly connect with the concept of gravity and engineering of aqueducts is the 'Aqueduct Challenge'. Students work in groups to create aqueducts that use gravity to transport water from a

Figure 14.2 Forth grade students complete the Aqueduct Challenge to move water via gravity. Photo by Yesenia Moreno

reservoir in a watershed to a New York City apartment (see Image 14.2). As they work in heterogeneous groups, they are able to question the quality of materials, the risk of leaks, wasting water and contamination. In a bilingual classroom setting, heterogeneous grouping is critical for the development of language and content, as students negotiate the language(s) they are using to troubleshoot and problem-solve. The groups created for hands-on learning consider the language dominance and prior knowledge of students. For example, any given group will have at least one or two students who are more confident as bilinguals in English or Spanish, and one or two emergent bilinguals in either English or Spanish that are still strengthening one language or another. Activities that allow students to problem-solve using the language(s) of preference, as they are challenged to use an additional language or leverage their bilingualism as a valuable language resource for their group members.

As previously mentioned, the culminating experience in this unit is to visit the Cross-River Reservoir located in the Croton Watershed. Students spend three days and two nights engaging in various activities that range from forest ecology to watershed connections. This is an unforgettable experience that every graduating 5th-grader will remember, as it is the first time many of them are away from home, and out in nature. This experience is a stretch for both students and families, especially for families where culturally it is not common to sleep away in any other place besides home. Taking students beyond the classroom is vital to developing the child as a whole learner. We are in the business of creating lifelong learners by providing *experiencias inolvidables* (unforgettable experiences) by way of bridges that connect language and cultures as a means to understand science as they expand their horizons.

Living With and Learning From Animals

At Dos Puentes Elementary we strive to create unforgettable experiences for our students. Another way we make science come alive is by including live animals to make learning engaging, connected to students' backgrounds and allow them to develop a sense of care. The science classrooms have always had a variety of animals which include hissing cockroaches, mealworms, crayfish, betta fish, walking sticks and a tarantula. The animals we chose were based on our FOSS curriculum, where it is important for the students to physically engage with what they are studying. FOSS provided animals such as mealworms which would allow us to physically see the life cycle from egg to beetle.

During the pandemic the students were not able to experience daily interactions with live animals. Upon our return to in-person learning, we thought that animals were critical to our students' learning as well as their socioemotional wellbeing. After some thought and asking for financial assistance from the Dos Puentes Parent Association, we decided on bunnies. Children are less likely to be allergic to bunnies, and they are low-maintenance and cute!

Nube East Puentes and Sombra West Puentes have been the most welcomed members of our school community. Nube resides in the east-side science classroom which serves grades 1–3 while Sombra is in the west-side science classroom which serves grades 4–5. They are brothers who have become loved and cared for by the students and staff of the school.

Nube and Sombra are the perfect fit for Dos Puentes, and especially for the science classrooms. They are naturally curious bunnies. They like to explore and after feeling safe with their surroundings, they become more interested in what is around them. Nube, being more of a risk taker, started to wander off into the hallway, dance room and music rooms on the fifth floor. Nube travels back and forth between the classrooms and knows that if he wants to eat, he needs to make his way back to the science room. Bunny crossing signs were put up in the stairways and hallways so that staff and students can be reminded that Nube is on the loose. Sombra is our more reserved bunny who likes to spend his time solely in the science classroom. The freedom we give to our bunnies has made students more aware and conscious of their surroundings as they must do their part to keep the environment safe.

At Dos Puentes we believe that students learn more when engaged in center-based learning. Nube and Sombra have been integrated into our science center rotation. During that time the students observe, write and read about bunnies, while also having a chance to pet and care for them.

The bunnies have not only been an integral part of science content, but for the students' social emotional health as we recover from the pandemic. Hendrick *dice* (says) *'me gusta cuando puedo cuidar a Nube, me siento como si lo estoy protegiendo* (I like when I can take care of Nube, I feel like I'm protecting him)'. Giving the students the opportunity to care for pets allows them to gain experience in responsibility, trust, compassion, respect and patience. Zoe once shared 'Getting the bunny was a great idea. My classmates and I were disagreeing about what to do our project on. We couldn't decide, but then Nube hopped by and we saw how cute he was and it calmed us all down'. A bunny hopping allowed this group of students to refocus their attention on what was important. It was the pause they needed to be able to create a project that displayed all their voices. David shared 'We should definitely do a project on how bunnies can calm you down'. Having bunnies in the classroom has encouraged students to ask questions and propose new content for us to explore and research during our science classes. Many students shared how they had a bunny in the Dominican Republic or in their homes. Stories ranged from the challenges of caring for a bunny in an apartment versus *en el campo* (in the countryside) or how some people eat the meat of the rabbits. These types of stories resulted in students researching how bunnies adapt to their environments and the creation of food webs based on both their personal experiences caring for bunnies and the research they conducted.

In recent months we have experimented with the bunnies being able to visit different classrooms outside of science for the day. Staff members have noticed that if a child is feeling upset and needs a break, petting the bunny has helped them calm down. It has also motivated the students during their English language arts block. Students are actively listening to read-alouds because they see it is one of the bunny's favorite times of day to come out and sit with them. It has also encouraged the students' writing. They are driven to write more and expand on their ideas because they know their best efforts mean more quality time with the bunny.

Having the bunnies at Dos Puentes has also provided a new way to engage families (see Image 14.3). During our holiday breaks or long weekends, families are welcome to fill out an application to care for the bunnies during the time off. Families have shared how it has been a bonding

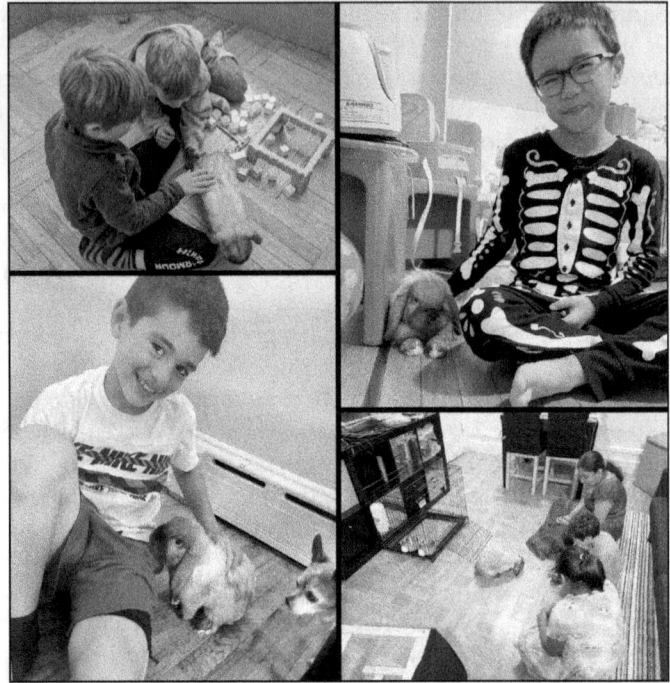

Figure 14.3 Sombra and Nube spending time with Dos Puentes families. Photos by Karín DeJesus

experience between them and their child. They are able to reflect upon what they have learned about bunnies with their parents, siblings and additional family members. I recall the first time a family picked up Sombra for the spring break and asked if they could feed him *lechuga* and *pepino* (lettuce and cucumber) because that is what they used to feed their bunnies in Mexico. It was at this moment that I (Karín) realized that this family probably knew more about caring for bunnies than I did! Additionally, some parents shared how the bunnies were a form of therapy for their children, and seeing their children care for the bunnies gives them a chance to see if they are ready for a pet of their own. The experience allows for added family and teacher communication before, during and after the bunny's stay.

Conclusion

The Dos Puentes science curriculum has promoted student engagement and enhanced student curiosity. We continue to learn on this journey of creating lifetime science enthusiasts. We want students to know that field trips, animals and hands-on activities are just the beginning, and that science is in the world all around them, connected to everything they see, hear, feel, think and do.

Researcher Commentary

Patricia Martínez-Álvarez

Teachers College, Columbia University

Researchers have been trying to understand how to make science more accessible for diverse learners for decades (Furman & Calabrese Barton, 2006). Including children's knowledge and languages in the science class is essential in this process. However, while we know that children bring experiences and understandings to the classroom that can be used for science learning, how to integrate these into instruction meaningfully is still not well understood (Calabrese Barton & Tan, 2009; Moje *et al.*, 2004). Karín DeJesus and Yesenia J. Moreno offer a practical illustration of the elements they center in their teaching and how to use them to create respectful science teaching and learning spaces.

Context

DeJesus and Moreno speak about how they build from students' linguistic and cultural strengths, cultivating their bilingualism and biculturalism. The value of incorporating the linguistic and experiential knowledge from the children's homes and communities supports development of new understanding that is privileged in the standard science curriculum (Brown & Ryoo, 2008; Stevenson, 2013). DeJesus and Moreno describe how they help children engage with science bilingually and, in their description, they speak of flexible language use. These teachers understand that bilingual children bring knowledge across their multiple languages, that language development is asymmetrical and always evolving, and that children need spaces to experiment with using their linguistic resources simultaneously (Flores, 2013). As they engage in science teaching, they help their young students feel like scientists and learn science while supporting them in meaning-making efforts inviting and integrating multiple languages, knowledge and modes (Poza, 2018).

Their understanding of the linguistic assets and needs of the children they teach translates into the inclusion of opportunities to use others as language resources and to challenge children to use an additional language with which they might not always feel comfortable. This is an important aspect in the strategies that DeJesus and Moreno describe as they encourage and embrace translanguaging while simultaneously providing opportunities to interact with language practices in Spanish and English, expanding children's linguistic repertoires and providing access to science concepts and language (Poza, 2018).

DeJesus and Moreno employ the idea of 'proximal representations' of science in their teaching (Hogan, 2000: 52). According to Hogan (2000), science can be made proximal to children's own experience and knowledge. These teachers, for instance, helped their young students understand complex concepts rooted in their everyday experiences with water. Children of immigrant backgrounds can carry understandings or can ask their families about where water comes from (beyond faucets) based on experiences in other countries. That connection then led to explorations about the transportation of the water they get in their own apartments in New York City, and to authentic connections to engineering practices. The importance of helping elementary students in engineering practices is emphasized in the most recent science education standards, the Next Generation Science Standards (NGSS Lead States, 2013). Similarly, DeJesus and Moreno incorporated animals in the students' science learning, connecting to their students' interests and natural curiosity. They embraced students' explorations through inquiries rooted in actual questions that surfaced when observing the two bunnies, Nube and Sombra. These 'real-life inquiries', including the experiences students had with the bunnies at home, can support the learning of science-standard content (Garza & Arreguín-Anderson, 2018: 5). For instance, understanding the flow of energy or articulating evidence-based arguments can be furthered as students document the animals obtaining food from energy sources like plants or exploring how the bunnies could calm the students down.

Through their science practices that are tied to students' cultural and linguistic backgrounds, DeJesus and Moreno create real life connections to complex science standards. They leverage children's proximal science representations and build pathways to connect them to more traditional or distal ideas that are typically emphasized in schools. In this way, they create possibilities for horizontal patterns of teaching and learning, where children can fluidly identify as experts and novices, as teachers and learners, within the same science unit (Martínez-Álvarez, 2017).

Discussion

Through the teaching of DeJesus and Moreno, we understand that science is, as they explained it, 'in the world all around them, connected to everything they see, hear, feel, think and do'. They exemplify how bilingual children can fall in love with science and act as scientists. Future research can continue to explore how children's everyday practices and the transnational knowledge their families carry can be integrated for sophisticated science learning in bilingual schools.

References

Brown, B.A. and Ryoo, K. (2008) Teaching science as a language: A 'content-first' approach to science teaching. *Journal of Research in Science Teaching* 45 (5), 529–553.

Calabrese Barton, A. and Tan, E. (2009) Funds of knowledge and discourses and hybrid space. *Journal of Research in Science Teaching* 46 (1), 50–73.

Flores, N. (2013) Silencing the subaltern: Nation-state/colonial governmentality and bilingual education in the United States. *Critical Inquiry in Language Studies* 10 (4), 263–287.

Furman, M. and Calabrese Barton, A. (2006) Capturing urban student voices in the creation of a science mini-documentary. *Journal of Research in Science Teaching* 43, 667–694. https://doi.org/10.1002/tea.20164

Garza, E. and Arreguín-Anderson, M.G. (2018) Translanguaging: Developing scientific inquiry in a dual language classroom. *Bilingual Research Journal* 41 (2), 101–116. https://doi.org/10.1080/15235882.2018.1451790

Hogan, K. (2000) Exploring a process view of students' knowledge about the nature of science. *Science Education* 84, 51–70.

Martínez-Álvarez, P. (2017) Multigenerational learning for expanding the educational involvement of bilinguals experiencing academic difficulties. *Curriculum Inquiry* 47 (3), 263–289. https://doi.org/10.1080/03626784.2017.1324734

Moje, E.B., Ciechanowski, K.M., Kramer, K., Ellis, L., Carrillo, R. and Collazo, T. (2004) Working toward third space in content area literacy: An examination of everyday funds of knowledge and discourse. *Reading Research Quarterly* 39, 38–70. https://doi.org/10.1598/rrq.39.1.4

NGSS Lead States (2013) *Next Generation Science Standards: For States, by States*. National Academies Press. https://www.nextgenscience.org/three-dimensions

Poza, L.E. (2018) The language of *ciencia*: Translanguaging and learning in a bilingual science classroom. *International Journal of Bilingual Education and Bilingualism* 21 (1), 1–19. https://doi.org/10.1080/13670050.2015.1125849

Stevenson, A.R. (2013) How fifth grade Latino/a bilingual students use their linguistic resources in the classroom and laboratory during science instruction. *Cultural Studies of Science Education* 8 (4), 973–989.

15 Field Trips as *Paseos* to Real World Connections

Peggy McQuaid and Kristen Minno-Bingham

Dos Puentes Teachers

In English, 'field trip' denotes a specific destination with a concrete curricular objective, much like a trip connotes a clear destination. In Spanish, field trips are called *paseos*, but *paseo* also translates to 'wandering' or a 'stroll'. In a sense, *paseo* has a slightly different connotation than a *trip*, in which there is space for unplanned stops and observations. We have found in our combined 14 years as educators at Dos Puentes across four grade levels that our field trips go beyond the standard curricular objectives to identify students' linguistic and social emotional strengths and address their needs. In this chapter we explore the ways educators can be open to multiple possibilities as they embark on a trip or *paseo* with their class, observing students closely for the sometimes unexpected and delightful ways they interact with the out-of-school environment.

Paseos for Student Agency

That teachers use field trips to support curricular goals will come as a surprise to no one reading this book. We draw on state standards to plan our units, but we utilize an inquiry-based approach by generating a broad essential question to start each unit and design a series of experiences – including field trips – for students to research and generate their own answers to the question. For example, for a science unit on the solar system, we brought students to the American Museum of Natural History to answer the question 'How do the components of our solar system move and interact with one another?'. As we made our way through the museum to the solar system exhibit, students' intellectual curiosity was sparked by other aspects of the museum. They gaze in awe at towering dinosaurs, request to see the big blue whale model, and eagerly share personal connections. On this particular trip, some of our Mexican American students found a case with Mixteco gold jewelry. They called their classmates over to the case excitedly, proud to show off a piece of their culture. We shortened our planned time at the solar system exhibit to show each other the things they found interesting and respond to their requests. We find that making space for student agency on these curriculum-driven trips enhances students' overall engagement in the inquiry process. In this way, the field trip does not always have to be a 'destination' with the sole intention of checking off a state-standard box. It can be a *paseo*, a wandering through the museum, thinking about our essential question, but also making time to stop at what piques our interest and connects with our diverse backgrounds.

Paseos as Linguistic Learning

Dos Puentes teachers also use field trips to address students' linguistic growth. In a bilingual program, linguistic objectives exist *alongside* but never *instead of* curricular goals. Linguistic objectives may be established for the entire class, or individual to the student – targeting English for a Spanish-dominant student or vice versa. In the classroom students can become disengaged from their language learning when it is not attached to an authentic purpose. However, field trips can provide authentic, tangible reasons to practice the emerging language forms in a low-stakes environment. One type of field trip that accomplishes this is a community walk, a walking tour of the area surrounding the school in which students have ample opportunity to share their observations orally with each other and interact with community members.

The Community Walk: A *Paseo* Right Around the Corner

Here we share a composite example of a 1st-grade community walk, mostly drawn from a project in collaboration with the CUNY-New York State Initiative on Emergent Bilinguals (CUNY-NYSIEB) (see Image 15.1). We started the year studying the essential question 'Who is part of a community?'. To answer the question, students went on a community walk and were given the task of orally naming what they saw to their walking partner. When we returned, students generated a word wall of this vocabulary accompanied by pictures (for example: *postal worker, sanitation worker, bus driver, peluquero/a, salón de belleza, esmalte de uñas, secadora, cliente*). In the integrated co-teaching (ICT) classroom, this was done in both languages. Later, the class studied the question 'How do community members use language?'. On a second community walk, students were tasked with asking community workers questions about how they use language. For example, Angelique asked the food cart operator 'What languages do you speak?'. We encouraged students to use the context clues around them to decide what language(s) to interview the worker. They were interested in asking them the languages they used at home and at work, and how they worked with customers with whom they did not have

Figure 15.1 Student maps of their family linguistic practices. Photo by Marguerite McQuaid

a common language. Back at school, students shared their observations orally and on post-its to answer the essential question. Tony noted that 'The food cart worker can count in English, French, and Arabic'. Liliana noted that the clinic worker only spoke English and wondered what patients do who speak languages other than English.

Leveraging the *Paseo* for Linguistic Learning

Our work with the community walk content did not stop after we returned to school. In younger grades, we have seen time and time again how having opportunities to practice new language orally leads to greater ease and engagement with writing, which is still developing for many 1st-graders. We took another look at a traditionally challenging unit on writing persuasive essays and adjusted the unit's task to write reviews of the community business and services we had observed on our walks. We wanted students to have more opportunities to practice their speaking skills with the domain-specific vocabulary turning to writing. We created dramatic play centers about the community businesses we had observed (see Image 15.2). In the hair salon center, Iolany was observed asking her *cliente* Amayah '*¿Qué color quieres que te lo pinte* (what color do you want me to dye it)?'. At the restaurant center, Yanira asked her customer David '*Do you want chile* (chili) *with your sopa*

Figure 15.2 Following a community walk, students re-enact the *salón de belleza*. Photo by Marguerite McQuaid

(soup)?'. These centers offered students the opportunity to practice and internalize the vocabulary and grammatical forms they had observed on their community walk in a low-stakes environment. Besides deciding what to say, students had a flexible space in which to decide what language(s) to re-enact based on what they observed (e.g. English at the food cart and Spanish in the hair salon).

Transferring Speaking Skills to Writing

Students then became immersed in writing primarily in one language although translanguaging was encouraged. The bilingual word wall created on our first walk became a resource for students to include at least some of their target language in their writing. For example, emerging Spanish learner Alex wrote: '*En mi opinión, the mejor restaurante es Malecon porque they prepare tu orden muy rápido y they llevar it to tu casa en una bicicleta* (In my opinion, the best restaurant is Malecon because ellos prepare your order very quickly and ellos take lo to your house by bicycle)'. Iolany wrote '*La mejor sala de belleza es Yvelisse Beauty Salon porque son muy amables y hablan inglés y español* (The best beauty salon is Yvelisse Beauty because they are very kind and they speak English and Spanish)'. The community walk provided a valuable front-loading opportunity for students to engage with the target language vocabulary orally and then utilize it in their content area writing. This was particularly successful for our students with speech and language Individualized Education Plan (IEP) classifications, which we attributed to them having a great deal of oral-language practice with the target vocabulary and grammatical forms before attempting to write. An additional benefit was for them to see multilingual people in action to deepen their understanding of themselves as multilingual students, and the benefits of learning languages to communicate with diverse community members.

Paseos to Foster Independence

Field trips offer opportunities for students to grow their independence. Our 4th and 5th grade students take trips outside of New York City to experience hands-on learning connected to the science curriculum. It can be challenging for families to entrust their children to school staff and allow them to participate in experiences that they might not have had themselves. The school staff works hard to build trust between us and families, starting from home visits before students enter kindergarten, so that most families eventually feel comfortable sending their students on our more adventurous multi-day trips. These trips provide many first-time experiences for students that go beyond the curriculum such as riding a chartered bus (and maybe even using its bathroom!) and traveling upstate to a New York State park. Students visit the Taconic Outdoor Education Center (TOEC) located an hour and a half north of NYC. TOEC is an educational sleep-away camp with a lodge, cabins, interactive exhibits, team-building nature course, and much more.

Students are often pleasantly surprised by their own resilience in the face of unfamiliar experiences. One responsibility for students at the TEOC was kitchen prep. Many children at first resisted the added responsibility of arriving early to a meal and serving their friends. But after their shift, students shared that they loved being in charge of the food, being of service to their friends and teachers, and making sure their classmates' needs were taken care of. Students even exhibited resilience in the face of the scary prospect of a night hike. Guided solely by the light of the moon, students were pushed to rely on other senses and face their fears as they walked through the darkness. Students gasped in horror and defiance as staff informed us that we would hike and play games outside without flashlights, and many were terrified at the prospect of being in the woods at night. By the time we were eating freshly baked cookies and drinking hot chocolate back at the lodge, many expressed that the night hike had been their favorite part of the trip. Longer-distance and multi-day trips allow students to develop independence from their families and discover their individual identities as they transition from the safety and security of elementary school to the greater world.

Paseos as Social Emotional Learning

As educators, we were well aware of the curricular and linguistic opportunities that abound on field trips, but we also wanted to know our students' perspectives. Our students shared how much they valued time spent with their friends outside of the classroom. Daniel said, '*Ir a un paseo significa disfrutar con la clase. Siento que estoy en Santo Domingo saliendo con mi familia* (Going on a field trip means having fun with the class. I feel like I'm in Santo Domingo going out with my family)'. Arianna shared, 'It's important to go on field trips because all the classes get to mix and meet new people'. We realized that field trips hold important possibilities for meeting students' social emotional needs. For this reason, all grades have gone on several field trips to our neighborhood park with our sole objective being for students to play together outside. Our schoolyard does not have any play equipment or space for a field, so trips to the park are special moments when the students can play together with fewer restrictions. Especially after the intense physical separation endured by students and staff during the pandemic, students have been eager to return to social activities. Furthermore, during play, affective filters are lowered and motivations are high to communicate and build bonds that transfer over into the classroom; thus the unstructured time offered on a park field trip offers excellent linguistic opportunities and connections.

Our students also shared how field trips create unexpected moments of wonder and joy. Second grader Ysabel shared that she likes field trips where she can 'learn about things that are mysterious to me like sea lions'. Luis, a 5th-grader, reflected that of all his trips at Dos Puentes, his first trip to the Bronx Zoo stands out in his memory. We have been visiting the Bronx Zoo multiple times a year ever since Dos Puentes opened. Just like community walks, the zoo is a *paseo* that provides a unique experience no matter how many times we visit. Through a partnership, teachers receive professional development and students are able to access paid experiences at the zoo for free. One of these was the Wild Asia Monorail, which accesses the far reaches of the zoo that are usually inaccessible on a short day trip. As we boarded the monorail, several students were nervous as they realized we would be riding on an elevated track above the animals. I (Kristen) observed their faces change from fear to fascination as we cruised above the enclosures. Ana expressed excitement at seeing the elephants, saying it was amazing to experience them in person. As we reluctantly exited the monorail, one of the girls called out, 'Ana is crying!'. I rushed over to her, asking if the monorail had been too high. Ana looked up at me, smiling, and said, 'No, I'm just so happy! Elephants are my favorite animal and I've never seen one in real life!'. I was stunned. Ana had been visiting the zoo for years but had never had the opportunity to see her favorite animal due to the 'paywall' it lived behind. More than teaching Ana the mammalian characteristics of elephants, this experience allowed her to feel the unexpected admiration of seeing a beloved animal (in New York City, no less) and created an unforgettable memory.

Conclusion

Field trips are essential experiences for students to work not only towards content and linguistic objectives in engaging, low-stakes environments, they also create spaces for socioemotional learning and exploring independence. When field trips are approached as *paseos*, they are no longer about the destination, but about the journey. Field trips begin with a teacher-directed curriculum, but they become a *paseo* by letting students be the guide. We end with the wise words of 2nd-grader Maya: '*Ir en un paseo significa aprender cosas para que cuando seamos grandes tengamos futuro*'. We wish you *un buen viaje* in your intellectual, socialemotional and linguistic travels with your students.

Researcher Commentary

Sara Vogel

The City University of New York

In this era of budget cuts, post-pandemic worry about health and safety, and policies holding schools accountable for narrow achievement metrics, the school field trip is on the chopping block (Watson *et al*., 2019). And yet, as Dos Puentes Elementary teachers, Peggy McQuaid and Kristen Minno-Bingham, point out in their chapter *Field Trips as Paseos to Real World Connections*, exploring beyond school walls might be key to holistic bilingual education. Peggy McQuaid and Kristen Minno-Bingham share joyful vignettes from walking trips in Washington Heights, monorail rides over the Bronx Zoo, and night hikes in upstate New York, demonstrating how going into and beyond the school's neighborhood can affirm students' linguistic identities, provide contexts for language practice and inquiry into curricular topics, and promote socioemotional development. Dos Puentes's field trips are worth protecting from external pressures.

Context

The authors' bilingual framing of *field trips/paseos* embodies dual possibilities: on the one hand, it orients us towards having a concrete destination, and on the other, to open-ended wandering and exploration. This metaphor is also useful for thinking about teaching and learning in general. When Dos Puentes educators guided students to engage with pre-planned essential questions about the solar system while also leaning into students' unique detours, they let their students help decide what is worth learning, and how learning happens without abdicating their own roles to frame, support and structure. I relate this dynamic to the research of Vossoughi *et al*. (2021), which traced long-standing debates in the literature around so-called 'child-centered' (discovery-based, inquiry-based) vs. 'adult-centered' (direct teaching, scripted activities) pedagogies. Rather than choose a side, those authors ask educators and researchers to consider the emergent ways educators 'tak[e] students' ideas, questions, and activity seriously' (2021: 3) and continually expand the goals of learning no matter the modality. McQuaid and Minno-Bingham report on moments when Dos Puentes teachers took their students' ideas and languaging seriously by structuring opportunities for students to notice, enact, re-enact and reflect upon interactions from 'the field'.

The philosophy embedded in the *field trip/paseo* duality also seems embedded in the teachers' approaches to language development. At Dos Puentes, there are explicit goals around learning particular kinds of language, but also, stock is placed in supporting students' translanguaging – or their deployment of their full language repertoires (García & Li, 2014). Translanguaging spaces are where 'children are given agency to act linguistically by being both creative and critical, and where teachers encourage those actions' (2014: 74). In translanguaging pedagogy (García *et al.*, 2017), educators intentionally leverage translanguaging to affirm students' bi/multilingual identities, dig into content and extend their language practices. Field trips like Dos Puentes's community walks are natural sites for translanguaging pedagogy, as children can experience a range of language models and purposes for using language. Back in the classroom, teachers can support learners to frame and make sense of what they saw and heard.

Opening the door to student wonderings and wanderings is not a simple task for teachers working in public school contexts – especially those serving language-minoritized emergent bi/multilingual students. Given school accountability and testing regimes, those students' English learning is often prioritized over all other values (Menken, 2013). Structuring field trips that advance linguistic and curricular goals while also providing open space to feel, relate, think, move, and translanguage freely requires teachers to simultaneously 'let go' and 'teach in' to what students bring. There is great intensity there. For teachers to mobilize this vulnerability productively, they must feel safe and supported (Lasky, 2005).

Discussion

At Dos Puentes, some of the most powerful field trip moments emerged from students' engagements with peers and the world around them. There is no need to 'over design' for a tearful discovery at the zoo, or the rush of self-empowerment that can come with achieving a difficult but meaningful task in an unfamiliar place. At the same time, given the environmental and economic precarity in places where racialized children and their families often live, place-based learning may also have the capacity to support collective, social and environmental justice goals. As teachers at Dos Puentes and elsewhere build on their students' language and cultural practices, they might also take cues from efforts like the Learning in Places collaboration, which supports place-based science investigations rooted in ethical decision-making for people, ecosystems, places and the planet. Tzou *et al.* (2021) summarizes one aspect of the collaboration's approach – asking 'Should We' questions:

> Asking questions such as: 'Should we move earthworms from the sidewalk? Should we put rat traps around our school? Should we remove invasive ivy from our school's wetlands? Should we attract more "wild" animals to our school's park?' requires investigations into ecosystem dynamics and relationships, community-based data collection, continuous deliberation using data and attention to histories of places, and learning that 'Should We' questions do not have straightforward answers. (Tzou *et al.*, 2021: 862)

Combined with McQuaid and Minno-Bingham's notion of the *paseo* as journey and destination, paying attention to the ethical dimensions and power dynamics inherent in 'taking children to the field' can further expand the possibilities of place-based education.

References

García, O. and Li, W. (2014) *Translanguaging: Language, Bilingualism and Education*. Palgrave Macmillan Pivot.

García, O., Ibarra Johnson, S. and Seltzer, K. (2017) *The Translanguaging Classroom: Leveraging Student Bilingualism for Learning*. Caslon Publishing.

Lasky, S. (2005) A sociocultural approach to understanding teacher identity, agency and professional vulnerability in a context of secondary school reform. *Teaching and Teacher Education* 21 (8), 899–916.

Menken, K. (2013) Restrictive language education policies and emergent bilingual youth: A perfect storm with imperfect outcomes. *Theory Into Practice* 52 (3), 160–168. https://doi.org/10.1080/00405841.2013.804307

Tzou, C., Bang, M. and Bricker, L. (2021) Commentary: Designing science instructional materials that contribute to more just, equitable, and culturally thriving learning and teaching in science education. *Journal of Science Teacher Education* 32 (7), 858–864. https://doi.org/10.1080/1046560X.2021.1964786

Vossoughi, S., Davis, N.R., Jackson, A., Echevarria, R., Muñoz, A. and Escudé, M. (2021) Beyond the binary of adult versus child centered learning: Pedagogies of joint activity in the context of making. *Cognition and Instruction*. https://doi.org/10.1080/07370008.2020.1860052

Watson, A., Greene, J., Holmes Erickson, H. and Beck, M.I. (2019) Altered attitudes and actions: Social-emotional effects of multiple arts field trips. *EDRE Working Paper* 2019-04. https://doi.org/10.2139/ssrn.3340163

Pillar 4 Introduction

Partnerships with Universities, Organizations *y* *La Comunidad*

Victoria Hunt

Founding Principal

The fourth pillar of Dos Puentes is Partnerships with Universities, Organizations *y La Comunidad*. It connects the school to the larger community, including local universities, professional development consultants and arts organizations. Each of these entities extend and expand our work for our students, but also support and push all adults within the school to continue their learning. Formal university partnerships support the whole school, and create spaces that build a learning community for adult educators. As the years have progressed, the school has used this pillar to expand connections to the larger community of Washington Heights, throughout New York City and nationally, as well as internationally. By building connections beyond our school, we expand opportunities for growth, collaboration and enrichment.

In this chapter we will consider our initial partnerships and their evolution over time. We will identify the elements that allowed for these partnerships to ignite conversations, unearth problems and find solutions within our school. Finding ways to work with adults outside of our staff requires leadership that can articulate the mission of the school, build trust, ensure the internal members feel that those from outside have their interests in mind and push everyone to be flexible in envisioning new opportunities. An added opportunity and advantage of staging the school as a full learning community (Fullan & Quinn, 2016) that includes adult learning is the modeling we do for children. As adults continue their own learning and growth, children see this and come to see education as a lifelong transformative process.

This pillar initially focused on local university partnerships with Teachers College, Columbia University and The City College of New York (CCNY) and expanded to include support for the arts, deepen our curriculum and work with the community surrounding our school and beyond. Expanding connections beyond our building supports our school just as it expands the growth of these organizations and institutions in mutually beneficial ways.

When developing the mission for Dos Puentes, the partnership pillar arose through experience in a prior school where Alcira Jaar, Rebeca Madrigal and I had been part of the Holmes Partnership for Professional Development Schools (PDS) (Polly, 2014). Through the PDS model, universities partnered with local schools to create symbiotic relationships and opened the doors for researchers to use the school as a lab site, in collaboration with school staff as active research partners to build upon their findings in their daily teaching practice. These partnerships brought the study of education to the school and allowed for greater opportunities for the work to be implemented in practice rather than remain isolated in the university (Frazier *et al.*, 2015). The concept of a learning community expands beyond students to include teachers, staff, families, and the wider community (Hunt, 2011).

Four of the five founding members of the school had a collective experience of being graduates of the Bilingual/Bicultural Program at Teachers College, Columbia University. We each studied under Professors María Torres-Guzmán and Ofelia García and developed deep ties to the program. This gave us a common understanding of bilingualism, biliteracy and multiculturalism and a learning stance that centered inquiry. Starting a new school poses many questions, but an inquiry approach provides a vantage point from which we can try out ideas, create space to reflect, adjust accordingly and then move forward. This partnership pillar allows us to facilitate the continued growth of Dos Puentes, grounded in an inquiry stance that extends learning for all members within the school from the youngest kindergartener to the most experienced staff member as well as to families. It also extends to all those with whom we partner, from universities to community organizations, to other schools and districts to international organizations. Learning is an ongoing process and an opportunity for everyone to grow.

Partnerships at Dos Puentes

As Dos Puentes has grown over the past decade, the partnership pillar has expanded to include a wide range of organizations. This chapter will include an overview of the development of university partnerships, professional development partnerships, partnerships with arts organizations and partnerships both within and outside of our community.

University partnerships

Our initial partnerships with both Teachers College (TC) and The City College of New York (CCNY) were integral to forming the mission of the school. As explained earlier, the collective experience of the majority of the founders with TC provided a lens to consider bilingualism and biliteracy, a constructivist approach to learning, and a commitment to social justice and equity. Dr Tatyana Kleyn, a founder who received her doctorate at Teachers College and now is a professor at CCNY, brought resources and deep connections from this program as well. When writing the mission for Dos Puentes, connecting with partners was important to ensure that learning went beyond our students and became an ongoing expectation for all members of the school community (see Image P4.1).

Our formal university partnerships include hosting student teachers, serving as a research site, and having some of our teachers teach undergraduate and master's courses at these institutions. Our university collaboration also supports us to extend learning for our teachers and staff to review curriculum from a bilingual perspective, to adapt monolingual English curriculum to include Spanish components, cultural connections and language learning goals.

From the moment we opened the doors of Dos Puentes we have hosted student teachers from numerous local institutions. These students come to understand our school, and have the experience of a dual language model with clear bilingual teaching structures. Student teacher candidates learn from their cooperating or host teachers as they also provide the teachers with additional support and new ideas for the classroom. As these candidates acclimate, they provide small group instruction, help with management, and are additional language models for Spanish and English. Because the host teacher is required to debrief with their student teacher, the cooperating teacher continues to have the opportunity to reflect on their own practices, as they are explaining their approaches and rationales to the student teachers (Martínez-Álvarez, 2021). Further, when the student teacher is observed by their university supervisor, the classroom teacher often participates in the debriefing sessions to provide the context of a lesson, set goals for the student teacher and support the growth of a future colleague in bilingual education. These student teachers are sometimes hired as full-time teachers as they have already been acclimated to the Dos Puentes community. Over the years we have hosted more than 100 student teachers and expanded our university partnerships to welcome student teachers from Bank Street College, Fordham University, Hunter College and Lehman College in bilingual education, (dis)ability education, childhood education and early childhood education.

Dos Puentes has also benefited from the recruitment of interns through a New York City Public School partnership called Bilingual

Image P4.1 A collaboration between Dos Puentes, The City College of New York (CCNY) and the NYC Public Schools Division of Multilingual Learners in the Dos Puentes library. From left to right: CCNY Dean of Education, Edwin Lamboy, CCNY Professor Tatyana Kleyn, Principal Victoria Hunt and NYC Public Schools Chief Mirza Sanchez-Medina. Photo by Alcira Jaar

Partner Services (BPS). These interns are bilingual childhood education undergraduate students at one of the City University of New York (CUNY) colleges. BPS interns work as paid paraprofessionals in the school during their degree program as they receive support from a BPS mentor and monthly professional development opportunities. Dos Puentes has three to five BPS interns each year. Because they are paid members of our staff, their role is extended to include supervising children at recess and lunch and participating in all staff activities. This professional relationship provides opportunities for candidates to work in their field to support their own education while reinforcing Dos Puentes with strong models of Spanish and individuals committed to becoming bilingual educators.

The university partnerships have led to research projects that have focused on early childhood approaches, the training of bilingual teachers, bilingual special education, immigration and translanguaging practices. In each of these projects university professors have met and organized projects with different groups of teachers, allowing them to build from existing research while also contributing to evolving findings (Espinet *et al.*, 2020; Espinet *et al.*, 2021; Espinet *et al.*, 2022; López & Makar, 2015; Martínez-Álvarez, 2021; Sánchez *et al.*, 2022; Souto-Manning *et al.*,

2015). These collective research projects have helped Dos Puentes to better envision play in our classrooms, allowed students to develop an understanding of their language practices built from children's sense of culture and family as they come to know others, supported the strengths and challenges related to immigration and belonging, and continued to value the benefits and gifts of multilingualism and the need to continue to push for social justice within our school and the larger society.

An additional benefit of our university partnerships is that our cooperating teachers are able to take classes at the hosting universities at no cost. While teachers cannot be paid to serve as cooperating teachers, the opportunity to take free university courses as a form of compensation for the time and effort they put into supporting their student teachers has provided for a number of teachers to earn additional certifications, take additional coursework, and even support their pursuit of doctoral studies. This opportunity brings outside learning to our building and provides additional environments for professional development to continue.

Lastly, several teachers serve as adjunct instructors at CCNY, Bank Street and Hunter College. As university faculty, the Dos Puentes teachers provide a practitioner's perspective to enhance the experience of future teachers. Occasionally, our teachers have their university students visit our school during the school day or after school to bring the university learning to an actual public elementary school site. We welcome these visits as we strive to help shape and prepare future educators and give them a strong vision for multilingualism and multiculturalism in their future careers. Additionally, our young students have visited different universities with their student teachers to have a better understanding of what a college and university look like and see the activities that take place there.

Educator professional development support and collaboration

While much of our professional development happens internally through teacher study groups and grade team collaboration, staff developers have been critical in deepening the curriculum and providing insight from practices throughout New York City. Dos Puentes works with staff developers who periodically come to the school to revise curriculum, model practices through lab sites, analyze student work and review pacing of curricular units for the following year. Existing curricula frequently need to be adjusted to support bilingual development but, as time has passed, many of our curricula also need to be tweaked to support the specific needs of our students across content areas. Some of these changes have evolved into a center-based approach that has organically developed. Currently our superintendent has Dos Puentes leading an initiative with staff developers called Facilitating Academic Centers for Inquiry-based Learning (FACIL) to support and partner with the elementary schools in our district (see Chapter 19 for more about FACIL).

We have worked with staff developers from the Teachers College Reading and Writing Project (TCRWP) nearly since the school's inception. While most of TCRWP school partners are not bilingual, over the years their program has changed to include resources in Spanish and attention to children's Spanish book titles. Through curriculum mapping and collaboration centering the needs of our program, students and teachers, the TCRWP staff developers have developed strategies to support students' literacy development in both English and Spanish. The staff developers provide insight from other schools to push us to negotiate with New York State Standards for students with a variety of strengths and needs.

Dos Puentes has always participated in the Math Collective, a group of NYC math educators who came together to consider child-centered practices and an inquiry approach toward the Engage New York State Math curriculum (also called Eureka Math). Through this partnership teachers have had the opportunity to participate in lesson studies, a practice that provides the construction, implementation and review of a particular lesson with input from a variety of participants (Cerbin & Kopp, 2006). These lesson studies include participants from different New York City public schools, thereby extending collaborative opportunities. Kate Abell, the staff developer at Dos Puentes and a member of the Math Collective, has brought lesson study practices and collective conversations that lay the groundwork for developing Math schoolwide.

We have added support from Anne Palmer, an educational consultant with two decades of special education experience to work with our special education teachers in our bilingual integrated co-teaching (ICT) classrooms, of which there is one per grade. Anne works collaboratively with these teachers to observe particular student behavior, consider students' individual academic needs and come up with structures or interventions for students who are having trouble functioning in the classroom. Anne's presence has created a deeper understanding of ways to consider children's strengths, and how to apply Universal Design for Learning (UDL) strategies to support students as they work to meet their Individual Education Plans (IEP) goals. This partnership expands special education resources and strategies and deepens the confidence and abilities of the teachers.

While Dos Puentes has always been committed to social justice, following the killing of George Floyd by police officers in Minneapolis, Minnesota in 2020, it became apparent that some of the internal work that was required within our community needed to be addressed by an outside person. While many members of our staff have equity training and strong skills in inclusivity and social justice practices, the nature of the topic was very personal for many. Staff input indicated that we needed a person from the outside to support conversations on race and provide tools to have these conversations with students. We began working with Arlène Casimir, initially from TCRWP, who went on to found the Awakened Teacher, strategies and supports for trauma-informed practices

Image P4.2 Dance teacher Clara Bello works with her students to prepare them for an upcoming visiting art residency. Photo by Gerardo Romo

in the classroom. Arlène has engaged teachers and staff in many personal conversations around race and trauma before working on ways to do this with children. This is an example of where the topic was too personal to begin developing internally and a person outside the organization felt more neutral and unbiased.

Over the past decade we have worked with a variety of staff developer partners. Given we are a dual language school that teaches its curriculum in Spanish and English, we have made it non-negotiable that any organization we work with understands this, and preserves this as we work with them. We value their work as they bring a particular expertise to our school that pushes our learning and provides support that is specially adapted to our bilingual context.

The arts

Located in New York City, one of the arts meccas of the world, it is imperative that our students have an awareness of, and access to, the richness of these resources. Too often communities lacking in financial resources are excluded from institutions and enrichment opportunities in their own backyard that people from around the world come to experience. To this end, identifying partnerships and experiences that are geared toward school children is critical in showing students that these resources are theirs as well. We have partnered with the New Victory Theater so children can visit Broadway and see live theater productions such as *Water on Mars* and *Elephant Piggie*. Children frequently visit museums and other cultural institutions and events. Our dance and music teachers organize family trips to Lincoln Center and Teatro Sea. Students have listened to live music at Carnegie Hall as well as venues in our neighborhood including the United Palace Theater. Extending the arts experience beyond the walls of our building ensures students are able to see art transcend their particular classes and see it as an integral extension of making meaning and a way to share ideas, feeling and expression.

Dos Puentes is fortunate to have full-time dance and music teachers who work with all our students weekly. However, we partner with community organizations to build upon the resources of our city to ensure our arts program is expanded exponentially.

Through partnerships and collaboration, dance has extended to Alvin Alley, Capoeira and a Hulah residency. Our music teacher works with a nonprofit called About the Swing that brings live jazz to our students and provides the opportunity for children to create their own jazz pieces. Our music teacher also brings children to Carnegie Hall to use their recorder skills to perform with other students with the full orchestra. Both the dance and music teacher leverage the funds of knowledge from our families and local community to bring in resident artists to share their crafts (González *et al.*, 2006). This has included a principal dancer from the American Ballet theater, a viola player and a McCarthy-winning jazz performer.

Image P4.3 Graduating 5th-graders 'cross the bridge' after learning about the New York Watershed that supplies water to New York City through a collaboration with the East of Hudson Forestry Program of the Watershed Agricultural Council. Photo by Victoria Hunt

Though we do not have a visual arts teacher on staff, our long-term partnership with Studio in a School ensures all children have the opportunity to draw, make prints, experience clay and sculpture in kindergarten through 5th grade. Through this partnership, Miguel Tio has been our resident teaching artist for more than nine years. The advantage of working through this collaboration is that we have all benefited from the Studio in a School organization by way of staff development and parent art workshops, as well as having our students' work displayed in art shows throughout the city. For the past five years, selected student work was shown at Christie's Auction House. Because Mr Miguel also sells his art and does his own shows, he models for our students the life of a working artist. Dos Puentes has helped the Studio in the School organization consider linguistic diversity as we have asked Mr Miguel, a Dominican immigrant from our community, to teach primarily in Spanish to support our dual language balance. Mr Miguel serves as a strong model of an artist and Spanish speaker to all our students.

Community enrichment organizations

While this fourth pillar began as collaboration with university partnerships, it has evolved to include a variety of relationships that deepen the learning throughout our school. Some examples of additional partnerships include the Leave It Better Foundation and the Taconic Outdoor Center, as well as the Watershed Agricultural Council (see Image P4.3). These partnerships help students develop a stronger understanding of their surrounding natural environment. Leave It Better, for example, is a gardening program that has provided the neighborhood with a flower and vegetable garden. Both children and families from the school work together to understand the composting, soil, planting and harvesting cycle as the process provides a garden that many community residents have noted brings them joy and beauty. There is a bench for the community right outside the garden where neighborhood residents can gather.

Dos Puentes is part of the International Academy of Spain (ISA), sponsored by the Spanish Consulate to promote and support Spanish around the world. Through ISA, the Queen of Spain, Letizia, made Dos Puentes her first stop on her first visit to the United States as reigning queen in fall 2014. This visit was hugely significant as our school neighborhood is far from the center of Manhattan. Washington Heights is predominantly filled with mostly Latinx residents from various parts of the Spanish-speaking world. This visit demonstrated an acknowledgement to many who have felt neglected and dismissed by European colonization of Latin America. During the visit, we had representatives from the US Congress, the Chancellor of the NYC Public Schools, our council member, our superintendent, the Manhattan Borough President and other elected officials, all bringing prestige and attention to our local community.

Partnerships also address other needs in the community. We have a partnership with the Corner Project, which is a needle exchange program for individuals addicted to intravenous drugs. As needle use is a large concern in our community, the Corner Project provides clean needles to those who need them. An unintended consequence is there are many used syringes with needles discarded around the school. This partnership has allowed us to ensure the syringes and needles are picked up safely and quickly so children are not exposed. While the solutions to addiction are multifaceted, this partnership is helping the most vulnerable members of our community and collaborating to ensure the safety of our children.

Additional community collaborations are set up to support our families. Dos Puentes has worked with local immigration organizations to ensure undocumented members of our community are clear on their rights, and we can ensure their protection in our buildings. During the COVID pandemic, we partnered with Columbia Presbyterian Hospital for information on vaccines, testing, and children's vaccines. Our partnership pillar facilitates collaboration with organizations and resources that enrich the community to work beyond our school. We become an integral partnering member of our local community in Washington Heights, NYC and beyond.

Overview of the Chapters

The following chapters provide specific examples of how partnerships have functioned in our community from the voices of teachers, families and researchers who have partnered with Dos Puentes. In Chapter 16, 'University Collaborations: Service and Research Projects', Wendy Barrales, Patricia Martínez-Álvarez, Maite T. Sánchez, Belinda Arana and I explain three projects conducted to support collaborative studies of translanguaging, bilingual special education students and immigration work conducted at the school. In Chapter 17, 'University Partners: Bilingual Student Teaching', Rebeca Madrigal, Silvia Peña and Jennifer Aquino Peña demonstrate the impact of being part of a strong bilingual community of future bilingual teachers. In Chapter 18, 'Expanding the Arts through Partnership and Passion', Clara Bello and Lorene Philips demonstrate how the arts come alive in the school when we collaborate with outside organizations and families. In Chapter 19, 'Center-Based Learning: Partnerships with Staff Developers and Schools', Queila Cordero and Joyce Veras present how our curriculum has been adapted with staff developers to be more meaningful through a center-based approach called FACIL, and how this work is shared with other schools in our district. Finally in Chapter 20, 'Connections with the Community and Beyond', Katherine Higuera-McCoy and Maggie Orzechowski explain how the school benefits and contributes to the resources within the neighborhood as an integral member of the Washington Heights community.

Dos Puentes exponentially grows when we collaborate and partner with others. We ensure our students see all that they are learning as part of a multilingual, multicultural community of future possibilities.

References

Cerbin, W. and Kopp, B. (2006) Lesson study as a model for building pedagogical knowledge and improving teaching. *International Journal of Teaching and Learning in Higher Education* 18 (3), 89–101.

Espinet, I., Aponte, G., Sánchez, M.T., Figueroa, D. and Busone-Rodríguez, A. (2020) Interrogating language ideologies in the primary grades: A community language inquiry unit. In CUNY-NYSIEB (ed.) *Translanguaging and Transformative Teaching for Emergent Bilingual Students* (pp. 219–238). Routledge.

Espinet, I., Sánchez, M.T. and Aponte, G.Y. (2021) Creating translanguaging inquiry spaces in bilingual classrooms. In E.J. Erling, J. Clegg, C.M. Rubagumya and C. Reilly (eds) *Multilingual Learning and Language Supportive Pedagogies in Sub-Saharan Africa* (pp. 175–192). Routledge.

Espinet, I., Sanchez, M.T., Poms, S. and Menendez, E. (2022) Exploring families' language practices through a social studies inquiry in kindergarten. *Young Children* 77 (4), 18–24.

Frazier, L., Brown-Hobbs, S., Civetti, L. and Gordon, P. (2015) PDS leadership team as community of practice: Implications for local school system and higher education partnerships. *School-University Partnerships* 8 (2), 41–52.

Fullan M. and Quinn, J. (2016) *Coherence: The Right Driver in Action for Schools, Districts and Systems*. Corwin Press.

González, N., Moll, L.C. and Amanti, C. (eds) (2006) *Funds of Knowledge: Theorizing Practices in Households, Communities, and Classrooms*. Routledge.

Hunt, V. (2011) Learning from success stories: Leadership structures that support dual language programs over time in New York City. *International Journal of Bilingual Education and Bilingualism* 14 (2), 187–206.

López, D. and Makar, M. (2015) The Common Core and the bilingual classroom: Findings from a New York City case study. *The Professional Journal of the New York Academy of Public Education* (4), 7–13.

Martínez-Álvarez, P. (2021) *Teacher Education for Inclusive Bilingual Contexts: Collective Reflection to Support Emergent Bilinguals with and without Disabilities*. Routledge.

Polly, D. (ed.) (2014) *Professional Development Schools and Transformative Partnerships*. IGI Global.

Sánchez, M.T., Espinet, I. and Hunt, V. (2022) Student inquiry into the language practices de sus comunidades: Rompiendo fronteras in a dual language bilingual school. In M.T. Sánchez and O. García (eds) *Transformative Translanguaging Espacios: Latinx Students and their Teachers Rompiendo Fronteras sin Miedo* (pp. 134–155). Multilingual Matters. https://doi.org/10.21832/9781788926065-010

Souto-Manning, M., Madrigal, R., Malik, K. and Martell, J. (2015) Bridging languages, cultures, and worlds through culturally relevant leadership. In S. Long, M. Souto-Manning and V.M. Vasquez (eds) *Courageous Leadership in Early Childhood Education: Taking a Stand for Social Justice* (pp. 45–56). Teachers College Press.

16 University Collaborations: Service and Research Projects

Wendy Barrales, Patricia Martínez-Álvarez, Maite T. Sánchez, Belinda Arana and Victoria Hunt

University Partners and Founding Principal

The fourth pillar of Dos Puentes's guiding philosophy is to work in partnerships with local universities to support ongoing learning and research for students and teachers. In this chapter, we consider some of the mutually beneficial relationships that Dos Puentes has with local higher education institutions. These projects include service projects and research conducted at our school, all of which benefit not only the universities and the researchers who work within our bilingual school setting, but also our students, staff and families. Research is an integral part of deepening understanding, connecting ideas and pushing learning forward both for bilingual and multicultural children and their adult educators.

Our university partnerships connect practice to theory, as they also help build theory from practice. The three collaborations described below support the continued growth of educators and students within Dos Puentes as they also deepen understanding of issues within the larger educational context.

The City University of New York – New York State Initiative on Emergent Bilinguals (CUNY-NYSIEB)

CUNY-NYSIEB was a professional development and research project that worked with schools in New York from 2012 to 2019 to better understand the dynamic language practices of emergent bilingual students, practices that are described by the term 'translanguaging'. The project's goals were to support schools to use translanguaging in instruction as well as integrate these practices into the schoolwide ecology (www.cuny-nysieb.org). In the past, dual language bilingual programs have had a policy of strict language separation. Such policies not only assume that bilingual people keep their languages separate, but they also perpetuate hierarchies of languages by implicitly and explicitly devaluing the dynamic language practices of bilingual students and families. CUNY-NYSIEB and Dos Puentes Elementary partnered to understand the ways in which translanguaging pedagogy could be enacted in dual language bilingual programs.

Translanguaging from the Classroom to the School to the Field

La colaboración (the collaboration) Dos Puentes-CUNY-NYSIEB started with the 4th-grade teachers (Jennifer Aquino Peña, Tim Becker, Jason Horowitz and Yesenia Moreno) who were curious and interested in incorporating translanguaging into their biliteracy lessons. After professional development sessions with the CUNY-NYSIEB team, the teachers designed book club units in which students considered social issues and explored translanguaging in books they were reading, as well as in their own writing and in classroom discussions. The teachers carefully chose mentor texts with authentic examples of translanguaging (for example, *My Name is Jorge* by Jane Medina, *Drita My Homegirl* by Jenny Lombard, *The Keeping Quilt* by Patricia Polanco and *My Name is Maria Isabel* by Alma Flor Ada). The teachers found that those units created translanguaging spaces centered on the multilingualism of the school community. Jason and Tim reflected that throughout this unit, their students 'demonstrated more confidence and autonomy when making linguistic choices in their speech and writing, while teachers became more aware of the intention of such choices' (CUNY-NYSIEB, 2021: 129). These teachers noted that months after the unit ended, 'translanguaging became a regular term in our classroom vernacular, as more students began to actively incorporate diverse language practices into their written work' (Horowitz & Becker, 2021: 130).

The following year, *la colaboración* became school-wide through the school's social studies curriculum, which created an instructional space for inquiry-based projects in which students' interests are at the core. Students work in collaborative groups to address social studies issues and create projects or presentations based on what they discover. At the time we began our collaboration, this inquiry time typically took place in the 'language of the day' (English or Spanish), but for our *colaboración*, teachers in each grade level and the CUNY-NYSIEB team designed a unit around the language practices of bilingual communities connected to their grade-level social studies curriculum. Students, teachers and families were encouraged to use all their linguistic resources, rather than just the language of the day. In Chapters 2, 12 and 15 teachers describe some of the projects they created for this unit. For example, in 1st grade, students played in classroom-based centers for the *salón de belleza* [beauty salon] and the *barbería* [barbershop] and they recreated the dynamic language practices they heard and observed in their communities. The teachers, Annabelle Maroney and Rebeca Madrigal, reflected on their experiences in the inquiry unit and noted that 'translanguaging is a powerful way to communicate'. They noted that their students' play showed 'sophisticated understanding of language use and gender roles ... and power ... and situatedness of culture' (Maroney & Madrigal, 2021: 235).

While teachers were designing and implementing the inquiry units, the researchers and teachers also met during and after school to discuss their learnings, questions and wonderings about incorporating translanguaging in dual language bilingual programs. They have collaboratively presented these learnings to other educators in the school as well as to families, in professional conferences and through publications (i.e. CUNY-NYSIEB, 2021; Espinet *et al.*, 2021; Sánchez *et al.*, 2022). Instructional videos and teachers' reflections of their work are also shared on the CUNY-NYSIEB webpage (www.cuny-nysieb.org). This *colaboración* has not only supported Dos Puentes's thoughtful engagement with translanguaging, but has also helped the CUNY-NYSIEB team and other researchers and educators – including future teachers – to better understand the ways in which translanguaging pedagogy can be planned and implemented in support of racialized bilingual students in dual language bilingual classrooms.

The Varied Ways of Knowing Afterschool Program (VWK)

The Varied Ways of Knowing (VWK) afterschool program developed in 2016 from the previously existing professional collaboration Dos Puentes had with the program in Bilingual/Bicultural Education at Teachers College, Columbia University. The larger project, partially funded by the New York State Education Department, aimed to promote cross-institutional collaboration, to serve bilingual children with and without disability and to prepare teacher candidates for inclusive bilingual programs.

During the four-year span of the VWK program, Patricia Martínez-Álvarez, a professor from the program at Teachers College, and two years later, Belinda Arana, a student teacher supervisor and instructor from the program, accompanied graduate students or candidates from Teachers College who came to Dos Puentes for two hours after the school day every week to teach and learn with bilingual students. The candidates designed and implemented literacy and science lessons guided by multimodal and digital texts, while exploring and building upon the knowledge and expertise of the children.

Supporting learning agency with bilingual children with and without disability

In VWK, we were all learners in the afterschool project space experiencing our histories, forms of learning and speaking and *conocimiento* (wisdom) that crossed contexts. *Conocimiento* surfaced during the VWK program in both of its Spanish senses, meaning both wisdom (*conocimiento*) and a verb (*conocer*) meaning the process of getting to know others.

Because of VWK's emphasis in understanding the children – particularly those carrying disability labels – as possessing extensive *conocimiento*, teacher candidates could more easily change the direction of activities to adapt to the learners, and this promoted children's agentive efforts or their pathways toward making decisions about their learning while in the VWK (Martínez-Álvarez, 2020). We knew that children with a disability might manifest agency in ways that are not always easily recognized, or are deemed inappropriate in school contexts (Gabel, 2002). The VWK aimed to understand these less traditional actions and promote agency.

One of the candidates recognized the value of the program through an example with a girl with a disability, sharing how, '*a veces también ha funcionado que dándole responsabilidad junto con esa agency* (sometimes it has also worked giving her responsibility together with that agency)'. That is, the afterschool program sought to foster children's agency by encouraging them to take even more volitional actions, such as in this case, taking the role of a teacher during the program. Children,

Image 16.1 A child's writing on a small whiteboard to agentively express intended actions *Translation*: We are ready. Can we please be the first ones? Please. Photo by Patricia Martínez-Álvarez

particularly those with a disability, enacted agency through many creative ways such as writing on small whiteboards to express their intended actions, both through writing and drawings. This is shown in Image 16.1, where a student was asking for her group to be first in acting out their mini play demonstrating how to use a *remedio casero* (home remedy).

The VWK afterschool program created a hybrid space involving *conocimiento* from the home, the community and the school. In our efforts to support the academic work children were doing during the school day, teacher candidates embraced the full humanity of the children as different forms of learning (traditional modes like reading and writing on paper with multimodal literacies like drawings or 3-D representations) and different knowledges from the home, community and school collided, transforming one another. While creating a 'superhero cape' through which children were invited to express their talents, for example, one girl drew and wrote to express herself multimodally. Her talents included being '*muy amorosa*' (very loving) and being an expert at painting. In another example, working on a representation of layers of identities using the faces of a cubed box made of cardboard, a boy included Sonic video games, and *historia de la vida* (life history) as some of the pivotal elements shaping who he was (see Image 16.2).

As one teacher candidate wrote, we took on the role of 'providers of material and activities that are inviting and interesting to [the children], to then engage [the children] in conversation that will provide us with valuable information about their funds of knowledge. We can *evoke* instead of *prompt*'. This allowed children to demonstrate in multimodal ways many types of knowledge and skills.

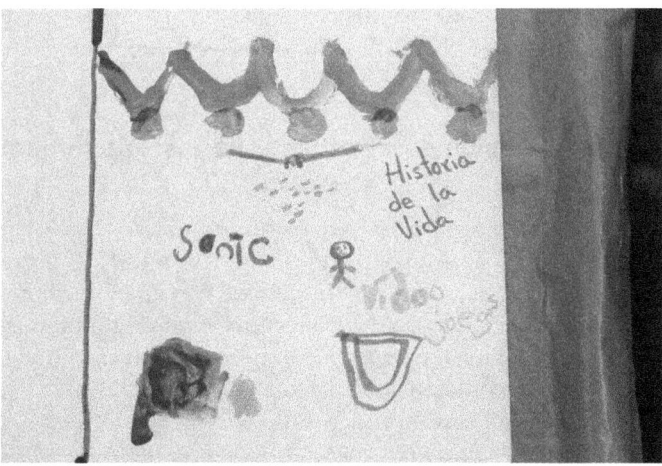

Image 16.2 A child's representation of layers of identities. *Translation*: Sonic. Super Sonic. Life History. Video games. Photo by Patricia Martínez-Álvarez

The cross-institutional partnership between Dos Puentes and the Program in Bilingual/Bicultural Education at Teachers College created a flexible space for exploring teaching and learning in inclusive bilingual programs. The project allowed children with and without disabilities, along with teacher candidates, to shine and learn from each other in humanizing ways.

The City University of New York – Initiative on Immigration and Education (CUNY-IIE)

The vision of CUNY-IIE states:

> Communities and schools are shaped and strengthened by the migration of people and ideas across the globe. CUNY-IIE creates opportunities for educational stakeholders to learn from immigrant students, families, and educators directly impacted by restrictive immigration policies and educational inequality. We aim to develop multimodal and multilingual resources that center the strengths of mixed-status immigrant communities that include undocumented, refugee, and asylum-seeking members. At CUNY-IIE, educators, researchers, families and local leaders work together to learn about, from, and with immigrant communities, act in ways that center our shared humanity regardless of legal status, and advocate for equitable policies and opportunities. (www.cuny-iie.org/about)

The work is firmly grounded in a set of principles (see www.cuny-iie.org/grounding-principles), all of which reflect several overlapping themes that inform our thinking and our work.

CUNY-IIE works at the intersection of immigration and education. One of the goals of the project was to connect historical realities such as the twin pillars of slavery and the dispossession of Native peoples, to the current realities of minoritized immigrant communities. A team of educators from Dos Puentes took on this challenge over two years, and sought to make connections to their students in order to improve their immigrant-focused practices.

¡Toma la palabra! Building an Authentic Partnership through *Testimonio*

The educators who participated in this initiative, Dr Alcira Jaar, Rebeca Madrigal, Sacha Mercier, Teresita Prieto and Kassandra Reyes Vizcaino, have strong personal ties to immigration and are committed to thinking of creative ways to support our immigrant-origin families. And, throughout the two years of partnership between Dos Puentes and CUNY-IIE, we met via videoconference, in person and with the entire CUNY-IIE partner school teams of educators across New York State. *Hemos compartido lágrimas y pensamientos profundos pero también hemos vivido momentos de alegría bailando cumbias y disfrutando pupusas. Es precisamente por estos momentos que tenemos una conexión y un calor familiar*

(We have shared tears and deep thoughts but we've also lived joyful moments dancing *cumbias* and enjoying *pupusas*. It's precisely for these moments that we have a connection and a family-like warmth). Our work is not solely about supporting our immigrant families; it is also based in the belief that self-care is community care. By creating a non-traditional professional development space where we center our experiences, our *testimonios* (testimonies), and ourselves, we are able to better show up for our *comunidad*. At a time when schooling, and in particular, schooling for immigrant families, has felt the extreme effects of the pandemic, we are able to hold space for venting, laughter and joy. We made sure to take moments to center *nuestras experiencias y nuestra comunidad* (our experiences and our community). Here is one of those stories:

It is 7 am on a Wednesday morning in April 2021. The Zoom room starts to populate with squares of bright smiling faces, albeit some of us with smiling eyes because we are in a shared space with masks on. We, the CUNY-IIE School Leadership Team (SLT), a group of teachers, counselors and administrators, are gathering to explore a virtual community walk of our neighborhood, Washington Heights. Weaving digital tools like Padlet, group-generated images and the In The Heights movie trailer, we are immersed in an experience of *el vecindario* (the neighborhood) that surrounds 185 Wadsworth Avenue (the school's address) (see Image 16.3). A member in our group, who is a lifetime resident of the Heights,

Image 16.3 *lo que sembramos* is a collage composed of artifacts that are often overlooked yet incredibly significant in creating spaces for care and professional development. Created by Wendy Barrales

guides us through a historical grounding of the original people who stewarded this land, the Lenni Lenape; we also learn about the Trujillo dictatorship which led to a large migration of Dominicans to New York City, and the looming worries of gentrification in the neighborhood. Despite our early start time, *nos reunimos con gusto* (we come together with pleasure) because our time together serves two purposes: professional development and a communal space of camaraderie.

Through the CUNY-IIE partnership we focused on *how* to support immigrant-origin families instead of solely identifying *what* they need. We also relied on the use of *testimonios*, a method with roots in Latin America that has been defined by Lindsey Pérez Huber (2009: 644) as 'a first person testimony representative of a collective, a verbal journey of a witness who speaks to reveal the racial, classed, gendered, and nativist injustices they have suffered as a means of healing, empowerment, and advocacy for a more humane present and future'. Y *aunque varios testimonios nos llenaron de lágrimas, el poder de nuestras experiencias y palabras nos ayudó a seguir pa'lante con nuestras comunidades inmigrantes* (and even though several testimonies filled our eyes with tears, the power of our experiences and words helps us to move onwards with our immigrant communities). Both the university partners and colleagues from Dos Puentes *compartieron las historias de cómo llegaron ellas y sus familias a los Estados Unidos* (shared their stories of how they and their families arrived to the United States). Many of their words still haunt us, like an educator in our community who shared, '... *con solo escuchar la palabra de inmigración me pongo nerviosa. Es un trauma que, aunque ya no estoy de ilegal, es difícil recordar* (... just hearing the word immigration makes me nervous. It's a trauma that, even though I'm no longer illegal, remembering is difficult)'. By co-creating a space where we could share intimate experiences, we were able to create a strong partnership where members of our team felt comfortable enough to be vulnerable. Before collecting data, implementing our curriculum and assessing growth, we centered our stories. It is through *testimonio* that we felt relational warmth to build a partnership that was rooted in care and trust.

Conclusion

Each university partnership is unique and has addressed different aspects of the school community, but all the projects were enhanced because scholars and student teachers were able to work within a bilingual space alongside bilingual educators who serve multilingual children. Dos Puentes benefited from the opportunity to learn from the research process, while also contributing to it. Research and service projects conducted at Dos Puentes take on a symbiotic relationship with our university partners that supports us to be a true learning organization for both children and adults.

References

CUNY-NYSIEB (ed.) (2021) *Translanguaging and Transformative Teaching for Emergent Bilingual Students. Lessons From the CUNY-NYSIEB Project*. Routledge.

Espinet, I., Sánchez, M.T. and Aponte, G.Y. (2021) Creating translanguaging inquiry spaces in bilingual classrooms. In E.J. Erling, J. Clegg, C.M. Rubagumya and C. Reilly (eds) *Multilingual Learning and Language Supportive Pedagogies in Sub-Saharan Africa* (pp. 175–192). Routledge.

Gabel, S. (2002) Some conceptual problems with critical pedagogy. *Curriculum Inquiry* 32 (2), 177–201.

Horowitz, J. and Becker, T. (2021) Teacher/Researcher Box #8.1. In CUNY-NYSIEB (ed.) *Translanguaging and Transformative Teaching for Emergent Bilingual Students. Lessons From the CUNY-NYSIEB Project* (pp. 127–130). Routledge.

Maroney, A. and Madrigal, R. (2021). Teacher/Researcher Box #14.1. In CUNY-NYSIEB (ed.) *Translanguaging and Transformative Teaching for Emergent Bilingual Students. Lessons From the CUNY-NYSIEB Project* (pp. 233–237). Routledge.

Martínez-Álvarez, P. (2020) Dis/ability as mediator: Opportunity encounters in hybrid learning spaces for emergent bilinguals with dis/abilities. *Teachers College Record* 122 (5), 1–44.

Pérez Huber, L. (2009) Disrupting apartheid of knowledge: Testimonio as methodology in Latina/o critical race research in education. *International Journal of Qualitative Studies in Education* 22 (6), 639–654.

Sánchez, M.T., Espinet. I. and Hunt, V. (2022) Student inquiry into the language practices de sus comunidades: Rompiendo fronteras in a dual language bilingual school. In M. T. Sánchez and O. García (eds) *Transformative Translanguaging Espacios: Latinx Students and their Teachers Rompiendo Fronteras sin Miedo* (pp. 134–155). Multilingual Matters.

Researcher Commentary

Nancy Stern

The City College of New York, CUNY

It is a consistent theme in the field of education that there is a need for partnerships between universities and schools. The Dos Puentes school-university partnerships described so lovingly in this chapter include three vibrant and innovative projects: the City University of New York-New York State Initiative on Emergent Bilinguals (CUNY-NYSIEB), Varied Ways of Knowing (VWK) and the CUNY-Initiative on Immigration and Education (CUNY-IIE). These collaborations provide many benefits to both Dos Puentes and to the participating universities.

These creative partnerships do just what Darling-Hammond (2006: 302) urges universities to do: 'venture out further and further from the university and engage ever more closely with schools in a mutual transformation agenda'. The mutual transformation here is key: these projects create bridges between universities and Dos Puentes that symbiotically impact students and teachers in the school, as well as university students and faculty. Through these collaborations, students have meaningful and effective school-based experiences, teachers and other school-based personnel continue to develop their own understandings and improve their practice, and universities gain insights into the needs and expectations of schools. University faculty can ground their understandings and ideas – both old and new – in the up-to-date realities of schools, and their own teaching can be informed by those experiences.

School-university partnerships are essential to research in the field of education, as new knowledge about teaching, learning and schools cannot proceed effectively without directly including students, teachers, families and communities. The collaborations also provide opportunities for university faculty – and for the teachers they work with – to pass on their new learnings through presentations and publication, leading to professional achievement for the presenters. As noted in the chapter, 'Research is an integral part of deepening understanding, connecting ideas and pushing learning forward both for bilingual and multicultural children and their adult educators' (p. 199).

Context

In the Principal's welcome on the Dos Puentes website, Dr Hunt writes, 'All of our staff is committed to collaborating in support of our children's various needs and strengths, our curriculum, and the overall growth of the school'. These school-university partnerships directly lead to supporting each of these areas. Through CUNY-NYSIEB, Dos Puentes further embraces the bilingualism of its students, recognizing, appreciating and building upon their creative and dynamic language practices. The VWK project leads teachers to recognize and build upon the talents, abilities and strengths of all students, including those labeled as having a disability. Through CUNY-IIE, educators who themselves may have had difficult immigration experiences, work to ensure that the school supports their own students and families.

These school-university partnerships are not unintegrated add-ons or disconnected extras; instead, the consistent, ongoing relationships that Dos Puentes has with local universities demonstrate that these collaborations are in fact, 'part of the institutional fabric of the school' (Watkins, 1990: A15; Yoon *et al.*, 2007) that demonstrate that 'high-quality professional development programs' (2007: 36) have a direct impact on student achievement. In fact, the characteristics of school-university partnerships identified as 'high quality' are exemplified in the Dos Puentes collaborations:

- focused on the learning and teaching of specific curriculum content;
- organized around real problems of practice;
- connected to teachers' work with children and linked to analysis of teaching and student learning;
- intensive, sustained, and continuous over time;
- supported by coaching, modeling, observation, and feedback; and
- connected to teachers' collaborative work in professional learning communities (Darling-Hammond 2012: 36).

Another important benefit of these collaborations is that they counter the deficit narratives that too often accompany discussions of multilingual learners. Instead, everyone involved – student teachers, teachers, school personnel, and university faculty and students can see just how much children can do and learn when they are challenged at high levels.

Discussion

The lessons learned from these three collaborations extend well beyond the participants. The CUNY-NYSIEB experience at Dos Puentes has illustrated what the effective use of translanguaging pedagogy looks like and can accomplish within a dual language bilingual program. There have been many conference presentations and publications that have resulted from CUNY-NYSIEB, some of which are mentioned in this chapter.

The VWK experience at Dos Puentes has led to improved instruction for emergent bilingual students who have been assigned the label of having disabilities, by helping teachers approach their students with respect, appreciation and recognition of their strengths. The findings of this program have recently been published in the book *Teaching Emergent Bilingual Students With Dis/Abilities* (Martínez-Álvarez, 2023), so that teacher educators, and teachers everywhere, can learn from these collaborations.

Furthermore, the work of CUNY-IIE is being shared across New York State and the rest of the country so that the hostile rhetoric and restrictive policies that create fear in immigrant-origin students, families and communities is neither replicated nor reinforced within schools.

The ongoing collaborations achieve what Jones *et al.* (2016: 109) call a 'delicate balance' between 'overly theoretical approaches' and 'the lack of theory-informed practice', a tension that is captured in the aphorism 'In theory, theory and practice are the same. In practice, they are not'. But the success of strong, solid school-university partnerships such as those at Dos Puentes show the opposite: good theory is informed by practice, and good practice is informed by theory.

References

Darling-Hammond, L. (2006) Constructing 21st century teacher education. *Journal of Teacher Education* 57 (3).

Darling-Hammond, L. (2012) *Creating a Comprehensive System for Evaluating and Supporting Effective Teaching*. Stanford Center for Opportunity Policy in Education.

Jones, M., Hobbs, L., Kenny, J., Campbell, C., Chittleborough, G., Gilbert, A. and Redman, C. (2016) Successful university-school partnerships: An interpretive framework to inform partnership practice. *Teaching and Teacher Education* 60, 108–120. https://doi.org/10.1016/j.tate.2016.08.006.

Martínez-Álvarez, P. (2023) *Teaching Emergent Bilingual Students with Dis/Abilities: Humanizing Pedagogies to Engage Learners and Eliminate Labels*. Teachers College Press.

Watkins, B. (1990) Education school reform group set to endorse plan that would alter teacher training, public schools. *Chronicle of Higher Education* 36 (21), A15–A20.

Yoon, K.S., Duncan, T., Lee, S.W.-Y., Scarloss, B. and Shapley, K. (2007) *Reviewing the Evidence on how Teacher Professional Development Affects Student Achievement* (Issues & Answers Report, REL 2007–No. 033). Regional Educational Laboratory Program, Institute of Education Sciences. http://ies.ed.gov/ncee/edlabs

17 University Partners: Bilingual Student Teaching

Rebeca Madrigal, Silvia Peña and Jennifer Aquino Peña

Dos Puentes Cooperating Teacher and (Former) Student Teachers

Dos Puentes is a learning place where aspiring bilingual teachers grow and practicing bilingual teachers evolve. We work to expand our knowledge as a school community by welcoming experts in the field who push us out of our comfort zone to try new initiatives and practices. Thus, we consider Dos Puentes to be a great place to host student teachers because our educators are well-qualified and passionate about teaching. We keep our classroom doors open as an invitation for researchers, evaluators, visitors, families and the focus of this chapter – student teachers – to observe and learn with us about quality practices for a bilingual school. Since our first year, we have been working with the Bilingual/Bicultural Program and the Early Childhood Program at Teachers College, Columbia University (TC), the Bilingual Program at Bank Street College and the Bilingual & TESOL Programs at The City College of New York (CCNY).

In this chapter we explain the variety of placements that exist for student teachers. We share the journeys of two former student teachers (Silvia and Jennifer) at Dos Puentes who are currently classroom teachers and also cooperating teachers, and a veteran cooperating teacher (Rebeca). Collectively we show how we are a lab for future teachers and continued learning for current teachers.

Bilingual Student Teaching Structures

At Dos Puentes, student teachers are placed in one of two different models for language development within the dual language structure. They are either placed in a side-by-side model or an Integrated Co-Teaching (ICT) model. In the side-by-side model there are two teachers and the children switch classrooms; one is the English classroom and the other is the Spanish classroom. Alternatively, student teachers can be placed in the

Table 17.1 Bilingual Program Student Teaching Model Advantages and Challenges

Model: Side-by-Side (Version A)
The student teacher (ST) is assigned only to one group of students or one class and follows them in the Spanish component and English component – essentially working with two cooperating teachers.

Advantages	Challenges
• ST exposed to two different teaching styles • ST witnesses how students are learning and behaving depending on the language • ST observes students' language development in Spanish and English and how one language can support the other in overall academic development • ST gets close to the students because this is the only person that follows them in both settings	• ST will not get to know the other class because they stay with one group • Difficult for ST to initially navigate the routines and schedules between the Spanish and English classes • Scheduling observations with supervisor can get complicated • Takes longer to establish a close relationship with the cooperating teachers because they split their time between two people • Takes longer for ST to take over the routines and teach the whole class

Model: Side-by-Side (Version B)
The student teacher (ST) is assigned only to one component (i.e. Spanish or English) and works with two groups of students.

Advantages	Challenges
• ST gets to know both classes (about 50 students in all/25 students per class) • ST is seen as a strong language model by students • ST develops a close relationship with the cooperating teacher because they spend more time collaborating • ST gets to know the routines and structures faster so they can take over as soon as they feel comfortable • If the placement is the ST's new/additional language, it is an opportunity for the ST to practice this language in all linguistic areas (reading, writing, listening and speaking)	• ST will not be able to observe students' use and development as bilingual speakers. • ST will get to know the other component teacher only during grade level meetings, planning meetings or by requesting a meeting to ask questions about specific students • ST will only develop a deep understanding of the curriculum in only one language

Integrated Co-Teaching Model (ICT)
The student teacher (ST) is in a classroom with a general and special education bilingual educator who alternate between teaching in two languages.

Advantages	Challenges
• ST exposed to two different teaching styles simultaneously • ST has the opportunity to get to know and work closely with both cooperating teachers • ST has the chance to establish a good rapport with students by staying with the class every day • ST observes the students' holistic language development and academic growth • ST learns how to differentiate lessons for students with disabilities in both languages • ST is exposed to the Individualized Education Student Program Plan (IEP) process and how teachers help students reach IEP goals • ST uses both languages for instruction	• ST needs more time to establish their own space to teach and/or take over in the classroom because there are more adults to negotiate with (two classroom teachers as well as paraprofessionals) • ST will not be able to develop deeply in one language because the languages alternate

ICT classroom with a general education bilingual teacher and a special education bilingual teacher where the students remain in the same classroom but alternate languages from day to day. Considering the differences across models helps to prepare student teachers for their own future bilingual classroom and the different models that exist. Table 17.1 outlines the advantages and challenges of each model.

Each of the three structures provides a strong understanding of what it's like to work in a dual language environment and the planning involved. Most importantly, student teachers see that a variety of structures exist depending on context, while each supports students to progress both academically and linguistically. Below, two student teachers who are now teachers and a veteran cooperating teacher each share their formative experiences with and reflections on bilingual student teaching.

Student Teacher *Testimonios*

Student teaching roles: A day in the life

A student teacher at Dos Puentes has many roles and responsibilities inside the classroom. Some of these include working with and learning from their cooperating teacher, writing lesson plans, supporting students and implementing their learning into the lessons they teach. As a student teacher, I (Silvia) had to balance college courses and university supervisor observations while working closely with my cooperating teachers and students. Additionally, as a student teaching in the side-by-side model, I had to adapt to the schedule of two different teachers. At times it was difficult. This is an example of how a typical observation played out for me:

'The time has come for another observation', my college supervisor announced and then shared some dates to visit. We met to decide which subject and language(s) I would be observed in to ensure I was teaching across the content areas and bilingually. After this meeting, I talked to my cooperating teacher (CT) to go over the calendar and curriculum to see if there were any scheduling conflicts (such as field trips or school events). Once the date had been cleared, I confirmed with my college supervisor. I then continued to plan and review the curriculum calendar to determine the topic for the lesson of the day. I also had to consider which class I would have that day. In a side-by-side model, it is important to understand that there are two classes, and students have different abilities, needs and personalities. What works for one class might not work for another. With logistics aside, 'Great! I have the date of the observation, the lesson, the class. Now I must write my lesson plan and share it with my CT ahead of time to make sure it makes sense' (see Image 17.1).

One of the best pieces of advice I received from my cooperating teacher was 'Remember, less is more'. Instead of making a highly complicated plan, a straightforward lesson with explicit instructions and enough time

Image 17.1 Cooperating teacher Rebeca Madrigal co-plans with her former student teacher Silvia Peña. Photo by Andrea Montero De Howitt

for the mini-lesson, independent practice and a share-out at the end was the way to go. On the day of the observation, that was all I thought about. I shared my lesson plan with my supervisor, the copies were made, my charts were finished and I even scripted my lesson plan in my sleep! The hardest part was the wait leading to the observation. Once I started the lesson, I just focused on my students and the lesson I put so much thought into. Even if things did not go exactly as planned, it was all part of the learning experience. To be able to make adjustments *during* the lesson based on the students and the environment is part of what teaching is about. After the lesson, we had time to debrief with my supervisor and, just like that, I would be planning for another visit soon.

My student teaching experience provided the time to learn, get feedback, feel vulnerable, coordinate multiple factors that affected planning and reflect. I learned that practice makes progress, so I continue to strive for improvement rather than perfection.

Image 17.2 Jennifer Aquino Peña, a former Dos Puentes student teacher, who is now a full-time teacher reviewing the daily schedule with her students. Photo by Gerardo Romo

Feedback as growth: A reflection on learning

A vital role of a student teacher is applying the learned training and knowledge from the college classroom to a real-world elementary classroom. During my semester as a bilingual student teacher at Dos Puentes, I (Jennifer) aimed to do just that. I was able to lead, teach and collaborate alongside my cooperating teachers in my journey to become an effective and reflective educator. Having the ability to go from theory to practice can be an overwhelming experience. However, at Dos Puentes, this experience provided me, and many others, a valuable opportunity to gain the needed teaching skills and put the theories I was learning into practice.

Throughout my experience as a student teacher, I was able to overcome many of my fears. The thought of being a young and inexperienced teacher was a frightening one to me. I learned the importance of being vulnerable and open to feedback. As an intern for a program called Bilingual Pupil Services (BPS) as well as a student teacher, I was consistently observed by BPS mentors and college supervisors. At times, it was nerve wracking; not everyone shared the same ideologies or teaching philosophy. I was constantly second-guessing my teaching pedagogy. It felt like I was in the middle of three different teaching philosophies from three different entities: my cooperating teachers, my BPS mentor and my college supervisor. Nonetheless, they always provided me with meaningful feedback from varied perspectives. For example, learning language progressions in a textbook is very different compared to when it is considered in the classroom. My professors taught me what the language progressions meant. My supervisor held me accountable to consider them. My cooperating teacher made me apply them to the multiple children at different levels in my class. Hearing all these different perspectives gave me the opportunity to grow, not only as an educator but as a human. I am more vulnerable and open to feedback because of it. This experience allowed me to receive and apply feedback in a constructive way by considering context. I am a strong believer that there is always room for improvement – and that is what Dos Puentes is all about, constant growth, application and innovation. During this period of time, I applied the teaching strategies I learned to the whole class and small group instruction. Additionally, I learned the importance of building a welcoming classroom environment where students' bilingual and multicultural voices are valued and cared for. Today, I work hard to replicate this type of experience in my role of a cooperating teacher to a bilingual student teacher (see Image 17.2).

Veteran Cooperating Teacher *Testimonio*

I (Rebeca) like to be called 'Maestra Madrigal or Sra. Madrigal'. In my 25 years as a bilingual teacher I had the honor of serving as a cooperating teacher many, many times to more than 60 different student teachers. It is a huge undertaking to share your space, class and thinking with someone else. However, I understand that as a bilingual teacher, it is my commitment to the field to continue supporting and modeling for new bilingual educators. I like to discuss current topics in bilingual education with my student teachers. Dr Victoria Hunt, founding Principal of Dos Puentes, was my cooperating teacher 25 years ago, and I was her student teacher. I still can vividly remember that experience and collaboration with Dr Hunt, so I try to reciprocate this experience with my own student teachers.

Beyond the Classroom: Student Teachers as Leaders

Student teachers at Dos Puentes have the opportunity to be part of the school culture outside of the classroom and participate in afterschool and summer programs. Student teachers have a unique opportunity to lead afterschool classes. Some programs where student teachers have taken the lead or have been active participants include Just Dance, math intervention, homework help, music, Zankel Fellows (a program led by student teachers from TC) and the summer school program. Lizbeth Cespedes, a student teacher and former BPS intern, became an assistant afterschool coordinator to lead the afterschool program in Just Dance. Lizbeth, who is now teaching at Dos Puentes shared: 'In 2014, Ms Consuelo (Parent Coordinator) and Dr Hunt had a meeting with all the BPS interns to introduce the idea of an afterschool program for the school'. We brainstormed different activities that we thought the students would be interested in. Another BPS intern and I pitched Zumba dance because we had seen students express their love for dance and music in the classroom. We thought, 'Well we like to dance too! Let's create a space where we can share our dance moves and love for music together'. We could never have imagined at that time that we would be recurring performers at United Palace, in Washington Heights, for the following three years! The performances were witnessed by the superintendent, administrators, political officials, families and other schools, which showcased the powerful performances of our Dos Puentes students that were led by our student teachers.

Conclusion

Bilingual student teachers need to be placed in different communities, schools and classroom settings to expand their knowledge about the population that they are going to be serving. At Dos Puentes, we try to provide different experiences to our student teachers by placing them in a side-by-side model or an ICT model. We work to integrate our student teachers in all our events and meetings, so they can visualize themselves as teachers and become familiar with all their future responsibilities. Student teachers see how language is negotiated and supported in different ways, and how to coordinate various supports to reflect on their practice. Student teachers are also the motors for cooperating teachers because they bring fresh ideas and energy. Thus, Dos Puentes trains future bilingual teachers by strengthening our collaboration with our university partners and continuing to reflect and grow.

Researcher Commentary

Sharon Chang

Teachers College, Columbia University

University partnerships provide ample mentored learning opportunities for student teachers, cooperating teachers, and field supervisors to reflect and grow together (Soslau & Alexander, 2021). Such mentored learning is a continuation of teacher development (Edwards & Collison, 1996), which is experienced both subjectively and objectively by teachers and teacher-educators. This development is subjectively interpreted based on an individual's cultural-historical context and is objectively negotiated when working toward future-oriented solutions.

Supporting bilingual teacher development, however, adds layers to the mentored learning practices due to the complexities of language, culture and identity (Chang *et al.*, 2020a). At Dos Puentes, school-based teacher-educators, like Maestra Madrigal, co-constructed teacher learning with bilingual student teachers (and current teachers), including Silvia Peña and Jennifer Aquino Peña. Drawing upon the testimonials and narratives of the bilingual teacher authors, I will contextualize the bilingual student teaching experience within broader teacher education literature and specifically through the lens of Cultural-Historical Activity Theory, referred to as CHAT (Engeström, 2022).

Context

When viewed from a CHAT perspective, student teaching is rule-governed and community-mediated (Douglas, 2014). In both side-by-side and ICT bilingual classrooms, student teaching requires continual negotiations about the division of labor – to delegate the different roles and responsibilities assumed by each bilingual (student) teacher. It is through such negotiations that tensions arise. For instance, Aquino Peña had to work with mentors who held different teaching philosophies, while Peña had to adapt to two different cooperating teachers' schedules in the school's dual language bilingual program.

Although tensions are typically considered negative and to be avoided in university partnership, when viewed through a CHAT lens, they are catalysts for mentored learning practice (Engeström, 2022). Aquino Peña and Peña, for example, demonstrated how they – with mediation by their cooperating teachers – turned these tensions and fears from threats to affirmations. Their collective understandings of these transformations validate their experiential reality as bilingual teachers (Chang *et al.*, 2020a), and are depicted in Table 17.1 as advantages and challenges that become sources of mentored learning practice.

Assessing and planning differentiated instruction that supports bilingual children's language and social emotional development also requires bilingual student teachers to assume additional roles and responsibilities. These threat-to-affirmation transformations can be derived from others' support and validation, such as when Rebeca Madrigal reminded Peña, 'Remember, less is more'. Additionally, when bilingual student teachers experience their students' language development, they gain critical language awareness of all linguistic areas (Chang *et al.*, 2020b). For example, Peña further embraced her bilingual teacher identity by valuing and caring for 'students' bilingual/multicultural voices'. In other words, student teachers develop themselves by acting as co-teachers and co-learners alongside other cooperating teachers and their students. This process establishes a feedback loop for bilingual student teachers that becomes an expansive learning cycle in which they name and engage in these tensions as micro-challenges (Engeström, 2022). In student teaching, we acknowledge that mentored learning is a vulnerable practice that situates teachers as learners. As Peña commented, 'Practice makes progress'.

Discussion

In bilingual student teaching, preservice teachers are learners who are socialized within a multicultural society that includes a history of contradictory ideas of bilingualism (Chang et al., 2020b). Mentored learning is thus constant and, with lifelong commitment, will continue. It is cumulative, re-energizing both mentors and mentees when they help one another – as Peña shared – 'make adjustments *during* the lesson based on the students and the environment'. Dialectically speaking, both school and university-based teacher-educators must move from a surface understanding of putting theory into practice toward an appreciation for appropriating a practical theory.

A linear application of theory to practice does not provide teachers with the tools they need for future-oriented actions. However, the non-linear appropriation of theory in practice equips mentors and mentees with everyday future-oriented actions that co-teachers can use to innovate as they become student-centered, multi-dimensional educators. Such appropriation of theory also promotes teacher learning via critical collaborations and leadership in various bilingual contexts, such as the afterschool and summer programs mentioned in this chapter, which allow student teachers to deploy their own interactional competences. In short, mentored learning practice should not be conceived as linearly transacted (Chang, 2021). Rather, it is a mode of social relations mediated by a group of teacher-learners/leaders as they enact their relational agency to visualize a co-construction of knowledge in teacher education (Chang et al., 2021).

References

Chang, S. (2021) Supporting expansive learning in preservice bilingual teachers' zone of proximal development of the activity system: An analysis of a four-field model trajectory. *Professional Development in Education* 47 (2–3), 225–242. https://doi.org/10.1080/19415257.2021.1879232

Chang, S., Martínez-Roldán, C. and Torres-Guzmán, M. (2020a) Struggling *to-be* or *not-to-be* a bilingual teacher: Identity formation in a Change Laboratory intervention. *Methodological Innovations* 13 (2), 1–19. https://doi.org/10.1177/2059799120921696

Chang, S., Torres-Guzmán, M. and Waring, H. (2020b) Experiencing critical language awareness as a collective struggle: Methodological innovations in language awareness workshops. *The Language Learning Journal* 48 (3), 356–369. https://doi.org/10.1080/09571736.2020.1740769

Chang, S., Martínez-Roldán, C. and Torres-Guzmán, M. (2021) The manifestation of Chinese preservice bilingual teachers' relational agency in a Change Laboratory intervention. *Mind, Culture, and Activity* 28 (1), 44–60. https://doi.org/10.1080/10749039.2021.1881125

Douglas, A.S. (2014) *Student Teachers in School Practice: An Analysis of Learning Opportunities*. Palgrave.

Edwards, A. and Collison, J. (1996) *Mentoring and Developing Practice in Primary Schools: Supporting Student Teacher Learning in Schools*. Open University Press.

Engeström, Y. (2022) Learning in activity. In R. Sawyer (ed.) *The Cambridge Handbook of the Learning Sciences* (pp. 134–155). Cambridge University Press. https://doi.org/10.1017/9781108888295.009

Soslau, E. and Alexander, M. (2021) *The Comprehensive Guide to Working with Student Teachers: Tools and Templates to Support Reflective Professional Growth*. Teachers College Press.

18 Expanding the Arts through Partnerships and Passion

Clara Bello and Lorene Phillips

Dos Puentes Dance and Music Teachers

Las artes is the soul of Dos Puentes in human form. The experiences we have, what we witness and are a part of on a daily basis, go beyond the scope of oral language. This chapter will attempt to put into words how the arts breathe life into the community of Dos Puentes. And because collaboration is at the heart of what we do, creating, developing and sustaining relationships between our school and the wider NYC arts community becomes second nature.

The curriculum for dance and music has been created by both of us to be interdisciplinary in nature, culturally relevant and responsive in our approach. The arts are a lens through which we view and experience the world. For this reason, making connections with other academic areas is not only feasible, it is the most logical approach. Moreover, when community and cultural partners are introduced, the learning comes full circle. The concepts we have been exploring in class start to come together through the arts. To create the richest artistic experiences for our students, we have cultivated several arts partnerships with music, dance, theater and art organizations. Here we examine two exceptional partnerships: A *capoeira* residency and 'About the Swing', a jazz-focused partnership.

Making Meaning through Movement

Within the dance/movement curriculum, kindergarten through 2nd grade focuses on creative movement, practicing how to use and share space and learning how to collaborate and use safe touch. Then, 3rd- through 5th-graders venture deeper into genre studies with a focus on social justice. By initially laying the foundation for a social justice unit, students were well positioned to capitalize on the partnership that evolved.

Image 18.1 5th-grade students practicing *capoeira* drills through the partnership with Professor Coco. Photo by Gerardo Romo.

One way social justice is addressed with upper-grade students is through the Brazilian dance form of *capoeira*, which is then extended by an overview of the transatlantic slave trade. I (Clara) lay the foundation for our partnership by asking students to look at the *ginga da capoeira*, the basic step, and how that one movement tells a story. As enslaved Africans often had shackles and chains around their ankles and wrists, the *ginga* step has epitomized this as the arms and legs do not stray too far from each other. The knees are bent, giving in to the ground, in keeping with African tradition. The soulful songs, music playing, dance and acrobatics all serve to keep the stories alive of those who were stolen from their land and suffered at the hands of enslavers. It also served to dupe the enslaver into thinking that this commotion was just wild entertainment. However, the *roda*, or circle, the *capoeiristas* made was kept tight to keep any foes from seeing what was going on as the enslaved were preparing to fight for their freedom.

Here enters Professor Coco of Abadá Capoeira Bronx for our *capoeira* residency. A free master class and a *capoeira* demonstration at our school led to a fruitful partnership, for both our students and for me as the dance teacher. We have been fortunate to have Professor Coco's two children at our school and his family as a part of our community. For many years, Dos Puentes has benefitted from his firsthand expertise with *capoeira* and Brazilian culture as someone who was born in Brazil and studied under *capoeira* experts. Moreover, the way he interacts with the children is unmatched. He possesses an uncanny ability to make *capoeira* – a martial art and multi-faceted art form rooted in a complex and serious history – an engaging, educational and enjoyable experience for all involved.

Witnessing the authenticity of Professor Coco's teaching style, his passion for *capoeira* and how the students immediately seemed to navigate to him, I pushed to have him back the following year. That first residency, paid for through the school's budget, was brilliant. We would touch base before, during and after each class with quick remarks or longer conversations depending on what was needed: for example, highlighting a technique further, occasional time checks or proposed next steps. Our flexibility and ability to see where students were, combined with our expertise in our individual areas, allowed the residency to shift, flow and best meet students' interests and needs.

The partnership evolved over the years. Professor Coco plays the *berimbau*, *pandeiro* and uses his booming, playful voice to give children a flavorful taste of *capoeira* life. This ranges from calisthenics where students are jumping over imaginary puddles to kicks and *esquivas* (dodges) to singing songs in Brazilian Portuguese and even playing some of the more rudimentary rhythms on the instruments. Students jump right in, embracing the fact that they are learning a new style of movement in yet another language (see Image 18.1). If students are ready to move further, he shows them the *Maculelê* – an Afro-Brazilian stick fighting – and then they move to the dance floor to experience *Samba de Roda*, the style of dance that gave birth to the modern samba. Throughout their experiences, students make connections to the slave trade, the African Diaspora and resistance to injustices.

As a lover and educator of languages, each year it has been my request that Professor Coco use as much of his home language – Brazilian Portuguese – as possible with students. As we progress through the residency, I write down common Brazilian Portuguese words and phrases as well as *capoeira* terms on a word wall which serves as a reinforcement, reminder and support of concepts learned in previous classes. Through repetition and with gentle support, students begin to greet, congratulate, thank and say farewell in Brazilian Portuguese, as well as ask questions using the *capoeira* terminology. In class discussions, students make connections between the Spanish they speak at home and/or in school and the words they learn in Brazilian Portuguese. Because the languages have similarities, students' faces would light up when they 'discovered' cognates and things suddenly 'made sense'.

To truly understand the roots of *capoeira* requires students to delve into the reason it exists in the first place. To do this our 5th-graders created a tableau around the transatlantic slave trade. We concluded that enslaved humans were stripped of their freedom, voices and power. Students kept saying how that was not fair and how they wished they could have done something. We used one of Augusto Boal's popular theater games, Image Theatre, to help. This approach involves creating a tableau, which is a picture people make using their bodies to show an image, issue or re-creation of a scene. Students first discuss what they want and what needs to change to achieve this. The first tableau shows the change that needs to take place and the final tableau depicts the result of the change. Over weeks, we created a series of tableaux featuring (1) the injustice suffered, in this case, the capture and enslavement of Africans, (2) their reaction to the injustice: resist, flee or hide and (3) the achievement of what they were seeking: freedom. In short, they embodied some of the realities of the African Diaspora through dance.

The *capoeira* residency provides students a way to extend their learning through a new form of dance, while at the same time exposing students to a new language. Working with a teaching artist like Professor Coco expands students' perspectives by learning about Brazilian culture from a Black man who hails from the country, speaks Brazilian Portuguese and shows children that movement in masculine and feminine ways is both possible and beautiful outside of gendered norms. Finally, the partnership provides me with the opportunity to collaborate and grow alongside Professor Coco and the children as we create an experience that uses *capoeira* to demonstrate understandings of freedom, liberty and resistance through an art form.

About the Swing

About the Swing is a non-profit program that has promoted jazz education to students throughout New York City for over ten years, bringing jazz to schools and collaborating with students to make their own music. The organization has shared live jazz performances with over 20,000 students. CEO Jay Seiden helps guide each school's music teacher in the partnership to build from their own musical strengths as they develop best practices to impact students' connections to jazz (see Image 18.2). The program came to us through Clara's personal connection to Mr Seiden, who in turn approached Dos Puentes about being an ongoing patron. Our partnership has gone through three phases over the eight years we have worked together.

In phase one of our partnership, the About the Swing program worked with our whole 3rd grade to incorporate the three modalities of teaching jazz: drumming, rhythm and vocals, and dance. The partnership provides a teaching artist – most of whom are bilingual in Spanish and English – to work alongside the music teacher. Students choose one modality to focus their work on for eight weeks and then combine them into a collective project. In phase two, the partnership culminates in a jazz social performance with a live jazz band and potluck dinner with families. This performance showcased the work of each modality through one song that encapsulated the theme of the program. Having the drumming group, the rhythm and vocal group, and the dance group all collaborate and having time for improvisation with the live jazz band, as well as audience

Image 18.2 Music teacher Lorene Phillips drumming to practice for the About the Swing performance. Photo by Gerardo Romo

participation, provided an authentic jazz experience for the whole community. Over the years we have explored such topics as Latin jazz, jazz funk and swing. These styles can be difficult to teach to 3rd-grade students who have a limited musical vocabulary. Yet, through hands-on learning, working with strong teaching artists, connecting to the rhymes of our families' cultures and traditions, and collaborating with our arts chair and dance specialist, students had a vibrant first experience with jazz that may stimulate further interest and experience in middle school and beyond.

The program has a significant impact on the students. Madison, a 3rd-grader, said she 'felt free and alive while performing on stage', while Jacob, also a 3rd-grader, shared that he 'loved the busy melodies and was inspired to listen to more jazz'. Families always enjoy the jazz social because it is not only a way to come together to see a wonderful performance, but also share a meal with the community. The jazz artists always share how much they learn from the students in the process and how they enjoy their energy, diverse linguistic repertoires, and variety of cultures. It feels like the full artistic feedback circle of sharing and receiving is completed through students, jazz artists and families' collaboration as audience members.

In phase three, this partnership has evolved to include an afterschool drumming ensemble of 15 students who created one of the first performance opportunities for our school as the COVID quarantine wound down. Students worked on different jazz drumming styles and did an intimate share with families and Mr Seiden to round out the experience. Our most recent engagement with About the Swing was a vibrant Louis Armstrong concert in which the Steven Bernstein Quartet performed the music of the Hot Five and told the history of Louis Armstrong. The students shared that they loved the solos, the trumpet, the storytelling and the beautiful live jazz band that came to our school. The children were invested in the story of Louis Armstrong, sharing facts with our performers that related to him as a New Yorker. They empathized with his story of getting into trouble with the law and then turning his life around when someone gave him a trumpet. Music brought him a new opportunity to engage with the world differently. We look forward to our students continuing to receive hands-on music skills and highly engaging performances from our About the Swing partnership.

Conclusion: Collaboration in the Arts is What We Do

From residencies with guest artists to masterclasses with artists within our families and student body, to inter-grade student partnerships and free events for our families to see live performances, Dos Puentes is a special place for the arts. It is a community filled with individuals, each with their own stories and talents such as Gabriel, a newly arrived 2nd-grader from the Dominican Republic who shared, *'Para mi, cuando yo bailo es algo como un poder que yo tengo y que me dio la vida* (For me, when we dance it's something like a power that I had and it gave me life)'. The arts at Dos Puentes is not just music and dance, it is about helping students connect with their inner superpowers and bringing students experiences that will stay with them well past their time with us. The arts is how we come together and welcome those stories and talents that make us individuals, make us special, but most importantly, make us one.

Researcher Commentary

Heather H. Woodley

New York University

I was once told by a mother that the most antiracist thing she could do was to raise a Black child surrounded by joy. As an educator, I considered this powerful statement in the classroom context. Where are connections between joy and antiracism for Black and brown students in schools? Responses consistently brought me to art – colors, creations, movement and music – as foundational to childhood joy. This art lives in the bodies and voices of children, and the role of art in Black and brown representation and resistance at Dos Puentes are living embodiments of how the arts team 'raises' or educates, their children in joyful, empowering engagement of culture, history and resistance through relationships with artists, communities, families and themselves.

Context

The arts at Dos Puentes are situated in myriad theoretical foundations including culturally relevant (Ladson-Billings, 1992) and culturally sustaining pedagogy (Paris, 2012), and a funds of knowledge approach (Moll *et al.*, 1992) as learning draws on community resources and knowledges. But these spaces go beyond cultural relevance into a deeply critical space of antiracist education.

Considering the intertwined nature of race and language, there is an antiracist call to action in our multilingual classrooms and schools. Looking deeper at these intersections, we see an 'erasing of the experiences of Afro-Latinxs' (Flores, 2016) that seeps into schools as whitewashed representations of Latinx communities, languages and histories infiltrate media and published materials. However, in choosing artistic mediums to explore in school, Dos Puentes partnerships made powerful decisions in *capoeira* and jazz – art forms that center blackness and resistance, allowing for joyful and creative spaces of childhood to flourish. *Capoeira* stems from the historical resistance of enslaved peoples in Brazil, and jazz is rooted in experiences and voices of US Black communities. These partnerships included exploring historical and political structures that surfaced and centered Afro-Latinx stories and representation (Nicola, 2016), while joyfully reclaiming it through art.

The arts at Dos Puentes are opportunities for all children to explore resistance while also engaging in it. These Black-centered arts fill young bodies with sounds and movement – two things they are often told *not* to produce, as 'still and quiet' are mostly (although falsely) equated with school success. But these arts are joy as an act of resistance (Engram, 2021) – resistance to stillness and silence assumed in learning, resistance to a curriculum that is increasingly white-washed and test-based, all of which tie into the arts' historical examples of resistance in diverse Black global communities. Art allows students to reclaim their childhoods as 'perceptions of the essential nature of children can be affected by race and … can mean they lose the protection afforded by assumed childhood innocence' (Goff *et al.*, 2014: 540). The art teams create spaces to push against the prevalent societal view of 'adultified' Black and brown children held to unrealistic and often dangerous expectations (Hagopian *et al.*, 2018). Art, movement and music are fundamental and foundational childhood activities that are too often cut short in schools. But at Dos Puentes the sounds and activities that are natural parts of childhood are celebrated and elevated as a regular part of the school curriculum.

Discussion

At Dos Puentes, the arts center diverse, multilingual Black experiences to create joyful spaces of criticality for all. Dos Puentes shows how art is a powerful entry point to issues of racism, resistance and cultural identity for younger students. Through arts, children learn history and empathy, immersed in experiences of enslaved people in connection with *capoeira* in Brazil, and jazz is framed as an empowering Black art form, when so much of Black history curricula are rooted in trauma. We see children thriving academically, creatively and socially in spaces where criticality meets joy and power, where they can engage in arts that explore oppression but center resistance and how art is used to fight back. Arts at Dos Puentes reminds us how children succeed when we engage their whole selves – their bodies, voices and hearts – and how deep learning can be when we make space for movement and sounds, and open intergenerational spaces where families and the community engage in arts with their children. We are left with many questions reflecting on these partnerships – how do we make artistic experiences that center blackness and joy accessible to more (if not, all) students in diverse communities? How do we normalize these artistic and creative practices as part of all academic subjects and content rather than relegated to 'enrichment' or 'specials'? And how can teachers engage with community partners in antiracist education that centers joy and resistance over trauma? Dos Puentes provides a blueprint to address these questions and a larger call to action as it illustrates the dramatic shift needed in the education of all students and reminds us that beautiful, powerful learning happens when we partner with artists from our communities and provide space for children to move, create sound, learn the truth about their histories, and dream of the futures they want to see.

References

Engram Jr., F. (2021) Black joy as an act of resistance. *TEDx Talks*, 5 May. https://www.ted.com/talks/dr_frederick_engram_jr_black_joy_as_an_act_of_resistance

Flores, N. (2016) Do Black lives matter in bilingual education? *The Educational Linguist: Examining Race and Language in Education*, 11 September. https://educationallinguist.wordpress.com/2016/09/11/do-black-lives-matter-in-bilingual-education/

Goff, P., Jackson, M., Di Leone, B., Culotta, C. and DiTomasso, N. (2014) The essence of innocence: Consequences of dehumanizing Black children. *Journal of Personality and Social Psychology* 106 (4), 526–545.

Hagopian, J., Au, W. and Y Watson, D. (eds) (2018) *Teaching for Black Lives*. Rethinking Schools.

Ladson-Billings, G. (1995) Toward a theory of culturally relevant pedagogy. *American Educational Research Journal* 32, 465–491.

Moll, L., Amanti, C., Neff, D. and Gonzalez, N. (1992) Funds of knowledge for teaching: Using a qualitative approach to connect homes and classrooms. *Theory into Practice* 31 (2), 132–141. https://doi.org/10.1080/00405849209543534

Nicola, M. (2016) Rethinking identity: Afro-Mexican history. *Rethinking Schools Magazine*, 30 (4).

Paris, D. (2012) Culturally sustaining pedagogy: A needed change in stance, terminology, and practice. *Educational Researcher* 41 (3), 93–97.

19 Center-Based Learning: Partnerships with Staff Developers and Schools

Queila Cordero and Joyce Veras

Dos Puentes Math Coach and Teacher

Over the 10 years that Dos Puentes has existed, partnerships between external organizations have extended and deepened our bilingual teaching and our students' learning. The curriculum has evolved with the help of staff developer partnerships in all areas. As we have grown within our school, we have also had the opportunity to share our learning and partner with other elementary schools in our district.

During the past three years our teacher learning has moved into a center-based approach, which has come to be known as FACIL, or Facilitating Academic Centers for Inquiry-based Learning. FACIL was a timely initiative that intersected with the academic struggles students were facing because of the COVID pandemic. Our data demonstrated that many children were not ready to move on to the next literacy or math unit because of the gaps in their skills. To address this reality, we worked with four staff developers to modify the curriculum across the school by incorporating literacy and math centers to supplement and extend our curriculum, ensure engagement and support students through multiple modalities in their specific area of need. These centers organized small groups of children that focused on a given activity for 7–20 minutes, before rotating to another center with a different focus. The work done through FACIL, coupled with the support from staff developer partners, such as Allyse Bader, Meghan McDonald, Anne Palmer and Kate Abell, has promoted student learning while simultaneously supporting our growth as pedagogues. In this chapter we, Joyce, an early-childhood classroom teacher and Queila, a former 5th-grade math teacher and current math specialist/Dean at Dos Puentes, explore the evolution of center development with our staff developers internally and then consider the subsequent partnership with district elementary schools that extended our work outward.

The FACIL Initiative

While remote and hybrid learning during the pandemic was hard for all of us (see Chapter 11), it did highlight that children were capable of much more independence than we might have assumed. A teacher working with smaller groups of children allowed them to better observe their students' learning. We also saw that children have a lot to teach each other. FACIL started at Dos Puentes as an initiative in our Integrated Co-Teaching (ICT) classrooms to meet the variety of children's needs, but following the pandemic it became a tool that was gradually transferred across the school. Centers are often used in a variety of classrooms but what made FACIL centers different from typical centers is that they are based in Universal Design for Learning (UDL) pedagogy. The UDL approach works to address and meet the particular learning needs of each individual student. Not all students do the same center rotation and centers are designed to support varied learning modalities and means of expression. For example, some children might read a particular text to gain information, while others listen to it or watch a video. Some children might use unifix cubes to show their thinking within a math problem and others may write a response or draw a picture. Although the curricula we were using – Teachers College Reading and Writing Project (TCRWP) and Eureka Math – were not designed for this structure, with the collaboration with our staff developers we were able to transition a lot of our teaching to this model. We now take you into the classroom to share how the FACIL centers were implemented by teachers who embraced this approach as they re-envisioned the workshop approaches to teaching literacy and math.

Literacy Centers through FACIL

After the school's FACIL committee introduced the concept of center-based learning based on UDL pedagogy, many teachers jumped in and created literacy centers in English and Spanish. We planned activities as grade-level teams across K-5 and also with our TCRWP staff developers. Through this partnership we received feedback and ideas for creating targeted activities to support students according to their areas of need. They also helped us deconstruct parts of the lesson from the TCRWP curriculum and create teaching points that the children could manage independently. We planned hands-on activities like puzzles, word sort games and drawing activities to address skills that supported phonological awareness, phonemic awareness, sight word recognition, letter identification, vocabulary and language development in students' language of dominance. For example, one game included ways to organize sequencing words such as *primero, después, luego y finalmente* (first, after, later and finally) that would make sentences students eventually join to create a story (see Image 19.1).

Image 19.1 A 3rd-grade class with FACIL centers focused on phonics. The centers include word games, small group instruction, sound practice and independent workbook practice. Photo by Ashley Busone-Rodríguez

The literacy centers disrupted our traditional literacy instruction. Previously I (Joyce) taught a mini-lesson that had all the students independently read, and then participate in partner reading while I conferenced with one or two individual children each class. Through FACIL literacy center time, the structure looks different. Students received a brief, whole-class mini-lesson, followed by a variety of hands-on centers where children practice targeted skills in small groups, often in their language of dominance, and according to their area of academic need. When available, an additional adult supports one of the centers. Teachers then focus on a small group in a direct way to assess for fluency or ask higher-order comprehension questions of students on their individual reading level, allowing time to teach directly to a needed skill, or to assess where the group of students are to determine next steps. The amount of time in literacy centers changes according to the age of the students. Large timers and a visual schedule are used to help the kids self-monitor to prepare to switch to the next center. Once children internalize the rotation schedule and their structures to support collaborative and independent work within the group, centers ensure that *everyone* is engaged in differentiated activities tailored to their individual academic goals.

FACIL led to significant academic growth through literacy centers in both English and Spanish. Because we were flexible with the language in certain centers, the linguistic demands of each center could be targeted towards the content and/or language objective. For example, English learners who required specific content vocabulary visited an English vocabulary center frequently as Spanish learners visited a Spanish vocabulary center. Early childhood students who struggled with initial literacy skills were given targeted practice in their language of dominance to develop a foundation in their home language. Upper-grade students who were concentrating on production of language in the new language were sent to centers with additional linguistic support by way of sentence starters for writing, or language prompts for conversations. Being purposeful but flexible with language within centers allowed opportunities to consider different children's linguistic needs while remaining focused on the overall literacy goals of the grade. As a result of the noticeable academic growth, we replaced the original centers with more challenging activities based on students' improved reading levels in both Spanish and English.

Math Centers through FACIL

As an educator I (Queila) find it essential to continue improving how I engage my students in meaningful learning. FACIL was incredibly influential in my growth as a math teacher, as it offered me a fresh perspective on centers. Although I had some experience with centers, this differed due to the large-scale focus placed on this teaching method that extended into other district schools. By seeing centers as a school-wide goal to increase student engagement, the planning and challenges became collaborative concerns. The clear and thoughtful math planning that took place, both in our grade teams and by observing other classrooms doing similar activities allowed us to implement math learning centers with a collective vision that led to meaningful discussions with colleagues who were going through the same process at the same time. For example, I learned what my grade partners were trying in their classrooms for literacy and we collaborated on what it might look like for a math lesson.

When planning for centers within the math classroom, I chose to deliver the different parts of a typical lesson through centers, which meant I did not have to plan everything from scratch. It was simply a new way of structuring the delivery in addition to the different learning activities for the children. For example, if the lesson called for basic facts practice, an open-ended task and a math game, these would occur simultaneously through three different centers. Students would essentially complete these tasks at different times and in a different order from their peers, all within the same math block. This small change in structure significantly improved student engagement. Building from traditional center-based teaching, over time the centers provided different ways for children to engage in the content depending on their needs. Something in particular that my students loved was that the math games were not always left towards the end of class time, but rather became part of the rotation schedule. Some students needed the game as a warm-up before their main task, others needed it as a challenge and, for some, the math games center served as a reinforcement of what they had just learned. This change also allowed my students to experience more success, which inevitably fed their excitement about the concepts we were learning and mathematics in general. In addition, the rotations provided me with an opportunity to differentiate for my students with more precision. However, this required strong organization skills and a significant amount of time dedicated to planning. The order in which the students completed each task greatly depended on what would potentially make each child most successful. Inevitably, I made errors that affected the flow of how children would move around the room. But once I understood what I had missed, I was able to easily adjust my plans. Math centers quickly became a routine I enjoyed planning for and was able to use on most days.

A concern I held was making sure that my students still learned the intended content deeply and completely. My fear was that I would compromise their learning for the sake of mine. I've been using a traditional workshop model for many years and I appreciated it because it provided a genuine space for learning through direct instruction, and exposure, practice and review. But admittedly, it did not always support deep, conceptual learning for every single one of my students, who are routinely at different levels of math proficiency. Through the FACIL partnership work and the conversations I was having with other educators, we saw how the content was not being sacrificed and most of our planning could remain the same. In fact, I was able to fit more meaningful pieces into the rotations because I could pick and choose which parts of the Eureka lesson were most needed for some students, and adapt them for others.

5th-grader Ana Sofía shared the following about centers:

> What I like about centers is that we get to switch around in our groups and experience different kinds of topics ... there's so much to learn about the subject, and it gets kids more engaged and [we] have more fun because we can do more hands-on projects.

How students experienced and perceived these centers, in addition to the intervisitations and peer learning, made a significant impact on the risks I took and the pedagogical learning that occurred for me as a math educator.

FACIL Centers as District Partnerships

As the FACIL centers developed in our school, Dos Puentes had the opportunity to share this approach with other schools in our district. At an observational visit during the pandemic, our Superintendent Manuel Ramirez observed how the 3rd-grade class of Ashely Busone-Rodríguez was using centers. He was impressed with the high level of engagement and differentiation of instruction. As he knew this was happening in other classrooms in our school, he wanted this approach to become a district initiative. He initially asked us to work with a cohort of five district elementary schools to grow FACIL. The goal was to share these center-based practices, building on our work with staff developers to ensure engagement and best meet the differences in strengths and needs of our students using a UDL lens. It was important to our superintendent that we explain the rationale for using this approach to our partners. The committee of teachers who piloted this approach supported growth in our school, but also created a structure to involve five self-selected elementary schools to meet monthly for intervisitations and planning time (see Image 19.2).

The partnerships with the other schools positioned our teachers as leaders. Our teachers reflected on their own development, which provided the tools for other schools to do the same. Differentiation, independence and opportunities to better know students through small groups impacted student autonomy, peer collaboration and engagement. Our teachers were able to reflect on the process and facilitate learning for teachers in other schools. Our teachers modeled the risks they took to implement the centers and constant adjustments they made with management, assessment and materials to ensure they continued to improve. Often these adjustments came through reflections about the curriculum with the staff developers.

Image 19.2 Principals and teachers from other District 6 New York City schools visit Dos Puentes to learn about the FACIL initiative and experience center-based learning to share with their schools. Photo by Victoria Hunt.

Due to the success of this first-year collaboration, each cohort school is now supporting the learning of an additional three schools. This is an evolutionary project that we hope will continue to promote differentiated strategies to support students as it empowers teachers to be leaders who continually reflect and collaborate. What started as support from outside staff developers and consultants helping Dos Puentes deepen and adjust our curriculum for our multilingual learners has evolved into an initiative where Dos Puentes has partnered with more than 20 schools to collaboratively support the engagement of students and teachers alike.

Conclusion

FACIL had a very positive impact on the students and teachers at Dos Puentes. The most significant change we observed at the classroom level was an increase in student engagement and participation. It also helped develop student independence, confidence, social skills and personal involvement in their learning. As teachers, we gained strategies that ultimately made us more effective without making very laborious changes. This, coupled with the feedback from our colleagues and partner schools, has helped elevate our teaching and learning to a new level. Teachers at Dos Puentes have seamlessly woven FACIL into the fabric of our school with internal support from peers and external support from staff developers and our district school partners. The vision of our superintendent has led to a structural change on a scale larger than we could have imagined as we've been able to share this learning with others through school and district based partnerships as we grow, learn and lead.

Researcher Commentary

Crissa Stephens
Georgetown University

This chapter presents partnerships which led to student learning, teacher action rooted in reflection and a sustainable, exponential network of support for other schools. These efforts centered students and teachers' knowledge to create a space for reflection and growth during the first wave of the pandemic. Through partnerships which supported the implementation of learning centers, teachers addressed student needs effectively, grew their pedagogical toolkits and became catalysts for others' learning in the district.

Context

As standardized testing requirements push schools further away from the responsive, student-centered approaches shared by Queila Cordero and Joyce Veras, the partnership with FACIL created a structure that allowed Dos Puentes teachers to implement pedagogy rooted in their students' strengths and needs. Their approach counters a shift away from the center-based curriculum in early childhood because of the requirements of standardized testing (NAEYC, n.d.). This has led to curricular practices that are neither responsive to the diversity of experiences and literacies in dual language settings nor to the desires, needs and knowledge of teachers within them.

So often, society frames teachers as passive implementers of a curriculum; however, in this chapter, we see how teacher-learning partnerships can drive educational change from the bottom up. The countermeasure against narrowing instructional practices and ideologies is an inquiry stance that positions teachers as knowledge producers and social change-makers (Cochran-Smith & Lytle, 2015). To sustain such a stance, systems and structures that protect and create space for ongoing learning and support are necessary. While teachers can exercise agency at the individual level, systemic support is crucial to foster and amplify their work. The partnerships at Dos Puentes were rooted in the experiences and knowledge of teachers and strengthened by partnerships that facilitate the space for inquiry. In turn, the teachers became knowledge producers whose collaboration with other schools led to transformation.

The kind of professional development that leads to educational and social transformation is dialogic, created in collaboration and focused on what teachers want and need to know about their students, teaching and classroom (Kohli *et al.*, 2015). Effective teacher learning structures also incorporate reflection, inquiry and structures that sustain growth over time (Guskey & Yoon, 2009). Often, professional learning for teaching emergent bilingual learners is top-down and couched in unsustainable, one-and-done models with detrimental effects (Stephens & Johnson, 2015). These approaches follow what Freire (2018) characterizes as a banking or transmission model where learning is deposited into a presumably empty vessel, rather than co-constructed upon teachers' and students' knowledge that responds to their educational realities.

By contrast, when teachers observe students' needs, strengths and skills through a critical inquiry lens, design curriculum around these observations and respond to the results within an overarching partnership structure that supports this, both student and teacher learning can be responsive and sustaining. At the classroom level, the partnerships at Dos Puentes create space for teachers to inquire and respond to students' lives and pedagogical growth. At the district level, the partnerships create a space for critical inquiry, learning and evaluation (Stephens *et al.*, 1996). In dual language education, research has long acknowledged that pedagogies must be formed in relationship to the lives, knowledge and circumstances of the unique social context of each learner, teacher and program

(Ascenzi-Moreno & Seltzer, 2021). Structures that go beyond the classroom level, such as these collaborative learning partnerships, are crucial to creating and implementing such pedagogy.

Partnership structures like these that support teacher learning and position them as knowledge creators and transformation agents are more important than ever in light of the increasing figures of teacher burnout related to the COVID-19 pandemic. In general, urban contexts like that of Dos Puentes see higher rates of teacher attrition and higher shortages of trained teachers for emergent bilingual students. These partnerships respond to what teachers elsewhere have voiced as a productive countermeasure to burnout in this time: intentional instructional support that allows them to serve their students and see them grow.

Discussion

So often we see top-down policies, programs and practices that are layered upon teachers, students and families by actors with more institutional power. In these accounts, we see a productive countermeasure – students and teacher knowledge and needs drive choices, and the partnerships provide an organizational structure that supports and expands this work. While the focus of this chapter is the instructional and transformative power of partnerships for learning, it starts with an observation about students: they were capable, during trying times, of much more independence than teachers initially thought. In partnership with staff developers, the teachers at Dos Puentes co-sharpen their lenses to see, respond to and amplify the strengths in students for learning. The partnerships create a structure to foment and solidify this asset-based stance and pedagogy. Through Cordero and Veras's accounts, we see a detailed example of what Cochran-Smith and Lytle (2015) call inquiry as stance, the kind of centering and amplification of practitioner knowledge and inquiry that can drive social and educational transformation in our schools.

References

Ascenzi-Moreno, L. and Seltzer, K. (2021) Always at the bottom: Ideologies in assessment of emergent bilinguals. *Journal of Literacy Research* 53 (4), 468–490.
Cochran-Smith, M. and Lytle, S.L. (2015) *Inquiry as Stance: Practitioner Research for the Next Generation*. Teachers College Press.
Freire, P. (2018) *Pedagogy of the Oppressed*. Bloomsbury Publishing.
Guskey, T.R. and Yoon, K.S. (2009) What works in professional development? *Phi Delta Kappan* 90 (7), 495–500.
Kohli, R., Picower, B., Martinez, A.N. and Ortiz, N. (2015) Critical professional development: Centering the social justice needs of teachers. *The International Journal of Critical Pedagogy* 6 (2), 9–24.
NAEYC (n.d.). DAP: Observing, documenting and assessing children's development and learning. www.naeyc.org/resources/position-statements/dap/assessing-development

Stephens, C. and Johnson, D.C. (2015) 'Good teaching for all students?': Sheltered instruction programming in Washington state language policy. *Language and Education* 29 (1), 31–45.

Stephens, D., Story, J., Aihara, K., Hisatake, S., Ito, B., Kawamoto, C., Mokulehua, J., Okayamashita, S., Omalza, S., Tsuchiyama, E., Yamate, F., Yoshioka, E., Yoshizaka, L. and Yoshizawa, D. (1996) When assessment is inquiry. *Language Arts* 73 (2), 105–112.

20 Connections with the Community and Beyond

Katherine Higuera-McCoy and
Maggie Orzechowski

Dos Puentes Community Coordinator and Mother

Creating authentic and sustainable connections across cultural, economic and linguistic differences is no easy feat. This work requires sensitivity, consistency, flexibility and patience to build bridges and be responsive to local issues and national politics as they directly impact the families in the Dos Puentes community. Some keys to fostering connection within a bilingual school with diverse families include creating opportunities for small-scale, regular gatherings where one-on-one relationships can be formed as well as organizing school-wide events where families and students can see that they are part of a larger bilingual and multicultural community.

Another aspect of connecting with the community is accessibility. This means ensuring that all events are truly bilingual in Spanish and English, rather than relaxing into English dominance. It requires having gatherings in the morning, evening, and weekends to accommodate various realities of the work and home lives of families. It means hosting some events outside so that our parents who are unvaccinated against COVID-19 can attend. It means that while there may be some events that are centered on fundraising and giveaways, others have no monetary requirement or push for a financial exchange. And while it should mean people with physical disabilities can access the building, Dos Puentes is in an old building (built in 1905) that does not meet the Americans with Disabilities Act (ADA) requirements.

Recognizing that building and sustaining connections and community partnerships will always be a work in progress, this chapter will highlight the foundations that have been and continue to be laid within and outside the school walls, and with the community at large.

Growing Connections: When Plants and Drug Needles Collide

Dos Puentes has many avenues for families to bond with the school's faculty and each other. Consistent gatherings in and outside the building let families know that they are always welcome and their presence is valued. Some of our offerings include the language exchange, Wellness in the Schools (WITS), Family Friday, Rincón Hispano, International Night, potlucks, and the garden committee. Just outside the school building, the Dos Puentes garden acts as a bridge from the school to the community, both physically and symbolically. The garden is a space for family plots, science exploration, storytelling, read-alouds, and street clean-up and beautification. The garden is a living laboratory offering hands-on opportunities for community building, collaboration and exploration (see Image 20.1). It naturally creates an environment for growth via partnerships. Our relationships with Leave It Better, Grow NYC, NYC parks, and the Washington Heights Corner Project have all been born out of this space.

The Dos Puentes garden is in its third generation. It started in 2013, the first year of the school, with two raised beds built by the Leave It Better Foundation and parent volunteers. The parents, teachers and students expanded this space by adding more beds and benches over the next few seasons. In 2015, the garden was torn up for construction and rebuilt. It was torn up again in 2019 due to construction access needs. Each time they have to rebuild it, the gardeners learn more about what they need and how to expand the space to its highest potential.

The community response and gratitude expressed by neighbors who enjoy having a shared green space in their neighborhood has been immense. Passersby are welcome to come in and sample lettuce leaves,

Image 20.1 Students doing observations in the school's garden in front of the building. Photo by Katherine Higuera-McCoy

pick a snap pea and smell the flowers. These simple exchanges often spark deeper connections. Sometimes neighbors reflect on happy memories from when they used to garden with their grandparents. Other times we have heard nostalgia for the scents and plants of their homelands. And in a most tender and vulnerable moment, a mother felt safe and supported while taking in the beauty of the space and opened up about her grief over the loss of her son.

Because the space is situated on the sidewalk with an open entrance, it became a night-time hangout for drug use (specifically injectable drugs) that resulted in used syringes discarded in this space, leading to a safety challenge for the gardeners and children. This led to a relationship with the Washington Heights Corner Project (WHCP). Because WHCP offers needle exchange and safe usage facilities, some community members feel that WHCP is contributing to and enabling the problem of injectable drug use in Washington Heights. WHCP is often on the receiving end of hostility and resistance to their mission. On their public Facebook page they state:

> WHCP is dedicated to improving the health, safety, and wellbeing of marginalized people who use drugs or engage in sex work. Their work addresses the intersection of stigma, policies, and practices that harm our participants and adversely impact the communities where we operate. WHCP is a leader in innovative and award-winning harm reduction and drug user health focused programs and services. In November 2021, they made history with the opening of the first two Overdose Prevention Centers in the United States, and again in March 2022 when the organization became the largest harm reduction service provider in the country.

This is not a traditional partnership to which schools and institutions are accustomed. WHCP's name or logo will not be featured on a newsletter or banner. It is a partnership based on the personal relationships of a few people that are being cultivated and grown. Therefore, many folks may not be aware that this 'underground' work is happening. Nevertheless, by forming a relationship with WHCP, parents and a few staff members were able to learn safe disposal techniques for syringes, request daily clean-ups from their team, and learn how to safely engage with the drug users to redirect them to safe usage sites where they can access care and practice harm reduction. Some of us went even further and were trained in how to administer the medication Narcan to individuals who are overdosing. The impact of this was a reduction of open drug use on the school campus and less syringe litter. But the problem has not gone away. By working alongside this often stigmatized organization, we were able to meet the needs of our school community without criminalizing or turning our backs on our neighbors who are suffering from drug addictions.

Image 20.2 America Scores students in fall 2021. Photo by Katherine Higuera-McCoy

Connection in Action: Bringing Together Sport, Poetry and Community

Dos Puentes's success and growth is deeply tied to its community partnerships. Over the years, the school has partnered with various youth organizations that have become a big part of the school culture. Some examples of community partners include America SCORES New York (ASNY), the Lego Robotics program, food and clothing drives, Know Your Rights training for immigrants, and the YM & YWHA's literacy program.

While there are many partnerships that have been a part of our school, the America SCORES New York (ASNY) has been with our school since the start (see Image 20.2). The ASNY program motto is to 'inspire urban youth to lead healthy lives, be engaged students, and have the confidence and character to make a difference in the world'. ASNY at Dos Puentes is a free after school program that serves students in grades 3 to 5 and focuses on ASNY's three main areas of building teamwork with the unique combination of (1) soccer, (2) poetry and (3) civic engagement. During soccer the students learn traditional skills such as passing, receiving, shooting, dribbling and ball control. In poetry they learn to be concise and share real or fictional stories with their own natural flow. The following is a heartfelt poem a student wrote in the ASNY program during the COVID pandemic:

I Wish Poem

I wish Covid would end
I want to be normal again

Ending Covid would be great
For everyone to be happy all day!

Let's end Covid
To stop people from dying and having to wear masks

I wish for no more violence
To have more peace with our families

Mi deseo es que no maltratan y humillan a los niños con hacerle bullying NO Importa el color de tu piel, si eres diferente a lo demás
Lo que sí importa el la clase de persona que eres

I wish we could bring back people that we've lost
So that our hearts grow with happiness

I wish for no more animal abuse
My favorite animal is a monkey. What is yours?

I wish for world peace

An infinite feeling of freedom to image incredible things like being able to speak to animals or a cake that regenerates after being eaten

Each year in the spring students come up with a community-based project. According to longtime coach, school partner and program coordinator, Leo Estrada, past projects in the Washington Heights area have included cleaning up local parks (such as Highbridge Park and Fort Tryon), planting a tree, walking around the neighborhood handing out goods to people in need, selling candy and donating the money to local shelters. Coach Leo, as he is known, said 'our student athletes choose their own project [because] they [want to] have a huge positive impact in their neighborhood, especially if they know it is a city that has a high crime rate. They want to make a difference. They want to set an example to their family/families of what to do to make your home a better place'. This program is something students look forward to each year. A 3rd-grade parent whose child participated in the program in 2021 said '*[e]l programa de America Scores es del agrado de mi niña, ella se divierte mucho allí y aprende a la misma vez. Como mamá siento que ha sido beneficioso para ella porque justamente el hacer deporte es algo que su doctora me había recomendado, después del tiempo que tuvo que pasar en casa encerrada por la pandemia* (My daughter likes the America Scores program, she has a lot of fun and learns at the same time. As a mother, I feel it has been beneficial for her because it's precisely doing sports that her doctor had recommended to me after the period of time she had to spend enclosed at home during the pandemic)'. As noted by this family's experience, it is a program that has helped students via a unique combination of physical, creative and social approaches. Students who participate in ASNY get to tackle real-life projects and make a difference to those around them whether it is in what they say or in what they do.

Connections Beyond the School: Advocacy for Immigrant Rights

National politics have a direct impact on our local community. In 2018, the Trump administration passed a family separation policy which took a 'zero tolerance' approach to undocumented immigration and enacted tougher legislation that criminalized migrants. In September 2018, Dos Puentes welcomed a family that was deeply affected by this policy. After some members of this family were separated at the border for almost six weeks, the family was reunited and subsequently relocated to NYC, where they took up residence in Holyrood Church, a local parish committed to social justice work that previously offered another family sanctuary from extreme immigration policies. During their time there the family fought to gain asylum in the US.

Shawna Mulcahy, a Dos Puentes parent, acted as a bridge of connection between the school and Holyrood, noting, 'because of their immigration status, it was difficult for the family to earn an income', so they were provided with financial and material support by members of the Dos Puentes community, as well as by members of the wider Washington Heights community. When the family was faced with the risk of imminent deportation, teachers and staff wrote beautiful letters of support advocating on their behalf. The family was ultimately granted a reprieve from deportation. As this family became integrated into the Dos Puentes and Washington Heights community, the connection between the school and Holyrood Church strengthened and the school was able to help support the church in other ways including through a clothing and food drive. Members of the Dos Puentes community continue to support Holyrood in their mission to provide vital assistance to all neighborhood residents.

Dos Puentes was uniquely positioned to welcome these Spanish-speaking immigrant children to their classrooms because of our dual language bilingual program. Beyond language, the school also looks for ways to support both undocumented and mixed-status immigrants by working in partnership with local organizations to provide trusted and pro-bono legal services. Immigration is also a topic that is discussed regularly in classrooms to normalize the experiences of its families, as highlighted by 1st/2nd grade teacher Rebeca Madrigal doing a read-aloud of the book 'El Muro' to address detention and separation of migrant families that was taking place at the US-Mexico border (see the CUNY-Initiative on Immigration and Education website for the video: www.cuny-iie.org/sis-videos).

Conclusion

Dos Puentes has many access points for families, students and teachers to connect within and outside school as well as in the community at large. These relationships enrich the lives of those involved, strengthen fellowship and deepen a sense of belonging. Dos Puentes is not perfect, but it will continue to put connection at the forefront and stay flexible to meet the changing needs of the families and Washington Heights. As famously put by Lin-Manuel Miranda in the Broadway show and movie *In the Heights*, '[O]nce upon a time, in a faraway land called Nueva York, *en un barrio* called Washington Heights everyone has a *sueñito*' – A dream where we create, expand and continue to grow from within a small place to a greater community and beyond.

Researcher Commentary

Kate Seltzer

Rowan University

In this chapter, authors Katherine Higuera-McCoy and Maggie Orzechowski describe how Dos Puentes approaches the vital and complex task of creating 'authentic and sustainable connections' with their communities 'across cultural, economic and linguistic differences'. In their discussion of the school's connections, Higuera-McCoy and Orzechowski provide examples of how the school engages in outreach and forms relationships with families and the broader community of Washington Heights. In this short commentary, I hope to demonstrate just how powerful these connections are and how well they align with what recent research tells us about the importance of centering critical consciousness and civic engagement in the education of bilingual students.

Context

In our book, *The Translanguaging Classroom: Leveraging Student Bilingualism for Learning*, Ofelia García, Susana Ibarra Johnson and I

(2017) put forth the concept of a translanguaging stance. This stance, or set of beliefs, that inform teacher practice and approaches to educating emergent bilingual students, is rooted in assets-oriented understandings of these students as well as their families and communities. Though the elements of the translanguaging stance will be different for different educators, we write that there are three beliefs that must be present:

(1) Students' language practices and cultural understanding encompass those they bring from home and communities, as well as those they take up in schools. These practices and understanding work *juntos* and enrich each other.
(2) Students' families and communities are valuable sources of knowledge and must be involved in the education process *juntos*.
(3) The classroom is a democratic space where teachers and students, *juntos*, co-create knowledge, challenge traditional hierarchies, and work toward a more just society. (García *et al.*, 2017: 50)

The second and third beliefs are clearly at the heart of Dos Puentes's approach to community engagement. In addition to ensuring that all school events are fully bilingual and accessible to families, Dos Puentes's work transcends the walls of the school and demonstrates how an institution that serves immigrant-origin youth must support and enrich their language development *and* their and their community's broader physical and socioemotional wellbeing. By partnering with local organizations devoted to this work, Dos Puentes is able both to serve the community and engage students in acts of service that situate them as civically engaged members of that community. Whether they are maintaining the Dos Puentes garden, which is open to the public, or participating in community-based projects such as 'cleaning up local parks ... planting a tree, walking around the neighborhood handing out goods to people in need, selling candy and donating the money to local shelters', the school's partnerships with community organizations ensure that students develop a critical consciousness as they develop their bilingualism (Palmer *et al.*, 2020).

The school's partnerships also reflect Dos Puentes's understanding of 'the unavoidable relationship between schooling and political life' (Mirra *et al.*, 2018, as cited in de los Ríos & Molina, 2020: 33), a fact that, as Higuera-McCoy and Orzechowski state and de los Ríos and Molina echo, was made particularly plain under the Trump presidency. In addition to normalizing students' immigration experiences and educating them bilingually, Dos Puentes supports students and their families by partnering with local advocacy organizations like Holyrood Church to resist draconian immigration policies. In this way, Dos Puentes's partnerships and advocacy efforts are a form of *sanctuary* for its surrounding immigrant community, which de los Ríos and Molina (2020), citing Patel (2018), describe as a space of refuge whereby schools 'work to provide concrete practices and networks that educators can engage to stand more deeply in solidarity with vulnerable communities' (2020: 33).

Discussion

The harsh policies of the Trump era and their ramifications did not disappear when he lost the 2020 presidential election. At the hands of Republican governors, for example, migrants who arrive in Florida and Texas, among other right-leaning states, are being bussed across the country with more thought given to gaining political points than to these individuals' humanity, safety and wellbeing. Many families who fell victim to the Trump administration's family separation policy still have not been reunited. And xenophobic, anti-immigrant rhetoric is poised to shape yet another election cycle. As such, it is incumbent upon schools to situate themselves as advocates, partners and *sanctuaries* for immigrant families as they navigate this often inhumane landscape.

Schools with bilingual programs located in communities where immigrant families live, like Dos Puentes, are uniquely equipped for this task. In its commitment to 'stay[ing] flexible to meet the changing needs of the families and Washington Heights', Dos Puentes demonstrates how bilingual education is – and has been since its inception – a political act (Flores & García, 2017: 16) aligned with 'the possibility of challenging the marginalization of Latinx and other minoritized students'. In this way, Higuera-McCoy and Orzechowski's chapter offers important examples of how schools can resist forces like gentrification and commodification that frame dual language bilingual education through the lens of 'economic interests and global human capital' (2017: 26) and instead align itself with movements for social justice and equity for racialized bilingual students their families, and their communities.

References

de los Ríos, C.V. and Molina, A. (2020) Literacies of refuge: 'Pidiendo posada' as ritual of justice. *Journal of Literacy Research* 52 (1), 32–54.
Flores, N. and García, O. (2017) A critical review of bilingual education in the United States: From basements and pride to boutiques and profit. *Annual Review of Applied Linguistics* 37, 14–29.
García, O., Johnson, S.I. and Seltzer, K. (2017) *Translanguaging Classrooms: Leveraging Student Bilingualism for Learning*. Brooks.
Palmer, D.K., Cervantes-Soon, C. and Dornier-Heiman, D. (2020) Bilingualism, biliteracy, biculturalism, and critical consciousness for all: Proposing a fourth fundamental goal for two-way dual language education. In P. Ramírez and C. Faltis (eds) *Dual Language Education in the US* (pp. 34–50). Routledge.

A Student's Closing Remarks

Raphael S. Kollin

Dos Puentes Graduate

SCR 1.1 Raphael Kollin giving his speech at the 5th grade graduation ceremony. Photo by Eric Kollin

Fifth-grader Raphael Kollin was selected by his peers to be one of the student speakers at the 2021 graduation. We end our book with his speech to conclude with the words and experiences of *un estudiante de* Dos Puentes:

Welcome graduates, Dr Hunt, Dr Jaar, Ms Consuelo, Dos Puentes teachers, families and staff! My name is Raphael Kollin, I have been going to Dos Puentes for five years. I joined Dos Puentes in 1st grade. It's been tough this past year, but I kept going. We all kept going, even before COVID, times were crazy but no matter how hard it was we kept working hard thanks to Dos Puentes. Thank you Dos Puentes, thank you for what you have done for me!

This school teaches many kids how to do so many things. Having an elementary school that teaches Spanish and English is so useful, not just for people to know the languages, but for people to figure out their family's language and not to forget them. If it wasn't for this school, I would not know Spanish as well as I do now. And thanks to Spanish it is easier to learn a third language, so that is why I am getting better at Hebrew.

Each day has gotten me ready for the next day. In math, I always came out with ten more pieces of information for my brain to learn. In literacy, I always learn a new strategy or idea. If music never was a subject, I would never know that I like playing the piano. I also learned what things I don't like doing very much. For example, I am not a crazy dancer, because of this school, I know who I am and how I could define myself as a person. All these five years I spent at Dos Puentes have prepared me for middle school and the next step to my journey of wanting to become an author.

Even the afterschool programs have helped me define who I am as a person. If America Scores were never a thing, I would not have known how fun it is to play soccer. Also, in chess class, I would never have learned how to play. Even the gardening class helped me because I now help plant plants in my backyard.

The most important thing about Dos Puentes is the friendships you make. My first ever friend from Dos Puentes was Tadeos, I'm still friends with him now. Then came Ethan, Henry, Anthony, Ama, Johan and Gabriel. I have a memory of a time I went bowling with Gabriel, Ethan, Ama and Anthony. I can't even explain how fun that was. Or what about the time I went to Adventure Land with Ethan, Anthony and Ama. It's not only the teachers that help me learn important information, it's my friends too. For example, the thing that pushed me to be a writer is the series that Ethan Lopez and I did. We also worked on a 2020 election article. Also we worked on slides about the short story *The Elevator*. This is the true meaning of the school, it's all about defining you as a person. We are all almost finished with 5th grade and moving into 6th grade. I think I have found out who I am as a person, I think you have too. All thanks to a school, Dos Puentes. *¡Nunca voy a olvidar está experiencia!*

Afterword

Carmen Fariña and Manuel Ramirez

NYC Department of Education Former Chancellor and Community School District 6 Superintendent

As a child of immigrants, I wish I had had an opportunity to see my home language honored and my culture celebrated. As former Chancellor of NYC Department of Education I (Carmen) am most proud of having opened up more than 150 dual language programs during my tenure. Dos Puentes is one of the best models of this type of school. It contains all the essential elements of a successful school: a great leader with clear vision; dedicated teachers who engage in deep professional development to accommodate various needs; and families who value bilingual education and are prepared to advocate for its existence. One of the largest worldwide movements in education are international schools where two or three languages are taught, and proficiency is expected in all aspects of literacy. Dos Puentes was ahead of its time when it opened in 2013 and truly is a shining star in this effort. Their students will excel anywhere academically, and more importantly socially and emotionally.

Dos Puentes is part of NYC's District 6, which has the highest number of Multilingual Learners of all the districts in the borough of Manhattan. To celebrate *una década* de Dos Puentes's dual language school and its commitment to building bridges *entre idiomas*, cultures *y mundos* by embracing *bilingüismo* and *biliteracidad* is a true gift to the Washington Heights community. Dos Puentes continues to serve as a model as we expand dual language programs, welcome immigrant families and fortify high-quality instruction in our district. They value and engage *la comunidad* in meaningful learning experiences anchored in culture, which is evident in this amazing publication which demonstrates their appreciation, understanding and approaches to strategically leveraging the community's diverse social and intellectual resources.

Although many people have a vision of the importance and benefits of a bilingual education – especially for immigrant families – they may not have a strategic plan to start a school or cultivate a community that will allow it to flourish. *Lessons from a Dual Language Bilingual School: Celebrando una década de Dos Puentes Elementary* takes you from the vision to the implementation. It takes you into the school, its classrooms and even the homes of the students and families they serve. It shows how the vision continues to grow and how programming, curricula and partnerships evolve and change over time. The book does not shy away from obstacles the school has encountered, it highlights how communities grapple with challenges and reflect collaboratively to find solutions. This is a book that can inspire, inform and support educators on their journey to starting and sustaining a bilingual program and/or school that centers the *bilingüismo, biliteracidad y multiculturalismo* of their unique *comunidad* to nurture access, growth and opportunities.

¡We celebrate Dos Puentes on their tenth *aniversario* and we hope they continue to build their sustainable dual language school while preserving the integrity of this important work in education as they embrace equity *y fortalecen la calidad, la implementación y el orgullo de la educación bilingüe!*

Index

50/50 Spanish/English split 11, 19, 49, 168

Abadá Capoeira Bronx 222–3
Abell, K. 192, 229
ableism 71
About the Swing 194, 224–6
accessibility of community events 239
activism 55–63, 244–5, 247
adjunct instructors 191
adult learning 187
advocacy 79–82, 84, 86–7
affective filters 50
Afro-Latinx communities 227
afterschool programs 201–4, 216–17, 219, 249
alegría de ser bilingüe 30–2, 33, 35, 53
Alexander, M. 217
Alim, S. 165
Alvarez, J. 49–50, 52
America SCORES New York (ASNY) 242–4
Americans with Disabilities Act (ADA) 239
Amplify Science 168
animals 139–41, 172–4
Anzaldúa, G. 55
Aponte, G.Y. 164–6
Aqueduct Challenge 170–1
Aquino Peña, J. 200, 211–17, 218
Arana, B. 199–206
Arreguín-Anderson, M.G. 176
artifacts 94, 138, 143, 205
arts 12, 33, 144, 159, 187–8, 193–5, 203, 221–8 *see also* dance; music; singing
Ascenzi-Moreno, L. 35, 44–6, 88, 237
ASPIRA Consent Decree 79
assemblies 20, 25
assessment
  science 169
  standardized testing 20, 53, 166, 235, 236
authentic experiences 79, 134, 139, 151–2, 160–5, 179, 225
authentic texts 23, 58
Awakened Teacher 192
Axelrod, Y. 154
Ayala, E. 115

Bader, A. 229
'bake sale' model of family involvement 74, 83, 112
Baker, C.N. 120, 121
balanced biliteracy approach 21–2
Balderrama, M.V. 52
Bank Street College 189, 191, 211
banking/transmission model of teaching 236
Barrales, W. 199–206
Bartolomé, L. 52
Bautista, K. 118–23
Becker, T. 200
Bello, C. 193, 221–6
belonging 52
bilingual ethnography 40
bilingual extension (bilingual teaching certification) 10–11
bilingual identities 19
Bilingual Pupil Services (BPS) 190, 215, 216–17
bilingual texts 23
Bilingual/Bicultural Program at Teachers College, Columbia University 188, 204, 211
bilingualism pillar 18–20
biliteracy *see also* literacy
  building 47–54
  child-centered biliteracy approaches 21
  pillar 20–3
Bishops, R.S. 48, 50

Black communities 2, 36, 55, 224, 226, 227, 228
blended learning 113
Bloomberg, Mike (Mayor) 4, 7
blue for English, red for Spanish 19, 158, 165, 168
Boal, A. 223
body language 36, 40
book club units 200
book fair 113
border spaces 55
brain development 153
Brazilian Portuguese 223, 224
Broadway divide 103–4
Bronx Zoo trips 144, 183
Brown, B.A. 175
Brown, S. 36
budgets 7, 78, 184, 223
building *comunidad* 109–17, 159–60, 165, 204–5
buildings and facilities 7–8, 183, 239
bulletin boards 93
bunnies 172–3, 176
Busone-Rodríguez, A. 55–61, 233–4

Calabrese Barton, A. 175
camping trips 145, 169, 170, 182
Cando, A. 32, 83–7, 89
capoeira 194, 222–3
CARES (Cooperation, Assertiveness, Responsibility, Empathy, and Self-control) assemblies 25
Caribbean Spanish 50
Carnegie Hall 194
Carrell Moore, H. 133
Cartledge, G. 70
Casado, A. 83–7, 89
Casimir, A.E. 120, 121, 192
Castilian Spanish 49
Castro Ramos, E. 109–14
Center on the Developing Child (Harvard University) 124
center-based approaches xx, 173, 191, 229–38
Cerbin, W. 192
Cervantes-Soon, C.G. 2, 52, 166
Cespedes, L. 216
Chang, S. 217–19
charter schools 7, 79, 116
Chávez-Moreno, L.C. 2, 10, 77
Chávez-Reyes, C. 73

Chen, L. 21
child-centered biliteracy approaches 21
Cioè-Peña, M. 2, 70–2, 133, 134
City College of New York (CCNY) 6, 188, 189, 191, 211
city landmarks visits 144–5
City University of New York (CUNY) 190
City University of New York – Initiative on Immigration and Education (CUNY-IIE) 204–6, 208, 245
City University of New York – New York State Initiative on Emergent Bilinguals (CUNY-NYSIEB) 39, 179, 199–201, 208, 209
civil rights movements 55, 56, 57
class (social) 18, 102
cluster subjects 111
Coalición Pro Educación Bilingüe 115
Cochran-Smith, M. 236, 237
Coco, Professor 222–3
co-construction of knowledge 18, 41, 219, 236
code switching 40
co-founders 6
cognates 48, 168, 223
collaboration *see also* integrated co-teaching classes (ICT)
 co-leadership models 77–8
 co-learning models 72, 218
 with families 74
 families as collaborators in children's learning 36–7
 juntos 88–9
 staff culture 47
Collison, J. 217
co-located schools 7, 100
color-coding 19
Columbia Presbyterian Hospital 196
commodification of bilingualism 61, 71, 247
Common Core Standards 21
communities of practice 97
community building project 159–60, 165
community enrichment organization partnerships 195–6
community of inclusion 101–3
community partnerships 195–6, 239–47, 250

community walks 42–3, 78, 179–86
Comprehensive Education Plan (CEP) 78
comunidad, building 109–17, 159–60, 165, 204–5
confianza 17, 85, 87–8
conocimiento 202–3
cooperating teachers 191, 213, 214, 216
co-planning 64, 66
Cordero, Q. 229–35
Corner Project 81, 196, 240, 241
counseling services 119, 125
country comparison inquiry 160–4, 165
COVID-19
   building *comunidad* 113, 115–16
   community enrichment organization partnerships 196
   computer access 128–9, 133
   Facilitating Academic Centers for Inquiry-based Learning (FACIL) 229–35
   Holding Space protocol 122, 124
   Manos Unidas 33
   parents 79
   poetry 243
   remote schooling 127–35, 205
creation of Dos Puentes 4–10
creative stations 58
critical consciousness 2, 18, 26, 61–2, 63, 106, 107, 166, 246
critical listening 62
critical pedagogy 62
cross-cultural conversations 24–5, 65, 70
Croton Watershed 169, 172
cruelty 25–6
cultural consciousness 30
cultural exchanges 57
cultural identities 30, 164, 228
cultural literacy 56–7
Cultural-Historical Activity Theory (CHAT) 218–19
culturally sustaining pedagogy 165, 227
curriculum
   activism 62–3
   adapting 48–51
   bilingual curriculum 20–1
   culturally responsive 21
   curriculum-driven trips 178–9
   Facilitating Academic Centers for Inquiry-based Learning (FACIL) 229
   historical activism 56
   professional development 191, 192
   site-specific bilingual curriculum 46
   university partnerships 189

dance
   arts partnerships 193, 194, 221–8
   bilingual out-of-classroom teachers 12
   building *comunidad* 111
   celebrating bilingualism 33, 36, 249
   country comparison inquiry 163
   school dances 32, 33
   student teachers 217
Darling-Hammond, L. 164, 207, 208
de los Ríos, C.V. 246
decentering whiteness 2
'decolonizing research' xix–xx, 3–4
deficit-oriented perspectives 71, 76, 88, 97, 209
DeJesus, Karín 168–74
Delavan, G. 3, 116
democratic values 89, 246
Di Camillo, Kate 48
Día de los Muertos 112, 163
differentiated instruction 218
digital divide 133
digital tools 128–9, 133, 137–8, 164, 201, 205 *see also* internet access; remote learning
disabilities 2, 64–72, 201–4, 239
   see also special-education students
district partnerships 233–4
Dominican community
   arts partnerships 195, 226
   bunnies 173
   country comparison inquiry 161–2
   history of migration to US 206
   ongoing cultural links with 9, 13, 50–1, 119, 169
   tribute to in colors of logo 9
   Washington Heights neighbourhood 2, 103, 105
Dominican Spanish 50
Douglas, A.S. 218
drugs 196, 240–1
drumming 225
Dryden-Peterson, S. 124
Duffy, P. 154
dynamic bilingualism 21, 26, 45, 78, 154, 199

Early Childhood Program, Teachers College, Columbia University 211
Earth Day 112
educators, families as 76–7, 83, 84–5
Edwards, A. 217
Ee, J. 115
Ellington, A. 8
emergent bilinguals 19, 45, 65, 154, 165, 171, 199, 236, 246
emergent bi/multilinguals with dis/abilities (EBwDs) 70
Engage New York State Math curriculum 192
engagement, importance of 50
Engeström, Y. 218
English
  power of 18, 25, 30, 47
  provision of English translations of Spanish 20
  standardized testing 20
'English Language Learners' 10, 45, 70, 79
English-only 39, 61
Engram, Jr, F. 227
environment 140
equity 52, 62, 106
Escalante Arauz, P. 138
Escamilla, K. 21
España, C. 62, 63
Espinet, I. 88–9, 106, 190, 201
Espinosa, C.M. 35–7, 45
Estrada, L. 243
Estrellita 23, 24
ethnic identities
  students/families 2, 8, 10–11, 14, 55
  teachers 11
ethnography 40, 44
Eureka Math 192, 230, 233
Every Student Succeeds Act (ESSA) 71
Except When They Don't (Gehl, 2020) 58
experiencias inolvidables (unforgettable experiences) 172
experiential learning 138, 175
explorations 142–3, 147–56
extended family 74, 92, 110

Facilitating Academic Centers for Inquiry-based Learning (FACIL) 191, 229–35

families *see also* Villegas, C.
  ethnic identities 2, 8, 10–11, 14, 55
  families as partners 76–7
  family coordinator role 74–5
  family diversity 100–8
  family engagement model 74, 98, 112–13, 173–4, 228
  family language inquiry 424
  pillar 73–82
family events xx, 25, 32, 77, 112, 240
Family Fitness Night 112
Family Fridays 24, 42–4, 76, 85, 109–12, 115, 159, 240
Fariña, C. 250–1
Ferlazzo, L. 97, 98
Fernandez, A. 100–5
field trips 112, 144–5, 169–72, 178–86, 193–4
50/50 Spanish/English split 11, 19, 49, 168
Figueroa, D. 38–44
Figueroa, M. 99
Fleischer, D.Z. 71
Flores, N. 3, 4, 18, 61, 88, 97, 166, 175, 227, 247
Floyd, George 192
folk tales 34
Fordham University 189
four Dos Puentes pillars 14–15
Frazier, L. 188
Freeman, Y.S. 11
Freire, P. 62, 106, 236
friendships 249
Full Option Science System (FOSS) 168, 172
Fullan, M. 187
Fundations 23
fundraising 74, 79, 102–3, 112, 113, 172, 239
funds of knowledge 89, 165, 169, 227
Furman, M. 175

Gabel, S. 202
García, O. 3, 5, 19, 36, 45, 61, 88, 115, 154, 165, 166, 185, 188, 245, 247
Garcia-Banguela, H. 157–64
gardening 81, 195, 240, 246, 249
Garrido, F. 36
Garza, E. 176
Gehl, L. 58
gender identities 58–9

gentrification 2–3, 10, 61, 70, 105, 106, 116, 166, 206, 247
gesture 36
'gifted and talented' students 100
Gillanders, C. 133
Ginsberg, L. 47–51, 53
Goff, P. 227
González, N. 88, 194
Gort, M. 154
graffiti 103, 104
grandparents 74
greetings 29, 67
Grosfoguel, R. xx
Grow NYC 240
guided reading 21
Guskey, T.R. 236

Hadi-Tabassum, S. 3
Hagopian, J. 227
Halliday, M.A.K. 134
Hammond, Z.L. 164
hands-on learning 138–40, 168–77, 225, 230
handwriting 23
Hao, L. 36
Harvest Festival 85, 103, 112
Hassinger-Das, B. 153
Hedrick-Shaw, D. 132–4, 161
Heggerty 23
Herrera, L.Y. 61–3, 63
Higuera-McCoy, K. 239–45
hiring committee 19–20
'Historia de mi lenguaje' 31
historical activism 56–7
historicization of schools 62
Hoffman, J. 153
Hogan, K. 175–6
Holding Space protocol 119–23, 125
Holmes Partnership for Professional Development Schools (PDS) 188
Holyrood Church 244, 246
home languages
  academic research on migration 125
  diversity 10
  Indigenous languages 31, 39
  kindergarten 25, 148
  maintenance of home language 35, 71, 85
  socioemotional learning and support 118
  student-driven inquiry 31
  translanguaging 19, 39
  visibility of 35
home visits 76, 84, 91–4
home-school partnerships 73, 76–7, 91–9
Horowitz, J. 29–37, 121–2, 131, 200
How Tía Lola Came To Visit Stay (Alvarez, 2002) 48–50, 52
'How To' unit 31
Howard, E.R. 106
humanizing pedagogy 35
Hunt, V. xix, 1–15, 100, 109, 111, 137, 187–206, 208, 216
Hunter College 189, 191
hybrid spaces 204

ice cream truck 113
identity
  activism 58
  bilingual identities 19
  cultural identities 30, 164, 228
  gender identities 58–9
  intersectional identities 39–40
  teachers' 41
  units to explore 25
Image Theatre 223–4
immigrant rights 244–5, 247
immigration organizations 196, 242
Immigrations and Customs Enforcement (ICE) 87
independence 182
independent reading 21
independent writing 21
Indigenous languages 31, 39
Individual with Disabilities Education Act (IDEA) 71
Individualized Education Plans (IEPs) 9, 13, 64–5, 68, 91, 95–6, 181, 192
inquiry units 143, 157–67, 201
inquiry-based learning
  celebrating bilingualism 31
  center-based approaches 229–35, 236
  Facilitating Academic Centers for Inquiry-based Learning (FACIL) 229–35
  family language inquiry 42–4
  inquiry as stance 237
  paseos 184
  pillar 3 137–40
  pillar 4 188, 192

translanguaging 39–40
integrated co-teaching classes (ICT)
  dual language bilingual approach 9, 11, 19
  educator professional development 192
  Facilitating Academic Centers for Inquiry-based Learning (FACIL) 230
  paseos 179
  special-education students 64–70
  student teachers 211–12, 213, 218
integrated language continuum 22
International Night/Talent Show 32, 77, 101, 240
international schools 250
International Spanish Academy (ISA) 195
internet access 129, 133
interns 189–90, 216–17
intersectional identities 39–40
interventions 13, 65, 66
investigations 142–3, 157–67
Ishimaru, A.M. 115
Isom, M. 101

Jaar, A. 6, 9, 52, 100, 137–46, 188
Jacobsen, L. 133
jazz 194, 224–6
Johnson, D.C. 236
Jones, M. 209
joy of being bilingual 30–1, 33, 35, 53
joyful moments 31–2, 33, 35, 36, 53, 182, 226–7
juntos 88–9, 246
Just Dance 216

Keselman, A. 137
kindergarten
  50/50 Spanish/English split 11, 19
  activism 56
  COVID-19 128
  explorations 147
  home languages 25, 148
  science 141–2
Kleyn, T. 1–15, 45, 73–82, 165, 189
Know Your Rights training 242
knowledge
  co-construction of knowledge 18, 41, 219, 236
  conocimiento 202–3
  funds of knowledge 89, 165, 169, 227
  'silenced knowledge' xx
  Varied Ways of Knowing (VWK) 201–4, 208, 209
Kohli, R. 236
Kolb, D.A. 138
Kollin, R.S. 248–9
Kopp, B. 192
Krashen, S.D. 50
KWL (Know, Want to Know, and Learned) charts 158

Ladson-Billings, G. 227
language exchange program 78, 112–13, 240
Lasky, S. 185
Lau v. Nichols 79
Lave, J. 97, 154
leaders
  families as 77–9, 83, 85–6, 107, 116
  student teachers as 216–17
learning communities 188
Learning in Places collaboration 186
Learning Policy Institute 124
Leave it Better foundation (LIB) 140, 144, 195, 240
Lee, H.-Y. 137
Lego Robotics 242
Lehman College 189
lemonade gathering 113
lesson planning 213–14, 233
lesson studies 192
Letizia of Spain, Queen 195
Li Wei 19, 185
libraries, classroom 22–3, 30–1, 35
lifelong learners 172, 187
linguicism 74
linguistic equity 3
linguistic maps 40–2
linguistic repertoires *see also* translanguaging
  combining with science 169
  expanding 145
  multimodal learning 165
  paseos 185
  purple time 158
  science 175
  social studies 200
  student-driven inquiry 31
  using full 38

literacy *see also* biliteracy; text selection
  community partnerships 242
  cultural literacy 56–7
  literacy centers 66, 67, 230–2
  literacy curriculum 21–2, 192
  March Reading Madness 33–4
  read-alouds 21, 50, 58, 130, 173, 245
  top-down literacy approaches 21
  voice recorders 68
  writing building on oral practice 180, 181–2
Lobo the puppet 130
location of Dos Puentes 8
Locura por la lectura 25, 32, 33–4
logo 9
Lopez, A. 29–37
López, D. 153, 190
López-Robertson, J. 37
Love, B. 35
Lowenhaupt, R. 74, 75
low-income families 18, 128–9, 239
lunchtime supervisors 190
Lunita 23, 24
Lytle, S.L. 236, 237

Madera Taveras, M. 60
'*Madre Tierra (Oye)*'(Chayanne) 33
Madrigal, R. 6, 33, 47, 188, 201, 211–17, 245
maintenance of home language 35, 71, 85
Makar, C. 97–9
Malik, K. 38–44
Manos Unidas 32, 33
March Reading Madness 25, 32, 33–4
Maroney, A. 201
Martinez, M. 80
Martínez-Álvarez, P. 175–6, 189, 190, 199–206
Martínez-Roldán, C.M. 50–1, 53
math centers 232–3
Math Collective 192
math programs (Eureka Math) 192, 230, 233
McDonald, M. 229
McQuaid, P. 178–84
meaning-making potential 36, 37
Mendenhall, M. 123–5
Menendez, E. 110, 147–53

Menken, K. 105–8
mentor texts 48, 52, 56, 200
mentored learning practice 218, 219
Mercier, S. 91–6, 97, 204
metacognitive awareness 48
metalanguage 22, 154
middle class 3, 18, 61, 106 *see also* gentrification
Mignolo, W.D. xix
migrants 11, 74, 79, 85, 87, 124–5, 204–6
Miguel, Mr. 195
Minahan, J. 118
Minecraft 132
Minno-Bingham, K. 162, 178–84
Moje, E.B. 175
Molina, A. 246
Moll, L. 73, 165, 227
Mollaei, F. 138
Mondol, K. 55–61
monolingual spaces/norms, disruption of 17, 35, 48, 65, 93, 189
Mora-Flores, E. 21
Morel, C. 157–64
Moreno, Y.J. 73–82, 168–74, 200
morning chant 29
morning meeting 67, 110, 119–21, 127
Mota, I. 118–23
movement breaks 67
movie nights 77
Muhammad, G. 35
Mulcahy, S. 244
multicultural community pillar 10, 23–6
multilingual community 10, 46, 181–2
multimodal learning 36, 62, 66, 165, 201, 202
music *see also* dance; singing
  arts partnerships 194, 221–8
  bilingual out-of-classroom teachers 12
  building *comunidad* 31, 33, 36, 111, 112, 249
  country comparison inquiry 163
  COVID-19 129–30
  socioemotional learning and support 119
  theme song 129–30, 133
Mystery Science 168

naming the school 9
needle exchange projects 196, 241

neighbors, relations with 240–1, 246
  see also building *comunidad*
neurodivergence 55
New School Institute 7
New Victory Theater 193
New York City Public School Partnerships 189–90
New York City Public Schools 21, 74–5, 129, 141–2
Next Generation Science Standards (NGSS) 176
Nicola, M. 227
Nieto, S. 5
No Child Left Behind (NCLB) 70
non-verbal language 36, 40
Nube East Puentes 172–4, 176

occupational therapy 13, 65
Office for Civil Rights 124
official languages of the US 30
Olivos, E. 88
online learning 127–35 *see also* remote learning
open-ended exploration 184
open-ended hypothetical questions 169
oracy 21
orgullo bilingüe 29
Orzechowski, M. 239–45
Otheguy, R. 36
outdoor learning 145
'out-of-school literacies' 36
'Own Voices' texts 58, 63

Palabra a Su Paso 23
Palmer, A. 192, 229
Palmer, D. 18, 52, 61, 62, 63, 106, 246
pandemic *see* COVID-19
parallel play 150–1
paraprofessionals 47, 65, 67, 190
Parent Association (PA) 77–8, 85, 101, 102, 172
parent coordinator role 74–5 *see also* Villegas, C.
'parental rights' 114, 116
parents
  families pillar 73–82
  family engagement model 74, 98, 112–13, 173–4, 228
  monolingual 20
  Rincón Hispano 20, 80, 240
  Spanish-first contact with 11, 20

Paris, D. 52, 165, 227
park clean-ups 243, 246
partnerships
  arts partnerships 221–8
  communities of practice 97
  community enrichment organization partnerships 195–6
  community partnerships 195–6, 239–47, 250
  district partnerships 233–4
  families as partners 76–7
  family engagement model 75–6
  home-school partnerships 73, 76–7, 91–9
  pillar 187–99
  staff developer partners 191–3, 229–38
  university partnerships 199–210, 211–20
paseos 144, 178–86
PDS (Holmes Partnership for Professional Development Schools) 188
PE (physical education) 111
peace corner 125
peer relations, supporting 120
Peña, S. 211–17, 218
Pérez, B. 21, 114–16
Pérez Huber, L. 206
Pero Like 40
personal versus academic benefits of bilingual programmes 106
Phillips, L. 221–6
phonics 21, 23, 231
Pimentel, C. 20
piñatas 31
place-based education 185–6
play 147–54, 154, 180, 182
poetry 242–4
Poms, S. 12, 64–70
Pontier, R. 154
potlucks xx, 25, 32, 77, 112, 240
Poza, L. 88, 175
Prieto, T. 64–70, 204
principal chats 77
principal's journey in establishing Dos Puentes 4–10
professional development 11, 190, 191–3, 205, 208, 236
proficiency, and the 'claiming' of languages 41
project-based learning 159–60

proposal for Dos Puentes 4–5
proximal representations 175–6
public speaking in Spanish 25, 32
Puerto Rican community 13, 79, 81, 92, 103, 109
puppets 130, 133
purple time 158, 165

Queen Letizia of Spain 195
Quinn, J. 187

rabbits 172–3, 176
race 2, 70, 226–7
raciolinguistics 4
racism 3, 74, 76, 102, 192, 228 *see also* white supremacy
Rahnama, H. 138
Ramirez, M. 233, 250–1
read-alouds 21, 50, 58, 130, 173, 245
Reading A to Z (Raz-Kids) 22
recruitment of teachers 13–14, 20
recycling project 86, 89
red for Spanish, blue for English 19, 158, 165, 168
referrals 125
reflective practice 215–16
refuge, spaces of 246–7
relational power 74, 206, 219
remote learning 113, 127–35, 230
resident teaching artist 195
resilience 182
resources in Spanish 21, 22–3, 30–1, 168, 192
respect/*respeto* 105–6
restorative spaces 39
Revolutionary Love 36
Reyes, K. 204
Rincón Hispano, El 20, 80, 240
Rosa, J. 4
Russ, S. 153
Ruth and The Green Book (Ramsey, 2010) 56
Ryoo, K. 175

Sánchez, M.T. 35, 36, 190, 199–206
sanctuary 246
Saunders-Stewart, K. 164
scaffolds 19
Schissel, J.L. 71
school choice 116
school counselor 119, 125
school dances 32, 33
School Leadership Team (SLT) 78, 85, 96, 205
schoolyard 183
science 12, 111, 112, 138–42, 168–77, 178, 186
Science, Technology, Engineering, Art and Math (STEAM) 140
security staff 29
See, Think, Wonder 158, 176
Seeger, P. 57
Seiden, J. 224, 225
self-regulation 119
Seltzer, K. 237, 245–7
semiotics 36
Shannon, S. 88
shared writing 21
Sheasley, C. 125
'Should We' questions 186
side-by-side model 11, 19, 211–12, 213, 218
Sidlo, A. 127–32, 133
signage 43
'silenced knowledge' xx
silent auction 102–3
siloed education policies 71
singing 25, 33, 57, 129–30, 133, 163
Sit-In How Four Friends Stood Up by Sitting Down (Davis Pinkney, 2010) 56
slavery 204, 222–3
small group support 21, 66, 68, 127, 131, 158, 171, 231
soccer 242
social justice
 activism 56, 62, 247
 arts 221
 biliteracy 52
 children with disabilities 72
 home-school partnerships 97
 inquiry-based learning 166
 partnerships 189, 191
social studies 11, 46, 142, 143, 157–8, 200
social workers 119, 125
socioculturally mediated process 154
socioemotional consciousness 30
socioemotional coping strategies 94
socioemotional learning and support 118–23, 151–2, 165, 173, 182–3, 246

socioemotional states 50
Solorza, C. 165
Soltero-González, L. 133
Sombra West Puentes 172–4, 176
Song, K. 76
Soslau, E. 217
Souto-Manning, M. 155, 190
Spanglish 85
Spanish texts 21, 22–3, 30–1, 168, 192
Spanish-first 11, 20, 24
Spanish-only 39
speaking practice 181
special education teachers 95
special-education students 9, 64–72, 95–6, 192, 201–4
speech and language services 13, 65, 181
sports 242–4
Spring, J. 2
staff developer partners 191–3, 229–38
standardized testing 20, 53, 166, 235, 236
Stanford, L. 118
Stefanski, A. 97
Stephens, C. 235–7
stereotypes 50, 102
Stern, N. 207–9
Stetsenko, A. 53
Steven Bernstein Quartet 226
Stevenson, A.R. 175
student body demographics 2, 8, 10–11, 14, 55
student choice 143, 147, 160
student council 56, 59–60
student teachers 189, 211–20
student voice 93–4, 99
'Student with Disabilities' (SWD) classifications 70
student-driven inquiry 31
student-led conference (SLC) 93–5
Studio in a School 144, 195
summer programs 216–17, 219
Sung, K.K. 115
Superintendent 191, 195, 217, 233

tableaux 224
Taconic Outdoor Education Center (TOEC) 182, 195
Tai Chi 111–12
Tan, E. 175
Taveras, M.M. 95, 157–64

teachers
 advocacy 79
 attrition rates 237
 bilingual extension (bilingual teaching certification) 10–11
 as bilingual models 30, 40–1, 168, 189, 195, 216
 bilingual out-of-classroom teachers 12
 collaborative culture 47
 cooperating teachers 191, 213, 214, 216
 Dos Puentes bilingual teachers 10–11, 12, 19–20
 ideological and political clarity 52
 joy of teaching 53
 as knowledge creators 236–7
 as learners 155
 professional development 11, 190, 191–3, 205, 208, 236
 recruitment 13–14, 20
 social change-makers 236
 special education teachers 65
 student teachers 189, 211–20
 teaching through inquiry 166
 timetabling 11–12
 training 166
 trust 52, 65
Teachers College Reading and Writing Project (TCRWP) 22, 23, 56, 192, 230
Teachers College (TC), Columbia University 5, 188, 189, 211
team teaching 65
testimonios 51, 52, 206, 213–16
text selection
 activism 58, 62
 bilingual texts 23
 high quality 49
 historical activism 56–7
 Spanish texts 21, 22–3, 30–1, 168, 192
 translanguaging 200
theater trips 193–4
theme song 129–30, 133
thriving 35
Tiger Rising, The (Di Camillo) 48
time allocation 11–12, 67
¡Toma la palabra! 204–6
top-down literacy approaches 21
Torres-Guzmán, M.E. 5, 6, 188
translanguaging 38–46

allowing space for 5, 19, 175, 200
CUNY-NYSIEB 199–201
explorations 142–3
Parent Association (PA) 78
paseos 185
play 149–50, 152, 154–5
purple time 158, 165
translanguaging stance 245–6
writing 181
translation
   English books translated into Spanish 4950
   IEPs 96
   Spanish-first with English translations (parent events) 11, 20
Trauma Responsive Teaching 118
trauma-informed practices 118, 192
trips/visits 112, 144–5, 169–72, 178–86
Trump, Donald 87, 244, 247
trust 52, 65, 182
t-shirts 93
two-way learning 18, 62, 73
Tzou, C. 186

Ubiera, Stephanie 83–7, 89
Ukraine 59–60
undocumented immigrants 196, 204, 244
unforgettable experiences (*experiencias inolvidables*) 172
Universal Design for Learning (UDL) 64, 66, 192, 230
university partnerships 187, 189–91, 199–210, 211–20
US bilingual education policies 3

Valdés, G. 20, 105, 106, 166
Valdez, V.E. 61, 70
Varied Ways of Knowing (VWK) 201–4, 208, 209
Velásquez-Leacock, C. 147–53
Veras, J. 229–35
video-making projects 131–2
Viernes Familiar 24, 42–4, 76, 85, 109–12, 115, 159, 240
Villegas, C. 6, 73–82, 84, 86, 87, 101, 109
visual arts 195
'*Vivir Mi Vida*' (Marc Anthony) 33

vocabulary development 22–3, 48–50, 58, 141, 145, 152, 179–81, 223, 230, 232
voice recorders 68
Vossoughi, S. 184
Vygotsky, L. 154

walking trips 144, 178–86
Warren, M. 74
Washington Height Corner Project (WHCP) 81, 196, 240, 241
Washington Heights neighborhood 7–8, 10–11, 44, 46
water unit (science) 112, 145, 169–70, 194
Watershed Agricultural Council 194, 195
Watkins, B. 208
Watson, A. 184
Wei, L. 19, 185
Welcome Potluck 25
Wellness in the Schools (WITS) 240
Wenger, E. 97, 154
white English-speaking majority, bilingual education seen to mainly serve 10, 18 *see also* gentrification
white normativity 2, 74
white privilege 5
white savior complex 18
white supremacy 2, 20, 100
whole-child approach 71, 76, 118, 124
'windows and mirrors' 48, 50
Withers, A. 91–6, 97
Woodley, H.H. 226–8
word study 21
Words their Way 23
working memory issues 68–9
Wynter-Hoyte, K. 36

xenophobia 20, 71, 76, 102, 247

'*Yo, yo, yo, leo*' 33–4
Yoon, K.S. 208, 236
youth-led movements 56–7, 62, 63

Zames, F. 71
Zankel Fellows 216